Student Stud

to accompany

Psychology
Frontiers and Applications

Michael W. Passer
University of Washington

Ronald E. Smith
University of Washington

Prepared by

David K. Jones
Westminster College

Boston   Burr Ridge, IL   Dubuque, IA   Madison, WI   New York   San Francisco   St. Louis
Bangkok   Bogotá   Caracas   Lisbon   London   Madrid
Mexico City   Milan   New Delhi   Seoul   Singapore   Sydney   Taipei   Toronto

McGraw-Hill Higher Education

*A Division of The **McGraw-Hill** Companies*

Student Study Guide to accompany
PSYCHOLOGY: FRONTIERS AND APPLICATIONS.
MICHAEL W. PASSER AND RONALD E. SMITH.

This book is printed on acid-free paper.

2 3 4 5 6 7 8 9 0 BKM BKM 0 3 2 1

ISBN 0-07-232398-1

www.mhhe.com

Table of Contents

Introduction

Welcome to the world of psychology! During this course you will study many aspects of the science of psychology, including
- the biology of behavior
- how people sense and perceive things
- how we learn
- how we store and use information
- how we develop over the lifespan
- what motivates us
- what causes us to experience emotion
- how we relate to each other
- how our personalities are structured
- how things can go wrong and how abnormal behaviors can develop
- and how therapy can help us with our problems.

It should be an exciting trip for you.

Michael Passer's and Ronald Smith's book is designed to help you understand how psychologists study and understand all of these topics and many more. It focuses on three major categories of explanations for human behavior and thought: biological, psychological, and environmental causes. As you read through the book, focus on understanding the behaviors of interest in the chapter from these three paradigms, or models, of behavior.

Psychology is a vast field. To get the most out of this course, you need to figure out how best to study for it so that you can learn and apply the information from it in the most efficient manner. Psychologists who study the process of learning have much to say about the best ways to study. On page 33 of your textbook, the authors have introduced four classes of strategies for enhanced academic performance: time management, study skills, test-preparation strategies, and test-taking skills. Let's consider each of those in turn.

It is extremely important when you arrive at college to develop solid time management skills. If you are new to college, you will soon find this out. If you are already a seasoned college student, you know what I'm talking about. There are so many things to do in college: classes, work, Greek organizations, clubs, student government activities, parties, sleep, a social life, and hopefully some free time. Therefore, you need to figure out how to schedule everything so that you can have a great college experience. Remember the main reason that you're at college is to learn and prepare for your future, but don't neglect the other things either! How, then, to balance everything? Get a planner. You have 168 hours in a week. Sit down with your planner or a written list of hours in each day of the week, and figure out how you're going to distribute your time. Put in time for studying. One of the major findings about studying is that it is far better to distribute study time than to try to cram for exams. Instead of waiting until the night before an exam to study, begin studying immediately upon starting a new chapter or unit. Keep up with the reading! It is much easier to understand what your professor is talking about in class if you are doing the reading that corresponds with the lecture. This is again another important psychological principle. To do that, though, you need to figure out how to fit plenty of reading and study time into your busy schedule. Use that planner and monitor your progress. If the schedule that you planned for yourself isn't working out, examine your priorities.

To study more effectively, there are a number of things that psychologists would recommend. First, find a quiet place to study. Studying in loud dorms with noisy roommates is not conducive to good learning. Do not study while lying on your bed. Your body has learned that lying down is conducive to sleep. Therefore, if you try to study while lying down, your body feels that it is sleep time, not study time. Do try to find a comfortable chair though. When you do find a good place for study, study <u>actively</u>. Too many students simply read the text. To study actively, you can use the SQ3R or PQ4R methods. First, preview the chapter to see what major topics it will explore. Develop some questions that you want answers to from the chapter. Then read the chapter and take notes on it. Highlighting sections of the chapter with a marker is not nearly as good a strategy as taking notes and <u>rewriting</u> sections of the chapter in your own words. You can try teaching the chapter to someone else. Often, people better understand material once they teach it to others. Finally, review the chapter to make sure that you understand the main points it is covering.

To prepare for tests, it is again good to distribute your studying. Don't cram! If you have kept up with the material as it was being presented, you won't need to learn everything from scratch come exam time. Use this study guide. The study guide contains the outline for each chapter, the directed questions that cover the key points of each chapter, a brief summary of each chapter, key chapter concepts where you can match the concept with the definition, a review where you can fill in key concepts, application questions, and practice tests containing multiple choice, true/false, short answer, and essay questions for each chapter. There is also a practice midterm, consisting of 150 multiple choice questions from the first eight chapters of the textbook and a practice final, which consists of 176 multiple choice questions from the last eight chapters of the textbook. You can find both of these practice tests on the book's web site (www.mhhe.com/passer) The study guide is, of course, designed to help you to review and to understand the key ideas in each chapter. Many of the multiple choice questions require application of the information, which is an important college-level skill to develop. If your instructor provides you with a study guide, use it! If there is a study session set aside, attend and ask many questions to make sure that you understand the material. Visit the professor or teaching assistant to get help! Talk to past students who have taken the course to try to anticipate what kinds of questions you're likely to get on your exam. As you're studying, develop your own questions, both multiple-choice and essay questions. Study with a partner or in a group and quiz each other. Prepare answers to mock essay questions. I know that this sounds like an awful lot of work, and it is. You will likely find, though, that success in college doesn't come without blood, sweat, and sometimes tears.

While actually taking the test, you can apply a few strategies as well. On multiple-choice items, try to anticipate the answer by reading the stem of the question first before looking at the answer alternatives. You can also try to eliminate as many items as you possibly can. If you've ever watched contestants on "Who Wants to be a Millionaire?" you'll know what I'm talking about. Beware of items that say "all" or "never." Don't be afraid to go against your first inclination. Many times the first guess is actually wrong. Don't outthink yourself, though! Sometimes students think the questions are more vague than they really are. On short-answer or essay questions, organize your thoughts in advance before you start writing. Make sure that you organize your time wisely on exams. Give yourself plenty of time to answer all of the questions. If you don't know an item, don't waste time while fretting over it. Go on and come back to it later. Don't leave anything blank though. Guess if you have to. Test anxiety can be a difficult thing with which to deal for many students. Try your best to relax. Take a deep breath. Stretch.

I hope that you find this study guide helpful to you as you complete this course. Psychology is an endlessly fascinating subject for me, and I hope that you will find it equally enjoyable and stimulating. I would appreciate any feedback you would care to send me about the study guide. Best wishes and good luck and you work your way through this course.

David K. Jones
Assistant Professor of Psychology
Westminster College
Fulton, MO 65251

Email: jonesd@jaynet.wcmo.edu

Acknowledgments

Preparing this study guide has been a major task. I would like to thank my wonderful editors at McGraw-Hill, Barbara Santoro and Mindy DePalma, for all of their wonderful help, advice, and patience as these chapters were completed. Thanks also to Michael Passer and Ronald Smith, without whose textbook this study guide would obviously not exist!

I would also like to thank a number of people who have helped me through the last couple of extremely rough years in my life. First of all, I would like to thank my family, including my parents, David and Brenda, and my brother, Tony. They are the best family I could ever hope for. I would also like to thank a number of friends for their help and support through difficult times: Danny Akarakian, Ann Bettencourt, Nancy Collins, Dick Freer, Sam Goodfellow, Keith Hardeman, Ted Jaeger, Kurt Jefferson, Amy Marcus-Newhall, Lynn Miller, Cathryn Pridal, Stephen Read, George and Helen Stone, Stephen and Erin Watson, and Patti Williamson. You guys are the best. You will never know how much I appreciate you. And, finally, I would like to thank my cats: Lexie and Sammy. I know that it is strange to thank one's cats, but I love them very much.

Chapter 1
PSYCHOLOGY: THE SCIENCE OF BEHAVIOR

Learning Objectives: *These questions, with a few additions (indicated with an asterisk), are taken from the directed questions found in the margins of the chapter. After reading the chapter, you should be able to answer these questions.*

1.   Define psychology and indicate what kinds of behaviors it studies.

2.   How do the goals of basic and applied research differ?

3.   How do the Robber's Cave experiment and the jigsaw classroom program illustrate the relation between basic and applied science?

4.   What are the four goals of psychology? How are these goals related to one another?

5.   How were the four goals of scientific psychology illustrated in the Robber's Cave study?

6.   At what three levels of analysis were possible causes for Charles Whitman's violent outburst explored?

7.   What are perspectives on behavior? Cite four ways in which they can influence psychological science.

8.   Contrast the positions of dualism and monism as they apply to the "mind-body" problem.

9.   What three classes of causal factors does the biological perspective focus on?

10.   What was the importance of Galvani's discovery for (a) the mind-body puzzle, and (b) the development of psychology as a science?

11.   What subsequent technical developments were important in the study of brain-behavior relations?

12.   What is meant by natural selection? What is its role in physical and behavioral evolution?

13.   According to evolutionary psychology, how do biological and behavioral evolution influence one another?

14.   According to sociobiology, what is the ultimate importance of evolved social behaviors? On what bases has this position been criticized by other theorists?

15.   What methods do behavior geneticists use to investigate the role of genetic factors in animal and human behavior?

16.   What is the conception of human nature advanced by the cognitive perspective?

17.   Compare the goals and methods of structuralism and functionalism.

18. What does gestalt mean? How does this meaning relate to the goals and findings of Gestalt psychology?

19. What were the methods used and the conclusions reached by Piaget in his studies of cognitive development?

20. How have Beck and Ellis advanced our understanding of emotional problems?

21. What is studied in the cognitive science areas of artificial intelligence and cognitive neuroscience?

22. What do social constructivists says about the nature of "reality?"

22.1* Summarize the "They Saw a Game" study by Hastorf and Cantril (1954).

23. What causal factors are the focus of the psychodynamic perspective?

24. What observations convinced Freud of the importance of unconscious and childhood determinants of adult behavior?

24.1* According to Freud, why are people afraid of and anxious about their sexual desires? What are defense mechanisms and what is repression?

25. In what sense is the human in continuous internal conflict, according to Freud?

26. What influences does Freud's theory have on contemporary psychology?

27. What are the important causal factors in behavior within the behavioral perspective? How was this school of thought influence by British empiricism?

27.1* What is behaviorism? What important people are associated with this movement?

28. What is cognitive behaviorism? How does it differ from radical behaviorism?

29. How does the humanistic conception of human nature and motivation differ from that advanced by psychoanalysis and behaviorism?

30. How does terror management theory draw on humanistic concepts? What are some of its major findings?

31. Define *culture* and *norms*. What functions does a culture serve?

32. Contrast individualistic and collectivistic societies.

32.1* Summarize the research of Margaret Mead.

32.2* What does the term eugenics mean?

33. Why is the distinction between originating and present causes important in the nature-nurture focus on evolutionary and cultural factors in behavior?

34.   In what sense has psychology come "full circle" from its early focus on mental events?

34.1* For each of the psychological perspectives, differentiate between their conceptions of human nature, major causal factors of behavior, and predominant focus and methods of behavior.

35.   What three levels of analysis allow us to incorporate causal factors suggested by each of the perspectives?

36.   What does the biological level of analysis tell us about the causes of depression?

37.   What kinds of psychological causal factors have been identified in depression?

38.   Which causal factors in depression are seen at the environmental level of analysis?

39.   What is meant by the interaction of causal factors?

40.   In what sense do depressive behaviors have biological, psychological, and environmental consequences?

40.1* What are the principles that are widely accepted by psychologists?

40.2* What are the four general classes of academic performance enhancement skills?

41.   Describe three important principles of time management.

41.1* What are two important suggestions for improving study habits?

42.   What does educational psychology research tell us about the effects of directions questions on retention of information? Why do they have these effects?

43.   What kinds of strategies are used by test-wise students when they take tests?

Chapter Overview

This chapter gives an introduction to some of the basic aspects of psychology. One of the most important things to understand is that psychology is both a basic and applied science, meaning that psychologists both search for knowledge about human behavior for its own sake and also use that knowledge to solve practical problems in personal lives, education, business, law, health and medicine, and other areas. As psychology is a science, psychologists use the scientific method to help satisfy their four basic goals: describing, understanding, predicting, and controlling behavior. Psychology is an empirical science, which means that it favors direct observations of behavior.

Psychologists use several different perspectives to understand behavior, including the biological, cognitive, psychodynamic, behavioral, humanistic, and sociocultural perspectives.
The biological perspective suggests that behavior is best explained by studying how the brain, biochemical processes, and genetic factors influence actions. A modern-day movement in psychology has pointed to evidence that evolutionary factors may influence current behaviors.
The cognitive perspective grew out of the early distinction between adherents of the structuralist

approach, which contrasted with the functionalist approach. The cognitive perspective views humans as information processors and problem solvers. Social constructivists believe that each person creates his or her own "reality" from his or her cognitive perceptions. Adherents of the psychodynamic perspective believe that unconscious conflicts and unresolved conflicts from the past influence our personalities and behavior. The behavioral perspective suggests that the environment, rather than individual characteristics such as cognitions or personality, is the primary determinant of our behavior. On the other hand, humanists stress the importance of motives, freedom, and choice as we move toward our full potential, or self-actualization. The sociocultural perspective suggests that cultural norms, or rules for behavior, shape our actions. Because it is likely that none of the perspectives provides a complete explanation for behavior, many psychologists stress the need to integrate the perspectives to provide a more complete explanation of human behavior.

There are a number of different specialty areas within psychology as a whole. These specialties include clinical, counseling, educational, experimental, industrial, developmental, social, personality, physiological, and quantitative psychologies.

Chapter Outline

The Nature of Psychology
    Psychology as a Basic and Applied Science
        From Robber's Cave to the Jigsaw Classroom
        Goals of Psychology

Perspectives on Behavior: Guides to Understanding and Discovery
    The Importance of Perspectives
    The Biological Perspective: Brain, Genes, and Behavior
        Discovery of Brain-Behavior Relations
        Evolution and Behavior: From Darwin to Evolutionary Psychology
        Modern Evolutionary Psychology
        Behavior Genetics
    The Cognitive Perspective: The Thinking Human
        Origins of the Cognitive Perspective
            Structuralism
            Functionalism
            Gestalt Psychology
            Piaget: Cognitive Development in Children
            Cognitive Approaches to Psychological Disorders
            Modern Cognitive Science
            Social Constructivism
    The Psychodynamic Perspective: The Forces Within
        Psychoanalysis: Freud's Great Challenge
        Current Developments
    The Behavioral Perspective
        Behaviorism
        Cognitive Behaviorism
    The Humanistic Perspective
    The Sociocultural Perspective: The Embedded Human
        Cultural Learning and Diversity

Psychological Frontiers
 Nature and Nurture: Biology, Culture, and Behavior
The Perspectives In Historical Context
 The Early Years
 The 1950s and 1960s
 The Current Situation

Integrating the Perspectives: Three Levels of Analysis
 Biological
 Psychological
 Environmental

Fields Within Psychology
 Clinical
 Counseling
 Educational
 Experimental
 Industrial
 Developmental
 Social
 Personality
 Physiological
 Quantitative

Applications of Psychological Science: Study Skills

Key Terms: *Write the letter of the definition next to the term in the space provided.*

1. ___ applied research
2. ___ artificial Intelligence
3. ___ basic research
4. ___ behavior genetics
5. ___ behavior modification
6. ___ behavioral perspective
7. ___ behaviorism
8. ___ biological perspective
9. ___ British empiricism
10. ___ cognitive behaviorism
11. ___ cognitive perspective
12. ___ collectivism
13. ___ culture
14. ___ evolutionary psychology
15. ___ functionalism
16. ___ Gestalt psychology
17. ___ humanistic perspective
18. ___ hysteria
19. ___ individualism
20. ___ insight
21. ___ interaction
22. ___ introspection
23. ___ jigsaw program
24. ___ levels of analysis
25. ___ mind-body dualism
26. ___ monism
27. ___ natural selection
28. ___ norms
29. ___ perspectives

a. idea that psychology should study the functions of consciousness
b. the reaching of one's potential
c. the idea that mind and body are one
d. a defense mechanism that keeps anxiety-arousing impulses in the unconscious mind
e. concerned with how elements of experience are organized into wholes
f. focuses on the role of the external environment in shaping our actions
g. the scientific study of behavior and the factors that influence it
h. the analysis of the mind in terms of its basic elements
i. techniques of behavior change from the psychology of learning
j. computer models of complex human thought, reasoning, and problem solving
k. the perspective that emphasizes growth and self-actualization
l. the quest for knowledge purely for its own sake
m. any inheritable characteristic that increases the likelihood that survival will be maintained in the species
n. emphasizes environmental control of behavior through learning
o. a classroom procedure requiring children to cooperate with one another rather than compete
p. sudden perception of a useful relationship or solution to a problem
q. the enduring values, beliefs, behaviors and traditions passed on from one generation to another
r. rules that specify what is acceptable and expected
s. research designed to solve specific practical problems
t. theory that complex social behaviors are products of evolution
u. the belief that the mind is a spiritual entity
v. emphasizes roles of unconscious processes & unresolved conflicts
w. holds that all ideas and knowledge are gained through the senses
x. an emphasis on personal goals and self-identity
y. the perspective that views humans as information processors and problem solvers
z. individual goals are subordinated to the group
aa. vantage points for analyzing behavior and its biological, psychological, and environmental causes
bb. biological, psychological, and environmental causal factors
cc. a method of describing inner experiences

30. ___ psychodynamic perspective	dd.	presence of one factor can influence the effects of other factors
31. ___ psychology	ee.	the viewpoint that believes that reality is our own creation
32. ___ repression	ff.	focuses on the manner in which culture is transmitted to its members
33. ___ self-actualization	gg.	suggests that an innate desire for continued life creates an anxiety called existential terror
34. ___ social constructivism	hh.	a discipline that focuses on the role of evolution in the development of human behavior
35. ___ sociobiology	ii.	a study of how behavioral tendencies are influenced by genetic factors
36. ___ sociocultural perspective	jj.	an attempt to bridge the gap between the behavioral and cognitive perspectives
37. ___ structuralism	kk.	a psychological disorder in which physical symptoms have no apparent organic cause
38. ___ terror management theory	ll.	focuses on the brain, biochemistry, and genetics as causes of behavior

Key People: *Write the letter of the ideas associated with the person in the space provided*

1. ___ Eliot Aronson
2. ___ Albert Bandura
3. ___ Charles Darwin
4. ___ Sigmund Freud
5. ___ Luigi Galvani
6. ___ Wolfgang Kohler
7. ___ Karl Lashley
8. ___ Jean Piaget
9. ___ Carl Rogers
10. ___ B.F. Skinner
11. ___ Wilhelm Wundt

a. developed psychoanalysis
b. proposed idea of natural selection
c. leading humanistic theorist
d. leader of Gestalt psychology
e. jigsaw program
f. believed that the real causes of behavior are environmental
g. discovered stages of cognitive development
h. severed leg of frog moved if electrical current applied
i. proposed idea of structuralism
j. cognitive behaviorist
k. interested in brain mechanisms of learning

Review at a Glance: *Write the term that best fits the blank to review what you learned in this chapter.*

The Nature of Psychology

Psychology is the scientific study of (1) _____ and the factors that influence it. Psychologists have a quest for knowledge for its own sake, which is called (2)_____ _____ and also pursue knowledge that is designed to solve specific practical problems, a type of research known as (3) _____ _____. The Robber's Cave study by Sherif et al. (1961) showed that hostility between groups could be reduced by having children work together in (4) _____ _____. This basic research was later used by Aronson et al. (1978) in the (5) _____ _____, which required that children had to cooperate in order to achieve a goal that neither could achieve alone.

As scientists, psychologists have four basic goals regarding behavior: to (6) _____, (7) _____, (8) _____, and (9) _____ it.

Perspectives on Behavior: Guides to Understanding and Discovery

(10) _____ are vantage points for analyzing behavior. The six different perspectives used by psychologists are the (11) _____, (12) _____, (13) _____, (14) _____, (15) _____, and (16) _____ perspectives. The ancient Greek belief that the mind is a spiritual entity not subject to the physical laws that govern the body is called (17) _____ _____ _____. The alternative view that mind and body are one is called (18) _____. The biological perspective emphasizes the roles of the brain, biochemical processes, and (19) _____ _____ _____. According to Darwin's evolutionary theory, any inheritable characteristic that increases the likelihood of survival will be maintained in the species because individuals having the characteristic will be likely to survive and reproduce. This process is known as (20) _____ _____. Psychologists in the field of (21) _____ _____ stress the ideas that an organism's biology determines its behavioral capacities and its behavior determines whether or not it will survive. Thus, behaviors may well be products of evolution. Similarly, (22) _____ suggest that complex social behaviors are also built into the human species as products of evolution. Another area within the biological perspective is (23) _____ _____, which is the study of how behavioral tendencies are influenced by genetic factors. The cognitive perspective views people as problem solvers and (24) _____ _____. Today's cognitive perspective has roots in the debate between the structuralist, functionalist, and Gestalt camps. The structuralists, who believed that sensations are the basic elements of consciousnness, attempted to study consciousness through the technique of (25) _____. In contrast, the approach that held that psychology should study the "whys" of consciousness, or (26) _____, was influenced by evolutionary theory. The study of how elements of experience are organized into wholes, or (27) _____ _____, suggested that the whole was greater than the sum of its parts. Modern cognitive psychologists study cognitive processes involved in things like decision-making and problem-solving. (28) _____ _____ was one of the most prominent theorists in the study of childhood cognitive development. A modern offshoot of the cognitive perspective studies complex human thought, reasoning, and problem-solving by developing computer models and is known as (29) _____ _____. Theorists who maintain that "reality" is in large part our own mental creation are known as (30) _____ _____. The perspective emphasizing the role of unconscious processes and unresolved past conflicts is known as the (31) _____ perspective and is most associated with (32) _____ _____. The behavioral perspective developed from (33) _____ _____, which held that all ideas and knowledge are gained empirically. Today, behaviorists emphasize the (34) _____ determinants of behavior. An attempt to bridge the gap between the behavioral and cognitive perspectives popularized by Albert Bandura, among others, is called (35) _____ _____. Humanistic psychologists stress the importance of conscious motives and free will and believe that we are motivated to reach our full potentials, a state called (36) _____. According to (37) _____ _____ _____, an innate desire for life despite the realized inevitability of death creates an anxiety called existential terror. The enduring beliefs, values, behaviors, and traditions shared by a large group of people, or (38) _____, also influences our behavior. The rules that society establishes to indicate what behavior is acceptable are known as (39) _____.

Integrating the Perspectives: Three Levels of Analysis

The three main levels of analysis that can be used to understand behavior are the (40) _____, (41) _____, and (42) _____ levels. These levels are usually combined to explain behavior. Indeed, the presence of one factor can influence the effects of other factors, a process called (43) _____.

Fields Within Psychology

There are a number of specialty fields within the larger field of psychology. For instance, (44) _____ psychologists are involved with the diagnosis and treatment of emotional disorders and abnormal behavior while (45) _____ psychologists study the biological foundations of behavior.

Apply What You Know

1. Explain each perspective's view of human nature and focus of study by using Study Sheet 1.1. The exercise should take about 20 minutes and it is well worth the effort.

2. Think of a self-help book that you've read recently. Which of the perspectives that you learned about in Chapter 1 does the book use? Give some examples of how the book uses those perspectives.

3. Choose one of the following (obesity, alcohol use, drug use, juvenile delinquency) and analyze the possible causes of the behavior by using each of the three levels of analysis (biological, psychological, and environmental). Use Study Sheet 1.2.

Stretching Your Geographies

1. Here's your chance to learn more about the diversity of psychology by engaging in an Internet scavenger hunt. Study Sheet 1.3 gives a list of questions to which you can find the answers on the WWW.

Practice Test

<u>Multiple Choice Items</u>: *Please write the letter corresponding to your answer in the space to the left of each item.*

_____ 1. According to the text, psychology is defined as the ____.

    a. study of people's subjective mental lives.
    b. scientific study of behavior and its causes.
    c. examination of unconscious factors.
    d. study of personality

_____ 2. Dr. Adams is a psychologist who works in the area of animal behavior. She has a particular interest in crows and her research is primarily aimed at gaining more information about the behaviors of these birds, such as their mating habits, eating rituals, and so on. Dr. Adams research is <u>best categorized</u> as ____ research.

    a. applied
    b. basic
    c. insight
    d. interaction

_____ 3. The jigsaw program (Aronson et al., 1978) worked in reducing inter-group conflict because ____.

    a. working together on jigsaw puzzles created more cooperation
    b. cooperative experiences only increase inter-group conflict
    c. the children were required to cooperate in order to reach a goal that neither group could reach alone
    d. groups almost always prefer to cooperate than to fight each other

_____ 4. Dr. Smith is a psychologist who is interested in studying aggression in sports. For her research, she attends high school basketball games and records the number of aggressive acts that she observes. Dr. Smith's research is <u>best viewed</u> as meeting the ____ goal of psychology.

    a. description
    b. understanding
    c. prediction
    d. control

_____ 5. Two psychologists are arguing over the causes of depression. One firmly believes that the disorder has a biological basis and that research should focus on identifying and treating these biological factors. In contrast, the other acknowledges the likely contribution of biology, but asserts that cognitions and thoughts are stronger causes of the disorder and believes that research should instead focus on identifying the key thoughts associated with depression and on effectively changing these thoughts. This difference in opinion can <u>most likely be attributed</u> to the psychologists' different _____.

    a.   personalities
    b.   educational backgrounds
    c.   family histories
    d.   psychological perspectives on behavior

_____ 6. In attempting to explain the violent behavior of Charles Whitman, some psychologists focused on the potentially important causal role of Whitman's unusual and irrational thoughts. These psychologists are attempting to explain Whitman's behavior in terms of the _____ level of analysis.

    a.   structural
    b.   psychological
    c.   environmental
    d.   biological

_____ 7. Monists believed that _____.

    a.   the mind is a spiritual entity not subject to physical laws
    b.   the biological perspective was wrong
    c.   mental events are a product of physical events
    d.   the love of money was the root of all evil

_____ 8. Karl Lashley investigated the brain mechanisms involved in learning by _____.

    a.   severing the leg of a frog and finding that the leg moved when he applied electrical current to it
    b.   studying the neurological differences between smart and dumb mice
    c.   measuring the EEG activity in trained an untrained animals
    d.   damaging specific brain areas of animals and observing how this impacted learning and memory

_____ 9. The idea that any inheritable characteristic that increases the likelihood of survival will be maintained in the species because individuals having the characteristic will be more likely to survive and reproduce is known as _____.

    a.   evolution
    b.   sociobiology
    c.   natural selection
    d.   behavioral genetics

_____ 10. Occasionally parents will sacrifice their lives in order to ensure the survival of their children. Someone associated with sociobiology would argue that these instances _____.

a. are due to innate altruistic drives within every human being
b. occur because genetic survival (of people who share your genes) is more important than individual survival
c. are due to the conflict between unconscious psychological forces and psychological defenses
d. occur because of the reinforcement of altruistic behavior by culture and society

_____ 11. The study of both identical and fraternal twins in an attempt to understand behavior is used most by _____.

a. behavior genetics
b. evolutionary psychology
c. sociobiology
d. the cognitive perspective

_____ 12. The approach known as _____ attempted to analyze the mind in terms of its basic elements.

a. functionalism
b. structuralism
c. Gestalt psychology
d. insight psychology

_____ 13. Gestalt psychology is concerned with _____.

a. the biological influences on behavior
b. the environmental determinants of behavior
c. how elements of experience are organized into meaningful wholes
d. artificial intelligence

_____ 14. Psychologists who study artificial intelligence are most interested in studying _____.

a. the environmental determinants of behavior
b. the biological influences on behavior
c. intelligence in nonhuman primates
d. computer models of complex human thought

_____ 15. A cognitive psychologist attempts to explain the long-term conflict between the Catholics and Protestants in Ireland in terms of the different "mental realities" that people in each group have created for themselves. This psychologist most likely adheres to the _____ cognitive viewpoint.

a. artificial intelligence
b. cognitive neuroscience
c. introspection
d. social constructivism

16. As a young Viennese medical student in the 1880's, Freud began to focus on the disorder called ____, in which physical disorders such as blindness develop without any organic cause.

a. repression
b. hysteria
c. psychodynamism
d. monism

17. The psychological defense mechanism of _____ is thought to protect people from anxiety by keeping anxiety-producing thoughts, feelings, memories, and impulses in the unconscious.

a. insight
b. psychoanalysis
c. hysteria
d. repression

18. Freud's psychoanalytic theory ____.

a. has had no effect on contemporary psychological theory
b. continues to influence both basic and applied psychology
c. continues to influence basic but not applied psychology
d. continues to influence applied but not basic psychology

19. People associated with the philosophical perspective of British empiricism ____.

a. view observation as a more valid approach to knowledge than reasoning
b. view reasoning as a more valid approach to knowledge than observation
c. believe that internal factors are the major determinants of human behavior
d. assume that most human behavior is motivated by unconscious forces

20. A psychologist is being interviewed on a local news program regarding the recent problems with school violence. The psychologist proposes that we need to significantly change the environments in which our children are being raised by more heavily reinforcing the behaviors we would like to see in our kids. This psychologist is most likely associated with the ____ psychological perspective.

a. humanistic
b. psychodynamic
c. cognitive
d. behavioral

21. The school of thought that emphasizes environmental control of behavior is known as ____.

a. behaviorism
b. cognitivism
c. psychodynamism
d. Gestalt psychology

_____ 22. Susan is having trouble with anxiety and is working with a psychologist to address this problem. As part of her treatment, the psychologist teaches Susan 1) how to change her anxiety-provoking thoughts and 2) how to change her environment so that it reinforces the new behaviors she wants to learn. Susan's therapist is <u>most likely</u> associated with the _____ area of psychology.

    a. humanistic
    b. psychodynamic
    c. sociocultural
    d. cognitive-behavioral

_____ 23. The _____ perspective tends to ignore mental processes because they are not directly observable. In contrast, the _____ perspective acknowledges the importance of both the environment and internal mental processes in determining behavior.

    a. cognitive-behavioral; behavioral
    b. humanistic; cognitive
    c. behavioral; cognitive
    d. behavioral; cognitive-behavioral

_____ 24. Nguyen is working with a psychologist who pays a great deal of attention to how he finds personal meaning in his life. The psychologist also focuses on the power of choice and free will. This psychologist <u>most likely</u> adheres to the _____ psychological perspective.

    a. behavioral
    b. psychodynamic
    c. humanistic
    d. biological

_____ 25. Terror management theorists believe that _____.

    a. people's unconscious desires motivate their behavior
    b. the best way to motivate children is to constantly punish them for their actions so that they live in terror
    c. people are motivated to support and defend their cultural worldview and to live up to its standards of value to allay death-related anxiety
    d. people are motivated by a "death wish"

_____ 26. Humanistic theorists believe that people are motivated to reach their full potential, a state called _____.

    a. self-actualization
    b. terror management
    c. existential anxiety
    d. existential bliss

27. Gabriella was raised in a family where individual achievement and accomplishment were stressed by both of her parents. She was constantly encouraged to set personal goals for her self and to strive to achieve them. The values emphasized by Gabriella's family are <u>most consistent</u> with ____.

    a. collectivism
    b. structuralism
    c. individualism
    d. functionalism

28. The enduring beliefs, values, behaviors, and traditions shared by a large group of people and passed on from one generation to the next is called ____.

    a. culture
    b. society
    c. norms
    d. collectivism

29. After scoring the game-winning penalty kick in the 1999 World Cup, U.S. player Brandy Chastain took off her jersey in her excitement and revealed her sports bra. Some people took offense to this, probably because Chastain violated ____.

    a. culture
    b. the principles of individualism
    c. the principles of collectivism
    d. cultural norms

30. Of the following, the one which is <u>not</u> a level of analysis for understanding the causes of behavior is the____ level.

    a. biological
    b. unconscious
    c. psychological
    d. environmental

<u>**True/False Items:**</u> *Write T or F in the space provided to the left of each item.*

1. The goal of basic research is to solve practical problems.

2. Psychologists are interested in controlling behavior.

3. Natural selection is a process that selects behaviors that have survival value, according to evolutionary psychology.

4. According to the biological perspective, evolution has not played a role in the development of modern human behavior.

5. Gestalt psychology is concerned with how elements of experience are organized into wholes.

6. According to the social constructivist view, there is a single "reality."

_____ 7. The perspective that emphasizes unconscious processes is the psychodynamic perspective.

_____ 8. An attempt to bridge the gap between the behavioral and cognitive perspectives is called cognitive behaviorism.

_____ 9. Individual goals are subordinated to those of the group in individualistic cultures.

_____ 10. In an interaction, the presence or strength of one factor can influence the effects of other factors.

Short Answer Questions

1. How do monism and dualism differ?

2. What are the basic principles of evolutionary psychology?

3. What kinds of factors do biological psychologists use to explain human behavior?

4. What kinds of factors do humanistic psychologists use to explain human behavior?

5. How do sociocultural factors affect behavior?

Essay Questions

1. **Why** would biological factors influence human behavior?

2. **Why** would environmental factors such as culture influence human behavior?

3. If we believe that behavior is affected by environmental factors, does that mean that people don't have personal control over their behavior? Explain your answer.

4. Although <u>both</u> biological and environmental factors are likely to affect behavior, would one set of factors be more likely to affect behavior than the other?

5. Why would evolutionary factors affect behavior?

Study Sheet 1.1 Psychological Perspectives on Behavior

Perspective	View of Human Nature	Focus of Study
Biological		
Cognitive		
Psychodynamic		
Behavioral		
Humanistic		
Sociocultural		

Study Sheet 1.2 Integrating the Perspectives

Behavior to be explained _____

Biological explanation for behavior

Psychological explanation for behavior

Environmental explanation for behavior

Study Sheet 1.3: Internet Scavenger Hunt

1. Who was the first woman to be elected president of the American Psychological Association?

2. In what year was she elected?

3. What percentage of doctorates in psychology are currently awarded to women?

4. What percentage of doctorates in psychology are currently awarded to African Americans?

5. What percentage of doctorates in psychology are currently awarded to Hispanics?

6. What percentage of doctorates in psychology are currently awarded to Asian Americans?

7. What percentage of doctorates in psychology are currently awarded to Native Americans?

8. Who was the first American woman to be awarded a doctorate in psychology?

9. Who was the first African American male to be awarded a doctorate in psychology?

10. Who became the American Psychological Association's first African American president?

Answer Keys

Answer Key for Key Terms

1. s	11. y	21. dd	31. g
2. j	12. z	22. cc	32. d
3. l	13. q	23. o	33. b
4. ii	14. hh	24. bb	34. ee
5. i	15. a	25. u	35. t
6. f	16. e	26. c	36. ff
7. n	17. k	27. m	37. h
8. ll	18. kk	28. r	38. gg
9. w	19. x	29. aa	
10. jj	20. p	30. v	

Answer Key for Key People

1. e	7. k
2. j	8. g
3. b	9. c
4. a	10. f
5. h	11. i
6. d	

Answer Key for Review at a Glance

1. behavior	16. sociocultural	31. psychodynamic
2. basic research	17. mind-body dualism	32. Sigmund Freud
3. applied research	18. monism	33. British empiricism
4. cooperative experiences	19. genetic factors	34. environmental
5. jigsaw program	20. natural selection	35. cognitive behaviorism
6. describe	21. evolutionary psychology	36. self-actualization
7. understand	22. sociobiologists	37. terror management theory
8. predict	23. behavior genetics	38. culture
9. control	24. information processors	39. norms
10. perspectives	25. introspection	40. biological
11. biological	26. functionalism	41. psychological
12. cognitive	27. Gestalt psychology	42. environmental
13. psychodynamic	28. Jean Piaget	43. interaction
14. behavioral	29. artificial intelligence	44. clinical
15. humanistic	30. social constructivists	45. physiological

Answer Key for Practice Test Multiple Choice Questions

1.	b	16.	b
2.	b	17.	d
3.	c	18.	b
4.	a	19.	a
5.	d	20.	d
6.	b	21.	a
7.	c	22.	d
8.	d	23.	d
9.	c	24.	c
10.	b	25.	c
11.	a	26.	a
12.	b	27.	c
13.	c	28.	a
14.	d	29.	d
15.	d	30.	b

Answer Key for Practice Test True/False Questions

1.	F	6.	F
2.	T	7.	T
3.	T	8.	T
4.	F	9.	F
5.	T	10.	T

Answer Key for Practice Test Short Answer Questions

1. Monists believed that the mind is not separate spiritual entity from the body and thus is subject to the same physical forces as the body is. Mind-body dualists, on the other hand, believed that the mind is a separate spiritual entity from the body and thus is not governed by physical laws. Most modern biological psychologists would agree with the monist position.

2. Evolutionary psychologists believe that evolution has played an important role in the development of human behavior. Behaviors that enhanced the abilities of individuals to adapt to their environment in turn increased the likelihood of survival of these individuals and their ability to reproduce. These behaviors were then selected through natural selection.

3. Psychologists using the biological perspective rely on four major factors in explaining human behavior. First, they study the structures and processes of the brain. Second, they study genetic factors through twin and adoption studies in the field of behavior genetics. Third, they study biochemical factors. Fourth, they study the influence of evolution on the development of modern human behaviors.

4. Humanistic psychologists emphasize a number of tendencies in their explanations of human behavior. They believe that people have free will, innate tendencies toward growth and self-actualization, and attempt to find meaning from their existence. This is a positive view of human nature, as it suggests that people will grow to their full potential if the environment is benign.

5. The sociocultural perspective emphasizes the roles of culture (enduring values, beliefs, behaviors and traditions shared by a group of people) and norms. Norms are rules that specify proper behavior for a particular culture or society.

Answer Key for Practice Test Essay Questions

1. Biological factors would likely influence human behavior for a number of reasons:

   a. We are biological creatures just as dogs, birds, and dolphins are, and we believe that biological factors affect the behaviors of members of those species
   b. Our brains control various behaviors, and the brain is a biological structure.
   c. Like other species, we are subject to evolutionary forces
   d. Genes and biochemical factors influence the development of our bodies, and we use our bodies to engage in behavior.

2. Environmental factors such as culture likely influence human behavior for a number of reasons:

   a. According to the ideas of British empiricism, we gain knowledge through our senses.
   b. The basic principles of learning apply to animal and human species.
   c. We are products of our culture and societies and thus behave in different ways from people in different cultures and societies.
   d. The nature of our environment determines what behaviors we need to engage in to adapt and survive

3. Even if we believe that environmental factors have a great deal of influence over our behavior, that does not mean that no other factors influence them. For instance, a person can learn to control biological factors through procedures like biofeedback. We can also alter many environmental factors. For instance, we may work to change cultural norms and other aspects of culture that influence our behaviors.

4. It is highly likely that both biological factors and environmental factors influence behavior. It is difficult to determine which would be a more important factor. They likely interact with one another in complex ways to produce complex human behaviors and interact as well with various psychological factors, such as cognition and personality.

5. Evolutionary factors likely affect human behavior because of two main reasons:

   a. First, we are biological creatures. There is a great deal of evidence that evolution has affected plants and other animals over millions of years through natural selection. Psychologists using the biological perspective have good reason to think similar procedures have applied to human behavior over millions of years.
   b. Second, all of the perspectives mentioned in the textbook stress the adaptability of human beings to their environment. As evolution works through the natural selection of traits and behaviors that promote survival, it is likely that evolutionary factors have affected the development of human behavior.

Chapter 2
STUDYING BEHAVIOR SCIENTIFICALLY

Learning Objectives: *These questions are taken from the directed questions found in the margins of the chapter. After reading the chapter, you should be able to answer these questions.*

1. What key scientific attitudes did Darley and Latané display?

2. How does Darley and Latané's research illustrate the basic steps of the scientific process?

3. What is a hypothesis?

4. What is a theory? How does it differ from a hypothesis?

5. Explain the major drawback of hindsight understanding?

6. What approach to understanding do scientists prefer? Why?

7. Describe the characteristics of a good theory?

8. Why are operational definitions important?

9. Describe the major ways psychologists measure behavior, and the limitations of each.

10. What is unobtrusive measurement?

11. What is a case study? Identify its advantages and drawbacks.

12. How can the findings of case studies mislead us in everyday life?

13. What is naturalistic observation, and what is its major advantage?

14. What biases can occur when conducting naturalistic observations?

15. Explain what random sampling is and why survey researchers use it.

16. What are some advantages and disadvantages of survey research?

17. Explain the main goal of correlational research, and how this is achieved.

18. Why are we unable to draw causal conclusions from correlational findings?

19. What do the terms "positive" and "negative" correlation mean?

20. How is a correlation coefficient interpreted?

21. Explain how correlational research can be used to predict behavior.

22. Describe the logic of experimentation.

23. What are independent and dependent variables? How are they related?

24. Why are control groups important?

25. How does random assignment in experiments differ from random sampling in surveys?

26. In experiments, identify an alternative to using random assignment.

27. Identify the independent and dependent variables in Rosenzweig's experiment.

28. Why do researchers manipulate two independent variables in the same experiment?

29. What are the primary differences between the experimental and descriptive/correlational approaches?

30. Explain why confounding decreases the internal validity of experiments.

31. What are demand characteristics? Why do they lower the internal validity of experiments?

32. Explain how the "placebo effect" can cloud the interpretation of research results.

33. Why do experimenter expectancy effects lower the internal validity of experiments?

34. How do researchers minimize experimenter expectancy effects?

35. How does external validity differ from internal validity?

36. Describe the purpose of meta-analysis.

37. Identify the major ethical issues in human research.

38. Why does some research involve deception? What ethical principle does deception violate?

39. What are the justifications for, and criticisms of, research in which animals are harmed?

40. As a critical thinker, what questions should you ask when someone makes a claim or assertion?

Chapter Overview

This chapter will help you to understand how to evaluate psychological research. The chapter opens with some basic steps in the scientific process, which apply to all scientific research, not just that in psychology. Once you start with an initial observation or question, you then form a hypothesis, or a tentative prediction or explanation about the phenomenon you are studying. Then you test the hypothesis by conducting research, analyzing the data, and determining if your hypothesis is correct or should be rejected.

Further research on the phenomenon then helps to build theory, a set of formal statements about how and why certain events are related. New hypotheses are then derived from the theory and tested. There are two major approaches to understanding behavior: hindsight understanding (after-the-fact explanations) and understanding through prediction, control, and theory building (the scientific approach). Psychologists study and measure variables, operationally defining them in terms of the procedures used to measure them. Psychologists rely on self-reports, reports by others, physiological measures, and behavioral responses to measure variables.

Psychologists use several methods of doing research. Descriptive research identifies how humans and animals behave. Case studies, which are in-depth analyses of individuals, groups, or events, are a type of descriptive research. Studies of animals or humans in natural settings are examples of naturalistic observation. Questionnaires or interviews are administered to people in survey research. It is important that the characteristics of the sample represent the population so that the researchers can make accurate conclusions about the population. This is often accomplished through random sampling. Associations between variables are measured through correlational research. If two variables are correlated, that does not necessarily mean that one variable causes the other variable. The correlation coefficient is a statistic that measures the association between the variables. A positive correlation occurs when higher scores on one variable are associated with higher scores on another variable. A negative correlation occurs when higher scores on one variable are associated with lower scores on another variable. The plus or minus sign of a correlation coefficient tells you the direction of the relationship, while the absolute value of the statistic tells you the strength of the relationship.

Correlations help researchers examine the relationships between variables. Experiments are used to determine cause-and-effect relationships. When performing experiments, researchers manipulate one or more variables (the independent variable[s]) and measure whether this manipulation produces changes in a second variable or variables (the dependent variable[s]). The researcher attempts to control for other factors (extraneous or confounding variables) that might influence the outcome. In many experiments, participants are randomly assigned to either an experimental group (receives the treatment) or a control group (does not receive the treatment). The two groups are then compared statistically to see if there is any difference between them. Another way to design an experiment is to expose each participant to all conditions of the experiment.

Psychologists are particularly interested in assuring others that their research is valid. Internal validity represents the degree to which an experiment supports clear causal conclusions. It is important to try to rule out other factors that may have influenced the results so that the researcher can conclude that it was the manipulation of the independent variable, rather than some other factor, that produced changes in the dependent variable. If the researcher cannot do that, he or she has a problem with the confounding of variables. Some problems that researchers try to control are demand characteristics, or cues that participants pick up about how they are "supposed" to behave, placebo effects, in which participants' expectancies affect their behavior, and experimenter expectancy effects, by which researchers subtly and unintentionally influence the behavior of their participants through their actions. External validity refers to the extent to which the results of a particular study can be generalized to other people, settings, and conditions. Researchers rely on replication, or the ability of a study to be repeated with the same results, to determine the external validity of the findings.

Ethical standards are very important in psychological research. The American Psychological Association (APA) guideline of informed consent states that participants should be given a full description of the procedures to be followed, should be informed of any risks that might be involved, and should be told that they have the right to withdraw from the study without penalty. Sometimes, psychologists use deception studies, in which participants are misled about the nature of the study. These experiments are controversial but may be necessary to obtain natural, spontaneous responses from people. Ethical standards are also applied to research with animals. Research with animals is controversial, but most research psychologists would probably argue that research with animals is necessary to further knowledge of both animal and human behavior.

Chapter Outline

Scientific Principles in Psychology
    Scientific Attitudes
    Gathering Evidence: Steps in the Scientific Process
    Two Approaches to Understanding Behavior
        Hindsight Understanding
        Understanding Through Predictions, Control, and Theory Building
    Defining and Measuring Variables
        Self-Report Measures
        Reports by Others
        Physiological Measures
        Behavioral Observations

Methods of Research
    Descriptive Research: Recording Events
        Case Studies: The Hmong Sudden Death Syndrome
        Naturalistic Observation: Chimpanzees, Tool Use, and Cultural Learning
        Survey Research: How Well Do You Sleep?
    Correlational Research: Measuring Associations Between Events
        A Correlational Study: Parenting Styles and Children's Adjustment
        The Correlation Coefficient
        Correlation as a Basis for Prediction
    Experiments: Examining Cause and Effect
        The Logic of Experimentation
        Independent and Dependent Variables
        Experimental and Control Groups
        Two Basic Ways to Design and Experiment
        Manipulating One Independent Variable: Effects of Environmental Stimulation on Brain Development
        Manipulating Two Independent Variables: Effects of Alcohol and Expectations on Sexual Arousal
    Experimental Versus Descriptive/Correlational Approaches

Threats to the Validity of Research
  Confounding of Variables
  Demand Characteristics
  Placebo Effects
  Experimenter Expectancy Effects
  Replicating and Generalizing the Findings
    Psychological Frontiers: Science and the Paranormal
  Meta-Analysis: Combining the Results of Many Studies

Ethical Principles in Human and Animal Research
  Ethical Standards in Human Research
  Ethical Standards in Animal Research

Critical Thinking in Science and Everyday Life
    Applications of Psychological Science: Evaluating Claims in Research and
    Everyday Life

Key Terms: *Write the letter of the definition next to the term in the space provided.*

1. ___ archival measures

2. ___ case study

3. ___ confounding of variables

4. ___ control group

5. ___ correlation coefficient

6. ___ correlational research

7. ___ demand characteristics

8. ___ dependent variable

9. ___ descriptive research

10. ___ double-blind procedure

11. ___ experiment

12. ___ experimental group

13. ___ experimental expectancy effects

14. ___ external validity

a. every member of the population has an equal probability of being chosen

b. defines a variable in terms of the specific procedures used to produce or measure it

c. the factor that is measured by the experimenter

d. cues that participants pick up about a hypothesis

e. an in-depth analysis of an individual, group, or event

f. the researcher measures two variables and then statistically analyzes whether they are related

g. both experimenter and participant are kept unaware as to which condition the participant is in

h. a tentative explanation or prediction

i. the group that receives a treatment

j. degree to which the results of a study can be generalized to other people, settings, and conditions

k. the observation of behavior in its natural setting

l. group that does not receive a treatment

m. a statistical procedure for combining the results of different studies that examine the same topic

n. a set of formal statements that explains how and why certain events are related to each other

15. ___ hypothesis

o. when participants have been given a description of experimental procedures, have been informed of risks, and have been given freedom of withdrawal

16. ___ independent variable

p. a statistic that indicates the direction and strength of the relation between two variables

17. ___ informed consent

q. already existing records or documents

18. ___ internal validity

r. an inactive or inert substance

19. ___ meta-analysis

s. occurs when higher scores on one variable are associated with lower scores on a second variable

20. ___ naturalistic observation

t. a method for examining cause-effect relationships

21. ___ negative correlation

u. represents the degree to which an experiment supports clear causal conclusions

22. ___ operational definition

v. information about a topic is obtained by administering questionnaires or interviews

23. ___ placebo

w. seeks to identify how humans and other animals behave, particularly in natural settings

24. ___ placebo effect

x. each participant has an equal likelihood of being assigned to any one group within an experiment

25. ___ population

y. when people receiving a treatment show a change in behavior because of their expectations

26. ___ positive correlation

z. individuals about whom we are interested in drawing conclusions

27. ___ random assignment

aa. any characteristic that can vary

28. ___ random sampling

bb. ways that experimenters influence their participants to act in ways that are consistent with the hypothesis

29. ___ replication

cc. the process of repeating a study to determine whether the original findings can be duplicated

30. ___ representative sample

dd. a subset of individuals drawn from the larger population of interest

31. ___ sample

ee. higher scores on one variable are associated with higher scores on a second variable

32. ___ scatterplot

ff. when two variables are intertwined in such a way that we cannot determine which one has influenced a D.V.

33. ___ survey research

gg. sample that reflects characteristics of the population

34. ___ theory

hh. graph that depicts the relationship between variables

35. ___ variable

ii. the factor that is manipulated by the experimenter

Review at a Glance: *Write the term that best fits the blank to review what you learned in this chapter.*

Scientific Principles in Psychology

Doing scientific research involves using the scientific process. Once a researcher has observed a phenomenon or formulated an initial question about it, he or she forms a (1) _____, or tentative explanation or prediction, about it. Researchers then test the idea, analyze the data, and determine if the hypothesis was correct or should be rejected. As additional evidence comes in, researchers attempt to build (2) _____, which are sets of formal statements that explain how and why events are related. There are two main approaches to understanding behavior. After-the-fact understanding used to explain a behavior is known as (3) _____ _____. Scientists, though, typically try to understand a phenomenon through (4) _____, (5) _____, and (6) _____ _____. Psychologists study (7) _____, which are characteristics that vary. Defining a variable in terms of the specific procedures used to measure or produce it is known as an (8) _____ _____. Psychologists measure behavior in a number of different ways. (9)_____ - _____ _____ ask people to report on their own knowledge, beliefs or feelings. Measures of heart rate, blood pressure etc. are known as (10) _____ _____. Already existing records of people's behavior that are used for research are known as (11) _____ _____.

Methods of Research

An in-depth analysis of an individual, group, or event is called a (12) _____ _____. Sometimes researchers are interested in describing behavior that occurs in its natural setting, a type of research called (13) _____ _____. Information about a topic is obtained by administering questionnaires or interviews to many people in (14) _____ _____. In survey research, researchers are interested in making conclusions about a (15) _____, which represents the entire set of individuals about whom we are interested in making conclusions. Because it is often impractical to study an entire population, researchers typically study a subset of that population called a (16) _____. To draw valid conclusions about the population, the sample must accurately reflect the characteristics of the population. Such a sample is known as a (17) _____ _____. When every member of the population has an equal probability of being chosen for the sample, the researcher has created a (18) _____ _____. When researchers are interested in measuring the associations between events, they conduct (19) _____ _____, though such research does not indicate causation. A statistic that measures the direction and strength of the relationship between two variables is called a (20) _____ _____. When higher scores on one variable are associated with lower scores on a second variable, the researcher has discovered a (21) _____ correlation. When higher scores on one variable are associated with higher scores on a second variable, the researcher has discovered a (22) _____ correlation. A type of research method that is used to determine cause-and-effect relationships is known as an (23) _____. In an experiment, the variable that is manipulated by the experimenter is known as the (24) _____ variable, whereas the variable that is measured by the experimenter is known as the (25) _____ _____ variable. Through (26)

_____ _____ , participants in an experiment are often assigned to groups. The (27) _____ group is the group that receives a treatment, while the (28) _____ group does not.

Threats to the Validity of Research

It is important for researchers to establish that their research is valid. (29) _____ _____ represents the degree to which an experiment supports clear causal conclusions. A problem with internal validity exists when two variables are intertwined in such a way that we cannot determine which one has influenced a dependent variable, a condition known as (30) _____ _____ _____. Cues that participants pick up about the hypothesis of a study are known as (31) _____ _____. Inactive or inert substances known as (32) _____ are often used to control for participant expectancy effects. When an experimenter subtly and unintentionally influences the behavior of participants so that it is consistent with the hypothesis of the study, the effects are called (33) _____ _____ effects. Researchers are interested in establishing not only internal validity but also in establishing (34) _____ _____, which is the degree to which the results of a study can be generalized to other people, settings, and conditions. To determine whether a tentative conclusion reached in one study is valid, the results of the study must be (35) _____. Research designed to statistically combine the results of many studies involves a statistical procedure known as (36) _____ _____.

Ethical Principles in Human and Animal Research

When research participants are given a full description of the research, are informed of risks, and are told that they are free to withdraw from the study without penalty, the participants have received (37) _____ _____. Studies in which participants are misled as to the nature of the study are known as (38) _____ studies.

Apply What You Know

1. Remember that operational definitions define a variable in terms of the specific procedures used to produce or measure it. Use Study Sheet 2.1 to write operational definitions for each of the following concepts: intelligence, "good memory," aggression, love, and happiness.

2. Famed psychologist Dr. Lena Onmee hypothesizes that stress and anger cause depression. However, having been out of school too long, Dr. Onmee has forgotten the basics of experimentation, so she turns to you, ace psychology student, for help in designing her experiment. Describe how you would advise her to set up the experiment by using Study Sheet 2.2.

3. Use Study Sheet 2.3 to find seven problems with the following study:

Space psychologist Spiff lands on the dreaded planet Zorg. Nothing much is known of the Zorgian people, but they are rumored to be vicious and dangerous to humans. To determine if this is the case, Spiff decides to do an experiment. He hypothesizes that the Zorgians are only likely to be vicious and dangerous when they are angered, so he defines anger as his dependent variable. A group of southern Zorgians, who are known to be quite different from the northern Zorgians, volunteer to participate in Spiff's study. He lets the angry Zorgians be in his control group and the non-angry Zorgians be in his experimental group and tells them the hypothesis of the study before it begins. He then measures the viciousness and dangerousness of both groups and compares them by using meta-analysis.

Stretching Your Geographies

1. Access the U.S. Census Bureau website (http://www.census.gov) and determine the percentages of males and females, racial groups, and age groups in the county in which your college or high school is located in the 1990 census. Describe how you, as a researcher, would draw a representative sample from that population.

Practice Test

<u>Multiple Choice Items:</u> *Please write the letter corresponding to your answer in the space to the left of each item.*

_____ 1. A tentative explanation or prediction about some phenomenon is called a ____.

    a. theory
    b. thesis
    c. hypothesis
    d. variable

_____ 2. Theories are ____.

    a. tentative explanations or predictions about some phenomenon
    b. formal statements that explain how and why events are related
    c. characteristics that vary
    d. definitions of variables in terms that they are produced or measured

_____ 3. One of the problems of after-the-fact or "hindsight" explanations is that ____.

    a. there are many ways of explaining past events and there is usually no way to know which of these ways is correct
    b. they fail to provide a foundation on which further scientific study can occur
    c. they are usually too theoretically complex and sophisticated
    d. they overemphasize the importance of external validity

_____ 4. Bored with a life of fighting supercriminals and trying to stay resistant to the charms of Lois Lane, Superman tries to find a way to occupy his time. Deciding to study superhuman powers, he defines such powers as being "faster than a speeding bullet, more powerful than a locomotive, and able to leap tall buildings in a single bound." Superman has created a(n) ____ of the variable.

    a. hypothesis
    b. self-report measure
    c. physiological measure
    d. operational definition

_____ 5. A researcher is interested in studying factors that influence interpersonal attraction. In a study designed to explore this variable, the researcher uses a very attractive person for an assistant. Interpersonal attraction is then assessed by whether or not the people participating in the study call up the attractive assistant to ask the person on a date. In this example, callin up the attractive assistant represents a(n) ____ of interpersonal attraction.

    a. correlational study
    b. hypothesis
    c. case study
    d. operational definition

_____ 6. A social psychologist is interested in studying aggression in sports fans. He goes to various sporting events and keeps track of the number of aggressive acts that occur between fans using a well-defined coding system. This psychologist is using _____ to measure behavior.

a. self-report measures
b. physiological measures
c. behavioral observations
d. reports by others

_____ 7. Trying to determine why men cheat on their wives, a research psychologist studies Bill Clinton in an in-depth analysis. This psychologist is using the _____ method of study.

a. correlational
b. experimental
c. archival
d. case study

_____ 8. In order to learn about the social behavior of children, a developmental psychologist goes to an elementary school, finds a seat near one of the windows in a classroom, and watches the children playing on the playground outside during recess. This psychologist is engaged in _____.

a. naturalistic observation
b. correlational research
c. a case study
d. experimental research

_____ 9. Putting his research plan to work, Superman decides to study Batman, Robin, Aquaman, and Spiderman, and apply his results to all superheroes. In this case "all superheroes" is how Superman is defining his _____.

a. sample
b. random sample
c. representative sample
d. population

_____ 10. Batman, Robin, Aquaman, and Spiderman make up Superman's _____ in this case.

a. sample
b. random sample
c. representative sample
d. population

_____ 11. Dr. Jones is interested in conducting a survey of all the college students at her university. She is careful when conducting her research to make sure that each student on campus has an equal chance of participating in her survey. To create her survey sample, Dr. Jones is using random ___.

a. sampling
b. assignment
c. preference
d. appointment

_____ 12. The use of a _____ sample best establishes _____ validity.

a. non-random; internal
b. representative; external
c. representative; internal
d. non-random; external

_____ 13. When it is not clear whether variable X caused variable Y or vice-versa, there is a(n) _____.

a. demand characteristic
b. bidirectional causality problem
c. third-variable problem
d. experimenter expectancy effect

_____ 14. Dr. Little has heard that people tend to become more politically conservative as they get older and decides to conduct a study to see if this is true. She conducts a telephone survey where she asks participants how old they are and their political identification. She then uses statistics to see if there is a relationship between age and political identification. The design that **best describes** Dr. Little's research is _____.

a. experimental research
b. correlational research
c. naturalistic observation
d. behavioral observation

_____ 15. Dr. Gonzalez has just completed a correlational study where he found a strong association between parental expectations and child academic achievement. In other words, children who perform well in school tend to have parents who have high expectations for their children. However, Dr. Gonzalez can't tell which variable causes the other. It may be that high expectations cause children to perform better but it may be that children who perform better in school cause their parents to have higher expectations. This particular problem is known as _____.

a. the bidirectional causality problem
b. the third variable problem
c. poor external validity
d. the experimenter expectancy effect

_____ 16. After years of experience, super researcher Dr. Yo G. Bear finds that the more food from stolen picnic baskets in Jellystone Park that bears eat, the sicker they get. Dr. Bear has observed a _____ relationship between the variables.

    a. negative correlational
    b. positive correlational
    c. zero correlational
    d. cause-and-effect

_____ 17. A "Survivor" contestant notices that the more worms a member caught for his or her tribe to eat, the less votes to be voted off the island he or she received in Tribal Council. This contestant is has observed a _____ relationship between the variables.

    a. negative correlational
    b. positive correlational
    c. zero correlational
    d. cause-and-effect

_____ 18. For psychologists, the most direct method for testing cause-and-effect relationships is ____.

    a. correlational studies
    b. archival studies
    c. surveys
    d. experiments

_____ 19. In its simplest form, an experiment has three essential characteristics. Of the following, the one which is <u>not</u> a characteristic of experiments is ____.

    a. an experimental manipulation of an independent variable
    b. an experimental manipulation of a dependent variable
    c. a measurement of a dependent variable
    d. attempts to control for extraneous factors

_____ 20. Dr. White wants to look at the impact of failure on self-esteem. Dr. White designs an experiment were half of the participants are led to believe that they have failed on an ambiguous task, while the other half of the participants are told that they have succeeded. Dr. White then has the people in his study complete a questionnaire measuring self-esteem, and she looks to see if there are any differences between the success and failure groups. In this example, self-esteem would be considered the ____ variable.

    a. dependent
    b. independent
    c. placebo
    d. confounding

_____ 21. Evil arch-criminal Lex Luthor, having discovered that kryptonite destroys Superman's powers, wonders if the substance will also cripple other superheroes. He thus assigns one group of superheroes to an experimental group, feeding them kryptonite soup, and assigns another group to a control condition that gets chicken soup. In this case, the type of soup is the _____.

a. dependent variable
b. placebo
c. independent variable
d. correlational variable

_____ 22. A clinical psychologist has developed a new form of psychotherapy to treat a particular personality disorder. In order to test its effectiveness, a group of people with the personality disorder is selected to receive the therapy for 8 weeks. A second group of people with the disorder is also created but this group receives no therapy at all. At the end of the 8 weeks, the mental health of the people in both groups is assessed to evaluate the new psychotherapy. In this study, the people who did **not** receive any therapy would be in the _____ group.

a. experimental
b. control
c. random
d. sample

_____ 23. Bored with life on Gilligan's island, the Professor decides to study the effects of rubbing coconut oil on people's skulls. He randomly assigns three castaways to his experimental group and the other three to his control group and measures the mean intelligence level of both groups. The rubbin of coconut oil on people's skulls is the _____ variable.

a. dependent
b. confounding
c. independent
d. correlational

_____ 24. In survey research, random _____ is typically used to insure that a sample is representative, while in experiments, random _____ is used to balance differences between participants across the various experimental groups.

a. sampling; assignment
b. assignment; sampling
c. sampling; appointment
d. appointment; assignment

_____ 25. Random assignment controls for important differences between individual participants by ____. This is in contrast to designs where each participant is exposed to each condition or group in an experiment. These designs control for individual differences by ____.

a. balancing them; randomly sampling them
b. holding them constant; balancing them
c. balancing them; holding them constant
d. randomly sampling them; holding them constant

_____ 26. A researcher is interested in interpersonal attraction and the factors that effect it. She designs a study where she looks at the effect of similarity and social warmth on interpersonal attraction. Participants in her study meet a target person who either is or is not similar to the participant (the similarity variable) and who is either friendly or is aloof (the social warmth variable). After interacting with the target person under these conditions, participants are then asked to rate how attractive they think the target person is. In this study, similarity and social warmth are the ____ variables and interpersonal attraction is the ____ variable.

a. independent; dependent
b. dependent; independent
c. confounding; dependent
d. independent; confounding

_____ 27. Sally has been suffering from depression and finally decides to seek help from a clinical psychologist. After a couple of months of therapy, Sally's depression starts to lift. However, her improvement really isn't due to any of the therapy she has received from her therapist but instead is a product of Sally's expectation that psychotherapy is supposed to be effective and therefore she should be getting better. This example is **best considered** an example of ____.

a. experimenter expectancy effects
b. the double-blind effect
c. the placebo effect
d. a study with high external validity

_____ 28. In a famous experiment by Rosenthal and Jacobson (1968), teachers at an elementary school were told at the beginning of the year that certain students were "late bloomers" and most likely these particular students were going to become strong students during the school-year ahead. Sure enough, by the end of the year, the identified students were doing much better in school. Interestingly, the researchers had selected these children randomly at the beginning of the year. The findings in this study are **most similar or analogous** to the problem of ____.

a. demand characteristics
b. experimenter expectancy effects
c. the placebo effect
d. random sampling

_____ 29. Bored with just encouraging Americans to have more and better sex, diminutive Dr. Ruth decides to study why so many more men than women have extramarital affairs. To study this question, she recruits Ted Kennedy, Frank Gifford, Marv Albert, and Bill Clinton for her study. However, her granting agency, worried that it is throwing its money down the proverbial rat hole, wonders why she has recruited such an unrepresentative sample of celebrities for her study. The agency is evidently worried about the _____ of Dr. Ruth's work.

a. internal validity
b. random assignment
c. experimenter expectancy effects
d. external validity

_____ 30. When research participants are given a full description of the procedures to be followed, are informed of any risks that might be involved, and are told that they are free to withdraw from the study at any time without penalty, they have been given _____ procedures.

a. informed consent
b. meta-analysis
c. psychological risk
d. social risk

True/False Items: *Write T or F in the space provided to the left of each item.*

_____ 1. A hypothesis is a tentative explanation or prediction about some phenomenon.

_____ 2. An operational definition is defined as any characteristic that can vary.

_____ 3. The tendency to respond in a socially acceptable manner rather than according to how one truly feels or behaves is called a demand characteristic.

_____ 4. Already existing records or documents used to study some behavioral phenomenon are called archival measures.

_____ 5. When every member of the population has an equal probability of being chosen for the sample, the sample is called a representative sample.

_____ 6. If I predict that the more questions from this study guide you get correct, the higher the score you will get on your next exam, I am predicting a positive correlation between the variables.

_____ 7. The variable that is manipulated by an experimenter is called the independent variable.

_____ 8. The degree to which an experiment supports a clear causal conclusion is known as the study's external validity.

_____ 9. Cues that participants pick up about the hypothesis of the study or about how they are supposed to behave are known as placebo effects.

_____ 10. The process of repeating a study to determine whether the original findings can be duplicated is known as meta-analysis.

Short Answer Questions

1. What types of physiological measures are used by psychologists to study behavior, and why are they subject to interpretive problems?

2. Describe what correlational research is used to study and what correlation coefficients mean.

3. How are independent and dependent variables and experimental and control groups used in experiments?

4. Distinguish between random sampling and random assignment.

5. What are some of the basic ethical standards used in human research?

Essay Questions

1. Why is it better to study behavior through prediction, control, and theory building than through hindsight understanding?

2. Describe the four types of measurements used by psychologists to measure variables.

3. Describe three major types of descriptive research.

4. Explain the logic of experimentation.

5. Describe three major threats to the internal validity of an experiment.

Study Sheet 2.1   Operational Definitions

Intelligence

"Good memory"

Aggression

Love

Happiness

Study Sheet 2.2   Designing an Experiment

Hypothesis: Stress and anger cause depression

Independent variables:

Dependent variable:

Operational definition of dependent variable:

Diagram the experimental design (experimental and control groups, random assignment etc.)

Study Sheet 2.3   Problems with the design

1.

2.

3.

4.

5.

6.

7.

Answer Keys

Answer Key for Key Terms

1. q	13. bb	25. z
2. e	14. j	26. ee
3. ff	15. h	27. x
4. l	16. ii	28. a
5. p	17. o	29. cc
6. f	18. u	30. gg
7. d	19. m	31. dd
8. c	20. k	32. hh
9. w	21. s	33. v
10. g	22. b	34. n
11. t	23. r	35. aa
12. I	24. y	

Answer Key for Review at a Glance

1. hypothesis	11. archival records	21. negative	31. demand characteristics
2. theories	12. case study	22. positive	32. placebos
3. hindsight understanding	13. naturalistic observation	23. experiment	33. experimenter expectancy
4. prediction	14. survey research	24. independent	34. external validity
5. control	15. population	25. dependent	35. replicated
6. theory building	16. sample	26. random assignment	36. meta-analysis
7. variables	17. representative sample	27. experimental	37. informed consent
8. operational definition	18. random sample	28. control	38. deception
9. self-report measures	19. correlational research	29. internal validity	
10. physiological measures	20. correlation coefficient	30. confounding of variables	

Answer Key for Practice Test Multiple Choice Questions

1.	c	16. b
2.	b	17. a
3.	a	18. d
4.	d	19. b
5.	d	20. a
6.	c	21. c
7.	d	22. b
8.	a	23. c

9. d	24. a
10. a	25. c
11. a	26. a
12. b	27. c
13. b	28. b
14. b	29. d
15. a	30. a

Answer Key for Practice Test True/False Questions

1. T	6. T
2. F	7. T
3. F	8. F
4. T	9. F
5. F	10. F

Answer Key for Practice Test Short Answer Questions

1. Psychologists use several different types of physiological measurements of behavior. Heart rate, blood pressure, respiration rate, and hormonal secretions are often studied. Electrical and biochemical processes in the brain are also studied. The problem in interpreting these measures is that it is often unclear how these physiological measures are linked to specific patterns of behavior.

2. Correlational research is used to study the relationships between variables. Two variables (X and Y) are measured and then are statistically analyzed to determine whether they are related. The statistic that is used to measure the association is called a correlation coefficient. The sign of the coefficient indicates if the variables are positively or negative correlated. A positive correlation means that as one variable increases the other also increases, while a negative correlation means that as one variable increases the other decreases. The absolute value of the correlation coefficient indicates the strength of the relationship.

3. In the simplest kind of experiment, participants are first randomly assigned to either an experimental group or a control group. The experimental group receives the treatment or active level of the independent variable while the control group does not. The independent variable is manipulated by the experimenter. The dependent variable is then measured by the experimenter for each group, and the groups are statistically compared to determine if there is a difference between them.

4. In random sampling, every member of the population has an equal probability of being included in the sample. Random samples are used to try to make the sample representative of the population and to increase the study's external validity. Random assignment is used in experiments to assign people to the various conditions of the experiment. Random assignment helps to increase the internal validity of the experiment.

5. According to APA's guidelines regarding informed consent, research participants should be given a full description of the procedures to be followed, should be informed about any

possible risks of the research, and should be told that they are free to withdraw from the study at any time without penalty. Researchers are also concerned with a participant's right to privacy, the psychological risk (e.g. emotional stress) to the participant, and the social risk (e.g. whether information about the individual might become known by others, and have detrimental effects) to the participant.

Answer Key for Practice Test Essay Questions

1. Hindsight understanding is problematic when used to explain human and animal behavior because past events can usually be explained in many ways such that it is not clear which explanation might be the correct one. It is better to use the scientific process to study behavior. Under controlled conditions, researchers can test their understanding of what causes a certain behavior by formulating hypotheses and determining whether those predictions are borne out in the lab. When research results support the hypotheses, researchers can create an integrated network of predictions in the process of theory construction.

2. Psychologists rely on four types of measurements to measure variables. Self-report measures are reports by people about their own knowledge, beliefs, feelings, experiences or behavior. Such measures are often used in survey research. Researchers can also ask other people to report on the behavior of the individuals under study (reports by others). Physiological measures such as heart rate, blood pressure, respiration rate, hormonal secretions, electrical and biochemical processes in the brain are also studied. A fourth measurement approach is to observe people's overt behaviors in laboratory or naturalistic settings. Finally, psychologists sometimes use archival measures, or already existing records or documents to study human behavior.

3. Case studies are in-depth analyses of individuals, groups, or events. The case study method enables intensive study of a particular case and the collection of a large amount of data. In naturalistic observation, the researcher observes behavior as it occurs in its natural setting. Survey research involves administering questionnaires or interviews to many people. Survey questions typically ask about people's attitudes, opinions, and behaviors.

4. In an experiment, there are three essential characteristics. First, the experimenter manipulates one variable. This is known as the independent. Second, the experimenter measures whether this manipulation produces changes in a second variable, known as the dependent variable. Third, the researcher attempts to control for extraneous or confounding variables that might influence the outcome of the experiment. Random assignment to groups is important to make sure that the experiment starts out with equivalent groups of people.

5. One major threat to the internal validity of an experiment is a demand characteristic. Demand characteristics are cues that participants pick up about the hypothesis of a study or about how they are supposed to behave. Placebo effects occur when a participant's expectancies about a treatment influence their behavior. Experimenter expectancy effects occur when experimenter's subtly and unintentionally influence their participants to respond in a manner that is consistent with the hypothesis of the study.

Chapter 3
BIOLOGICAL FOUNDATIONS OF BEHAVIOR

Learning Objectives: *These questions, with a few additions (indicated with an asterisk), are taken from the directed questions found in the margins of the chapter. After reading the chapter, you should be able to answer these questions.*

1. Name and describe the functions of the three main parts of the neuron.

2. Which structural characteristics permit the many possible interconnections among neurons?

3. How do glial cells differ from neurons? What three functions do they have in the nervous system?

4. What causes the resting potential of neurons? Under what condition is a neuron said to be in a state of polarization?

5. What chemical changes cause the process of depolarization that creates graded and action potentials? How do the latter differ from one another?

6. What is the nature and importance of the myelin sheath? Which disorder results from inadequate myelinization?

6.1* What are neurotransmitters? What are the five steps of the process of chemical communication?

7. How do neurotransmitters achieve the processes of excitation and inhibition of postsynaptic neurons?

8. Describe two methods by which neurotransmitter molecules are deactivated at the synapse.

9 Describe the roles of (a) acetycholine; (b) dopamine; (c) serotonin, and (d) endorphins in psychological functions.

10. What are the three major types of neurons in the nervous system? What are their functions?

11 Differentiate between the central nervous system and the peripheral nervous system. What are the two divisions of the peripheral nervous system?

12. Describe the two divisions of the autonomic nervous system, as well as their roles in maintaining homeostasis.

13. How do the structural characteristics of the spinal cord permit spinal reflexes?

14. Describe four methods used to study brain-behavior relations.

15. How are CAT scans, PET scans and MRIs produced, and how is each used in brain research?

16. In what sense might the structure of the human brain mirror evolutionary development?

17. Which behavioral functions are controlled by the hindbrain structures, namely, the medulla, the pons, and the cerebellum? What occurs with damage to these structures?

18. Describe the roles played by the ascending and descending reticular formation. Why is it called the "brain's gatekeeper?"

19. What is the role of the thalamus in sensory input, and, possibly, in thought and perceptual disorders?

20. What role does the hypothalamus have in motivated behavior, hunger, pleasure-pain, and hormonal functions?

21. What is the possible relation between the hypothalamus and the limbic system in relation to emotion and motivation? What roles do the hippocampus and amygdala play in psychological functions?

22. What are the four lobes of the brain, and where are they located?

23. Differentiate between sensory, motor, and association cortex.

24. How are the somatic sensory and motor cortexes organized?

25. Where are Wernicke's and Broca's areas? How are they involved in speech?

26. What is the role of the association cortex, the "silent areas?"

27. Describe the role of the frontal cortex in higher mental (including "executive") functions.

28. What is hemispheric lateralization and what do we know about the functions that are concentrated in the left and right hemispheres?

29. What roles have (a) the corpus collosum and (b) the optic chiasma played in "split brain" research? Is it reasonable to speak of separate "right" and "left" brains in normal people?

30. How is language lateralized in the brain? Are there sex differences?

31. What is neural plasticity? How do age, environment, and behavior affect plasticity?

32. Why do children typically show better recovery of function after brain injury?

33. How are axon repair, brain grafts, and neural stem cell injections being used to improve the functioning of damaged brains? What kinds of ethical issues arise in the use of these procedures?

34.   How does the endocrine system differ from the nervous system as a communications network?

35.   What are some ways in which the nervous and endocrine systems affect and interact with one another?

36.   What physiological explanation did Cannon offer for death by "black magic?"

37.   In what ways does the immune system have sensory, response, and memory capabilities?

38.   How do under- or overreactivity to internal or external antigens give rise to four varieties of immune dysfunction?

39.   Cite four pieces of evidence that the immune and nervous system communicate with and affect one another.

40.   Which psychosocial factors have been shown to influence immune functioning?

41.   What can be done to enhance immune functioning?

42.   Differentiate between genotype and phenotype.

43.   How does genetic transmission occur from parents to offspring?

44.   Compare dominant, recessive, and polygenic influences on phenotypic characteristics.

45.   Describe the methods used in recombinant DNA research.

46.   What is the knockout procedure and how is it used by psychologists to study behavior?

47.   What is the percentage of genetic resemblance between parents and children, identical and fraternal twins, brothers and sisters, and grandparents and grandchildren?

48.   How are adoption and twin studies used to achieve heritability estimates? What have such studies shown?

49.   Why are studies of twins raised together and apart especially informative? What findings have occurred in such studies?

Chapter Overview

After reading this chapter, you should have a better idea of the biological influences on human and animal behavior. The chapter covers the neural bases of behavior, the nervous system (including the structures and functions of the brain), nervous system interactions with the endocrine and immune systems, and genetic influences on behavior. Specialized cells called neurons are the building blocks of the nervous system. Each neuron has three main parts: the cell body, which contains the biochemical structures that keep the neuron alive, the dendrites, which collect information from neighboring neurons and send it on to the cell body, and the axon, which conducts electrical impulses away from the cell body to other neurons, muscles, and glands. Glial cells support neurons by holding them in place, manufacturing nutrient chemicals, and absorbing toxins and waste materials. An action potential is a sudden reversal in the neuron's membrane voltage. The shift from negative to positive voltage is called depolarization. The depolarization process occurs when the dendrites of the cell are stimulated, resulting in small shifts in the cell membrane's electrical potential, a shift called a graded potential. If the graded potential is large enough to reach the action potential threshold, an action potential occurs. Either an action potential occurs or it does not, according to the all-or-none law. When a neuron is stimulated, tiny protein structures called ion channels are activated. Sodium ion channels allow positively charged sodium ions to enter the interior of the cell, leading to the process of depolarization. Immediately after an impulse passes any point on the axon, a time period called a refractory period occurs, during which another action potential cannot occur. The myelin sheath is a tubelike insulating substance covering some axons in the brain and spinal cord.

Neurons communicate through synaptic transmission. The synapse is a tiny gap between the axon terminal and the next neuron. Chemical substances called neurotransmitters, which are stored in synaptic vesicles, carry messages across the synapse and bind to receptor sites. Once a neurotransmitter molecule binds to its receptor, it continues to activate or inhibit the neuron until deactivation occurs. One method of deactivation is reuptake, in which the transmitter molecules are taken back into the presynaptic neuron. There are many types of neurotransmitters. One involved in memory and muscle activity is acetylcholine. Abnormally high concentrations of dopamine have been found in the brains of schizophrenics. A class of neurotransmitter that is involved in reducing pain and increasing feelings of well-being are called endorphins. Serotonin may be involved in mood, eating, sleep, and sexual behavior.

There are three major types of neurons in the nervous system. Sensory neurons input messages from the sense organs to the spinal cord and brain, motor neurons carry impulses from the brain and spinal cord to the muscles and organs, and interneurons perform connective or associative functions within the nervous system. The division of the nervous system containing the brain and spinal cord is called the central nervous system. The division that consists of all neurons connecting the CNS with the muscles, glands, and sensory receptors is called the peripheral nervous system. In turn, the PNS is divided into two systems. The somatic nervous system consists of sensory and motor neurons while the autonomic nervous system regulates the body's glands and involuntary functions such as breathing, circulation, and digestion. The autonomic nervous system consists of two branches. The sympathetic branch activates or arouses bodily organs while the parasympathetic branch slows down body processes. Most nerves enter and leave the CNS via the spinal cord. Some simple stimulus-response sequences such as pulling away from a hot stove typically don't involve the brain and are known as spinal reflexes.

Psychologists have used a number of methods of studying the brain. Neuropsychological tests measure verbal and nonverbal behaviors that are known to be affected by brain damage. Sometimes researchers destroy neurons under controlled conditions or stimulate them with electrical current or with chemicals. The activity of large groups of neurons is often studied via an electroencephalogram (EEG). The newest tools of discovery involve brain imaging. X-ray technology used to study brain structures are called computerized axial tomography (CAT) scans. Pictures of brain activity involve the use of positron emission tomography (PET) scans. A technique to measure both brain structures and functions is called magnetic resonance imaging.

The brain historically has been divided into three main divisions. The hindbrain consists of the brain stem and cerebellum. The brain stem is involved in life support. The medulla plays a major role in vital body functions such as heart rate and respiration is the. The pons is a bridge carrying nerve impulses between higher and lower levels of the nervous system. The cerebellum is concerned primarily with muscular coordination, learning, and memory. An important relay center for the visual and auditory systems is contained in the midbrain. Within the midbrain is the reticular formation, which is involved in brain arousal, sleep, and attention. The size and complexity of the forebrain separates humans from lower animals. An important sensory relay station in the forebrain is the thalamus, while the hypothalamus plays a major role in motivational and emotional behavior. The limbic system helps to coordinate behaviors needed to satisfy emotional and motivational urges. Within the limbic system are the hippocampus, which is involved in the formation and storage of memories and the amygdala, which is linked to aggression and fear. The outermost layer of the brain is called the cerebral cortex. Each hemisphere of the cortex is divided into the frontal, parietal, occipital, and temporal lobes, each of which is associated with particular sensory and motor functions. Lying at the rear of the frontal lobe is the motor cortex, which is involved in controlling muscles. The somatic sensory cortex receives sensory input. Two specific speech areas are also located in the cortex. Wernicke's area is involved in speech comprehension while Broca's area is involved in the production of speech. The association cortex is involved in the highest levels of mental functions. People who suffer from agnosia, the inability to identify familiar objects often have suffered damage to their association cortex. Executive functions such as goal setting, judgment, and planning may be controlled by the prefrontal cortex. The brain is typically also divided into two hemispheres: the left and the right. The corpus callosum is a bridge that helps the two hemispheres communicate and work together. When a function is located more in one hemisphere than the other, it is known as lateralization. "Split-brain" research designed to look at the relative functions of the hemispheres involves studying the roles of the corpus callosum and the optic chiasma. The brain as a structure develops over time. The ability of neurons to change in structure and function is known as neural plasticity.

The endocrine system consists of numerous glands distributed throughout the body. The system conveys information via hormones, which are chemical messengers secreted by the glands into the bloodstream. The adrenal glands secrete stress hormones, which mobilize the body's immune system. When foreign substances known as antigens invade the body, the immune system produces antibodies to destroy them. Problems arise with both an underactive and an overactive immune system. An overactive response known as an autoimmune reaction results when the immune system incorrectly identifies part of the body as an enemy and attacks it. A relatively new field called psychoneuroimmunology studies how psychological factors affect health and illness.

The specific genetic makeup of the individual is known as the person's genotype, while the observable characteristics produced by that genetic endowment is known as the person's phenotype. Some genes are dominant and some are recessive. If a gene in the pair received from both the mother and the father is dominant, then the characteristic it controls will be displayed in the phenotype. If the gene received from one parent is recessive, then the characteristic will not show up unless the gene received from the other parent is also recessive. When many gene pairs combine to create a single phenotypic trait, the process is called polygenic transmission.

Geneticists today are mapping the human genome and studying how the genes affect human behavior. Genetic engineering involves duplicating and modifying the structures of genes. In recombinant DNA procedures, enzymes are used to cut DNA into pieces, after which the DNA is combined with DNA from another organism and then is inserted into a host organism. Behavior geneticists study how hereditary and environmental factors work together to influence human behavior. Researchers will often try to determine a characteristic's concordance, or co-occurrence in people who are genetically related to each other. A type of study in which a person who was adopted early in life is compared on a characteristic with biological and adoptive relatives is called an adoption study. Studies of the concordance rates of twins are called twin studies. Such studies help researchers to understand the relative influences of heredity and environment on behavior by comparing concordance rates for identical (monozygotic) twins with those for fraternal (dizygotic twins).

Chapter Outline

The Neural Bases of Behavior
  Neurons
  Nerve Conduction: An Electrochemical Process
      The Action Potential
      The Myelin Sheath
  How Neurons Communicate: Synaptic Transmission
      Neurotransmitters
      Excitation, Inhibition, and Deactivation
      Specialized Transmitter Systems

The Nervous System
  The Peripheral Nervous System
      The Somatic Nervous System
      The Autonomic Nervous System
  The Central Nervous System
      The Spinal Cord
      The Brain
      Unlocking the Secrets of the Brain
          Neuropsychological tests
          Destruction and stimulation techniques
          Electrical recording
          Brain imaging
  The Hierarchical Brain: Structures and Behavioral Functions
      The Hindbrain
          The brain stem: life support systems
          The cerebellum: motor coordination center
      The Midbrain
          The reticular formation: the brain's gatekeeper
      The Forebrain
          The thalamus: the brain's sensory switchboard
          The hypothalamus: motivation and emotion
          The limbic system: memory and goal-directed behavior
      The Cerebral Cortex: Crown of the Brain
          The motor cortex
          The sensory cortex

Speech comprehension and production
Association cortex
The frontal lobes: the human difference
Hemispheric Lateralization: The Left and Right Brains
The split brain: two minds in one body?
Hemispheric specialization of language
Research closeup: Are language functions localized differently in men and
women?
Plasticity in the Brain: The Role of Experience and the Recovery of Function
The role of early experience
Recovery of function after injury
Applications of Psychological Science
Healing the Nervous System

Nervous System Interactions With the Endocrine and Immune Systems
Interactions with the Endocrine System
Interactions Involving the Immune System
Psychological Frontiers: How Psychological Factors Affect the Immune System

Genetic Influences on Behavior
Chromosomes and Genes
Dominant, Recessive, and Polygenic Effects
Mapping the Genetic Code
Genetic Engineering: The Edge of Creation
Behavior Genetics Techniques

Key Terms: *Write the letter of the definition next to the term in the space provided.*

The Neural Basis of Behavior

1. ___ acetylcholine		a.	a sudden reversal in the cell membrane's voltage
2. ___ action potential		b.	an insulation layer covering the axons in the brain and spinal cord
3. ___ action potential threshold		c.	a neurotransmitter involved in memory and muscle activity
4. ___ all-or-none law		d.	collect messages from other neurons and send them to the cell body
5. ___ axon		e.	an excitatory neurotransmitter found in excess in the brains of schizophrenics
6. ___ cell body		f.	a shift from negative to positive voltage inside the neuron
7. ___ dendrites		g.	a neurotransmitter involved in mood, eating, sleep, and sexual behavior
8. ___ depolarization		h.	cells that are the basic building blocks of the nervous system
9. ___ dopamine		i.	small shifts occurring in the cell membrane's electrical potential
10. ___ endorphins		j.	a time period during which the membrane is not excitable and cannot discharge an action potential

11. ___ glial cells

12. ___ graded potential

13. ___ ion channels

14. ___ myelin sheath

15. ___ neurons

16. ___ neurotransmitters

17. ___ receptor sites

18. ___ refractory period

19. ___ reuptake

20. ___ serotonin
21. ___ synapse
22. ___ synaptic vesicles

k. chemical substances that carry messages across the synapse

l. contains the biochemical structures to keep the neuron alive

m. where neurotransmitters bind themselves in the postsynaptic neuron

n. the required level of intensity needed to fire the neuron

o. action potential occurs with maximum intensity or does not occur at all

p. neurotransmitters are taken back into the presynaptic axon terminal

q. conducts electrical impulses away from the cell body to neurons, muscles, and glands

r. a tiny gap between the axon terminal and the next neuron

s. neurotransmitters involved in reducing pain and increasing well-being

t. support cells that hold neurons in place
u. where neurotransmitters are stored
v. allow specific ions to flow back and forth across the cell membrane

The Nervous System

1. ___ agnosia

2. ___ amygdala

3. ___ association cortex

4. ___ autonomic nervous system

5. ___ Broca's area

6. ___ central nervous system

7. ___ cerebral cortex

8. ___ computerized axial tomography

9. ___ corpus callosum

10. ___ electroencephalogram

11. ___ forebrain

12. ___ frontal lobe

13. ___ hippocampus
14. ___ hypothalamus

a. simple stimulus-response sequences that do not involve the brain

b. plays a major role in motivational and emotional behavior

c. a sheet of unmyelinated cells that form the outermost layer of the brain

d. part of the ANS that has an activation or arousal function

e. a test that measures verbal and nonverbal behaviors that are affected by particular types of brain damage

f. a structure in the brain stem that plays an important role in heart rate and respiration

g. comprises all the neurons that connect the central nervous system with the muscles, glands, and senses

h. a measurement of the activity of large groups of neurons

i. part of the cortex that controls muscles involved in voluntary body movements

j. carries input messages from the sense organs to the brain and spinal cord

k. helps to coordinate behaviors needed to satisfy motivational and emotional urges

l. an area in the frontal lobe involved in the production of speech

m. uses X-ray technology to study brain structures
n. the lobe in which the area governing body sensations is located

15. ___ interneurons

16. ___ lateralization

17. ___ limbic system

18. ___ magnetic resonance imaging

19. ___ medulla

20. ___ midbrain

21. ___ motor cortex

22. ___ motor neuron

23. ___ neural plasticity

24. ___ neuropsychological test

25. ___ occipital lobe

26. ___ optic chiasma

27. ___ parasympathetic nervous system

28. ___ parietal lobe

29. ___ peripheral nervous system

30. ___ pons

31. ___ positron emission tomography

32. ___ prefrontal cortex

33. ___ prefrontal lobotomy

34. ___ reticular formation

35. ___ sensory neuron

36. ___ somatic nervous system

37. ___ somatic sensory cortex

38. ___ spinal reflex

39. ___ sympathetic nervous system

40. ___ temporal lobe

41. ___ thalamus

42. ___ Wernicke's area

o. transmits messages from the sense organs to the spinal cord and brain

p. involved in the formation and storage of memories

q. a structure that carries impulses between the lower and higher levels of the nervous system

r. part of the ANS that slows down body processes

s. part of the cortex that receives sensory input that give rise to sensations of heat, touch, and cold

t. the inability to identify familiar objects

u. perform connective or associative functions within the nervous system

v. the seat of the so-called "executive functions"

w. a neural bridge acting as a communication link between the two hemispheres

x. organizes emotional response patterns

y. consists of the sensory neurons that are specialized to transmit messages from sensory receptors and motor neurons to the muscles

z. contains clusters of sensory and motor neurons connecting higher and lower portions of the nervous system

aa. the lobe where the brain's visual area is located

bb. scans that measure brain activity

cc. when a function is located more in one hemisphere than in the other

dd. the ability of neurons to change in structure and function

ee. consists of all the neurons in the brain and spinal cord

ff. an area in the temporal lobe involved in speech comprehension

gg. can be used to measure both brain structure and activity

hh. the lobe where messages from the auditory system are sent

ii. involved in brain arousal, sleep, and attention

jj. the lobe where speech and skeletal motor functions are located

kk. a sensory relay station

ll. an area of the cortex involved in the highest mental functions, including perception, language, and thought

mm. controls the glands and the smooth muscles of several organs

nn. consists of two large cerebral hemispheres that wrap around the brain stem

oo. where fibers from the optic nerve cross over

pp. a procedure that severs the nerve tracts that connect the frontal lobe with the subcortical regions involved in emotion

Nervous System Interactions with the Immune System

1. ____ adrenal glands
2. ____ antigens
3. ____ autoimmune response
4. ____ endocrine system

5. ____ hormones

6. ____ psychoneuroimmunology

a. consists of numerous glands distributed throughout the body
b. secrete hormones regulating many metabolic processes
c. chemical messengers secreted from the glands into the bloodstream
d. foreign substances that trigger a biochemical response by the immune system
e. an overactive response occurring when the immune system mistakenly identifies part of the body as an enemy and attacks it
f. a discipline that studies how psychological factors affect health and illness

Genetic Influences on Behavior

1. ____ adoption study
2. ____ concordance
3. ____ gene
4. ____ genotype
5. ____ phenotype

6. ____ polygenic transmission
7. ____ recombinant DNA procedure

8. ____ twin study

a. the specific genetic makeup of an individual
b. the observable characteristics produced by a genetic endowment
c. contains DNA
d. when a number of gene pairs combine their influence to create a single phenotypic trait
e. when DNA is combined with DNA from another organism and inserted into a host organism
f. co-occurrence of a characteristic in people
g. a study in which a person who was adopted early in life is compared on some characteristic with both biological parents
h. a study in which monozygotic and dizygotic twins are compared

Review at a Glance: *Write the term that best fits the blank to review what you learned in this chapter.*

The Neural Bases of Behavior

Specialized cells called (1) _____ are the building blocks of the nervous system. Each neuron has three main parts. The (2) _____ _____ contains the biochemical structures that keep the neuron alive, and the genetic information that controls cell development and function is in its nucleus. (3) _____ collect information from neighboring neurons and send it on to the cell body. The part of the neuron that conducts electrical impulses away from the cell body to other neurons, muscles, and glands is called the (4) _____. Cells known as (5) _____ _____ support neurons by holding them in place, manufacturing nutrient chemicals, and absorbing toxins and waste materials. A sudden reversal in the neuron's membrane voltage is called an (6) _____ _____ and the shift from negative to positive voltage is called (7) _____. The depolarization process occurs when the dendrites of the cell are stimulated, resulting in small shifts in the cell membrane's electrical potential, a shift called a (8) _____ _____. If the graded potential is large enough to reach the (9) _____ _____ , an action potential occurs. Either an action potential occurs or its does not, according to the (10) _____ _____ _____ _____. When a neuron is stimulated, tiny protein structures called (11) _____ are activated. Sodium ion channels allow positively charged sodium ions to enter the interior of the cell, leading to the process of depolarization. Immediately after an impulse passes any point on the axon, a time period called an (12) _____ period occurs, during which another action potential cannot occur. A tubelike substance covering some axons in the brain and spinal cord is known as the (13) _____ _____. Neurons communicate through synaptic transmission. Chemical substances called (14) _____ carry messages across the synapse and bind to (15) _____ _____. Once a neurotransmitter molecule binds to its receptor, it continues to activate or inhibit the neuron until deactivation occurs. One method of deactivation is (16) _____, in which the transmitter molecules are taken back into the presynaptic neuron. There are many types of neurotransmitters. One involved in memory and muscle activity is (17) _____. Abnormally high concentrations of (18) _____ have been found in the brains of schizophrenics. A class of neurotransmitter that is involved in reducing pain and increasing feelings of well-being are (19) _____.

The Nervous System

There are three major types of neurons in the nervous system. (20) _____ neurons input messages from the sense organs to the spinal cord and brain, (21) _____ neurons carry impulses from the brain and spinal cord to the muscles and organs, and (22) _____ perform connective or associative functions within the nervous system. The division of the nervous system containing the brain and spinal cord is called the (23) _____ nervous system. The division that consists of all neurons connecting the CNS with the muscles, glands, and sensory receptors is called the (24) _____ nervous system. In turn, the PNS is divided into two systems. The (25) _____ nervous system consists of sensory and motor neurons while the (26) _____ nervous system regulates the body's glands and involuntary functions such as breathing, circulation, and digestion. The autonomic nervous system consists of two branches. The (27) _____ branch activates or arouses bodily organs while the (28) _____ branch slows down body processes. Most nerves enter and leave the CNS via the spinal cord. Some simple stimulus-response sequences such as pulling away from a hot stove typically don't involve the brain and are known as (29) _____ _____. Psychologists have used a number of methods of studying the brain. (30) _____ tests measure verbal and nonverbal behaviors that are known to be affected by brain damage. Sometimes researchers destroy neurons under controlled conditions or stimulate them with electrical current or with chemicals. Such techniques are known as (31) _____ _____ _____ techniques. The activity of large groups of neurons is often studied via an (32) _____. The newest tools of discovery involve brain imaging. X-ray technology used to study brain structures are called (33) _____ _____ _____ scans. Pictures of brain activity involve the use of (34) _____ _____ _____. A technique to measure both brain structures and function is called (35) _____ _____ _____. The brain historically has been divided into three main divisions. The hindbrain consists of the brain stem and cerebellum. The brain stem is involved in life support. A structure that plays a major role in vital body functions such as heart rate and respiration is the (36) _____. The (37) _____ is a bridge carrying nerve impulses between higher and lower levels of the nervous system. The cerebellum is concerned primarily with muscular coordination, learning, and memory. An important relay center for the visual and auditory systems is contained in the (38) _____. Within the midbrain is the (39) _____ _____, which is involved in brain arousal, sleep, and attention. The size and complexity of the (40) _____ separates humans from lower animals. An important sensory relay station in the forebrain is the (41) _____, while the (42) _____ plays a major role in motivational and emotional behavior. The (43) _____ system helps to coordinate behaviors needed to satisfy emotional and motivational urges. Within the limbic system are the (44) _____, which is involved in the formation and storage of memories and the (45) _____, which is linked to aggression and fear. The outermost layer of the brain is called the (46) _____ _____. Each hemisphere of the cortex is divided into four lobes, the (47) _____, (48) _____, (49) _____, and (50) _____ lobes, each of which is associated with particular sensory and motor functions. Lying at the rear of the frontal lobe is the (51) _____ cortex, which is involved in controlling muscles. The (52) _____ sensory cortex receives sensory input. Two specific speech areas are also located in the cortex. (53) _____ area is involved in speech comprehension while (54) _____ area is involved in the production of speech. The (55) _____ is involved in the highest levels of mental functions. People who suffer from (56) _____, the inability to identify familiar objects often have suffered damage to their association cortex. Executive functions such as goal setting, judgment, and planning may be controlled by the (57) _____ cortex. The brain is typically also divided into two hemispheres: the left and the right. The (58) _____ _____ is a bridge that helps the two hemispheres communicate and work together. When a function is located more in one hemisphere than the other, it is known as (59) _____. "Split-brain" research designed to look at the relative functions of the hemispheres involves studying the roles of the corpus callosum and the (60) _____ _____. The brain as a structure develops over time. The ability of neurons to change in structure and function is known as (61) _____ _____.

Nervous System Interactions with the Endocrine and Immune Systems

The (62) _____ system consists of numerous glands distributed throughout the body. The system conveys information via (63) _____, which are chemical messengers secreted by the glands into the bloodstream. The (64) _____ glands secrete stress hormones, which mobilize the body's immune system. When foreign substances known as (65) _____ invade the body, the immune system produces antibodies to destroy them. Problems arise with both an underactive and an overactive immune system. An overactive response known as an (66) _____ reaction results when the immune system incorrectly identifies part of the body as an enemy and attacks it.

Genetic Influences on Behavior

The specific makeup of the individual is known as the (67) _____, while the observable characteristics produced by that genetic endowment is known as the person's (68) _____. Some genes are dominant and some are recessive. If a gene in the pair received from both the mother and the father is (69) _____, then the characteristic it controls will be displayed in the phenotype. If the gene received from one parent is

(70) _____, then the characteristic will not show up unless the gene received from the other parent is also (70) _____. When many gene pairs combine to create a single phenotypic trait, the process is called (71) _____ _____. Geneticists today are mapping the human genome and studying how the genes affect human behavior. Genetic engineering involves duplicating and modifying the structures of genes. In (72) _____ _____ _____, enzymes are used to cut DNA into pieces, after which the DNA is combined with DNA from another organism and then is inserted into a host organism. Behavior geneticists study how hereditary and environmental factors work together to influence human behavior. Researchers will often try to determine a characteristic's (73) _____, or co-occurrence in people who are genetically related to each other. A type of study in which a person who was adopted early in life is compared on a characteristic with a biological relative is called an (74) _____ study. Studies of the concordance rates of twins are called (75) _____ studies. Such studies help researchers to understand the relative influences of heredity and environment on behavior by comparing the concordance rates for identical (monozygotic) twins with those for fraternal (dizygotic) twins.

Apply What You Know

1. Describe what is occurring in the diagram on Study Sheet 3.1.

2. Label the parts of the neuron shown on Study Sheet 3.2. (The myelin sheath is already indicated for you!)

3. Label the parts of the brain shown on Study Sheet 3.3.

Stretching Your Geographies

1. Do males and females have different brain structures? Do they use their brains in different ways? Do some library research to determine what researchers have found regarding sex differences in brain structures and functions. What differences do you find?

Practice Test

Multiple Choice Items: *Please write the letter corresponding to your answer in the space to the left of each item.*

_____ 1. Specialized cells that are the basic building blocks of the nervous system are called _____.

    a. axons
    b. dendrites
    c. neurons
    d. glial cells

_____ 2. A sudden reversal in the cell membrane's voltage, during which the membrane voltage moves from −70mv to +40mv is called _____.

    a. the action potential threshold
    b. the all-or-none law
    c. a graded potential
    d. an action potential

_____ 3. The changes in the electrical potential of a neuron that are proportional to the amount of incoming stimulation from other neurons are called _____ potentials.

    a. resting
    b. action
    c. graded
    d. polarized

_____ 4. When a neuron is stimulated, tiny protein structures on the cell membrane called _____ are activated.

    a. ion channels
    b. neurotransmitters
    c. synaptic vesicles
    d. myelin sheaths

_____ 5. Multiple sclerosis occurs when a person's own immune system specifically attacks _____.

    a. the dendrites
    b. the glial cells
    c. the myelin sheath
    d. the ion channels

_____ 6. A tiny gap between the axon terminal and the next neuron through which the neurotransmitters pass is called the ____.

a. synapse
b. synaptic vesicle
c. myelin sheath
d. ion channel

_____ 7. Neurotransmitters that depolarize the postsynaptic neuron are called ____.

a. excitatory transmitters
b. inhibitory transmitters
c. receptor sites
d. synaptic vesicles

_____ 8. The neurotransmitter most associated with mood is ____.

a. dopamine
b. aceytlcholine
c. serotonin
d. GABA

_____ 9. The ____ nervous system consists of all the neurons of the brain and spinal cord.

a. sympathetic
b. parasympathetic
c. peripheral
d. central

_____ 10. The sympathetic and parasympathetic nervous systems play complementary roles in maintaining ____, which refers to a balanced or constant internal state.

a. homeosynthesis
b. homeostasis
c. neural plasticity
d. a resting potential

_____ 11. During brain surgery, a physician places a small electrode on various portions of the patient's exposed cerebral cortex. Though the patient is anesthetized, he is still conscious and the physician asks him to report what he experiences when different parts of the brain arc electrically activated. This physician is using ____ to study the relation between the brain and behavior.

a. neuropsychological tests
b. stimulation techniques
c. brain imaging
d. electrical recording

_____ 12. CAT scans, PET scans, and MRIs are all examples of ____.

    a. electrical recording
    b. destruction and stimulation techniques
    c. brain imaging
    d. neuropsychological tests

_____ 13. A new born baby is having trouble regulating her breathing and heart rate and doctors are forced to place her on life support. Given her symptoms, it is **most likely** that this infant may have some abnormalities in or damage to her ____.

    a. thalamus
    b. hypothalamus
    c. cerebellum
    d. medulla

_____ 14. A male rat has a particular area of its brain destroyed and it subsequently loses its sex drive (i.e., the rat is no longer interested in sex). It is **most likely** that the rat's ____ was the site of the damage.

    a. hippocampus
    b. thalamus
    c. hypothalamus
    d. amygdala

_____ 15. The ____ system helps to coordinate behaviors needed to satisfy motivational and emotional urges produced by the ____.

    a. parasympathetic; thalamus
    b. sympathetic; thalamus
    c. limbic; hypothalamus
    d. hippocampal; hypothalamus

_____ 16. Control of voluntary body movements is localized in the ____.

    a. temporal lobe
    b. motor cortex
    c. association cortex
    d. occipital lobe

_____ 17. The sensory cortex ____.

    a. is not involved in sensation
    b. contains the association cortex
    c. receives input from our sensory receptors and gives rise to sensations of heat, touch, cold, and our senses of body movement and balance
    d. performs the same functions as the motor cortex

_____ 18. As a result of a head trauma, a man loses his ability to create speech and talk but can still understand what people say to him. He has **most likely** suffered damage to ____.

a. Broca's area
b. the amygdala
c. the cerebellum
d. Wernicke's area

_____ 19. Scientists have suggested that the entire period of human evolution could be labeled "the age of the ____ lobe."

a. occipital
b. temporal
c. parietal
d. frontal

_____ 20. The neural link between the two hemispheres that allows them to act as a single unit is called the ____.

a. Broca's area
b. corpus callosum
c. aphasia
d. agnosia

_____ 21. For many years, scientists have known that language is largely a ____ function.

a. frontal lobe
b. parietal lobe
c. left hemisphere
d. right hemisphere

_____ 22. Research demonstrating that rat pups raised in stimulating environments had larger neurons with more dendritic branches and that musicians who do complex string work with their left hands tend to have larger corresponding somatosensory areas were both discussed as examples of ____.

a. neural plasticity
b. split-brain research
c. what happens when the corpus callosum is cut
d. functions influenced by Wernicke's area

_____ 23. Immature, "uncommitted" cells that can mature into any type of neuron or glial cell needed by the brain are called ____.

a. neural plastic cells
b. neural stem cells
c. interneurons
d. motor neurons

_____ 24. The _____ system consists of numerous glands distributed throughout the body.

   a. endocrine
   b. immune
   c. central
   d. parasympathetic

_____ 25. Hormones are the primary method of communication for the ___.

   a. nervous system
   b. endocrine system
   c. immune system
   d. cerebral cortex

_____ 26. When an _____ invades the body, the _____ system creates _____ to destroy it.

   a. antibody; endocrine; antigen
   b. antigen; endocrine; antibody
   c. antigen; immune; antibody
   d. antibody; immune; antigen

_____ 27. A dominant gene is one that _____.

   a. interacts with multiple gene pairs to determine the expression of a single phenotypic characteristic
   b. determines the expression of the trait it controls only if its gene partner is also dominant
   c. determines the expression of the trait it controls only if its gene partner is recessive
   d. directly determines the expression of the trait it controls

_____ 28. Both of Bob's parents have blue eyes and Bob himself also has the gene for blue eyes yet Bob's eyes are actually brown. This means that the gene for blue eyes would be considered _____.

   a. polygenic
   b. phenotypic
   c. recessive
   d. dominant

_____ 29. The probability of a child sharing any particular gene with his or her parents is _____.

   a. .05
   b. .25
   c. .50
   d. 1.0

_____ 30. The co-occurrence of a characteristic in people that is measured in twin and adoption studies is known as _____.

    a. the heritability coefficient
    b. concordance
    c. genetic relatedness
    d. genotype

True/False Items: *Write T or F in the space provided to the left of each item.*

_____ 1. The basic building blocks of the nervous system are dendrites.

_____ 2. Positively charged sodium ions flow into the interior of the neuron, creating a state of partial depolarization, when the ion channels are activated.

_____ 3. Neurons communicate via neurotransmitters.

_____ 4. The two divisions of the central nervous system are the parasympathetic and sympathetic.

_____ 5. PET scans measure brain structure.

_____ 6. The cerebellum is concerned primarily with muscular movement coordination, but it also plays a role in learning and memory.

_____ 7. The hypothalamus acts as a sensory relay station in the brain and is known as the "switchboard" of the brain.

_____ 8. The association cortex is involved in the highest levels of mental functions, including perception, language, and thought.

_____ 9. Hormones are secreted by glands in the endocrine system.

_____ 10. When a number of gene pairs combine their influences to create a single phenotypic trait, that process is known as a recombinant DNA procedure.

Short Answer Questions

1. Describe the functions of the different parts of neurons.

2. Describe the divisions of the peripheral nervous system and their functions.

3. Describe four methods of study that attempt to unlock the secrets of the brain.

4. Describe how Broca's and Wernicke's areas are involved in speech comprehension and speech production.

5. How do dominant and recessive genes interact to produce phenotypic traits?

Essay Questions

1. Describe the process that occurs to create an action potential.

2. Describe the process by which neurons communicate with each other.

3. Describe the functions associated with the different areas of cerebral cortex.

4. Describe how split-brain research is used to study the lateralization of function.

5. What evidence indicates that the nervous, endocrine, and immune systems interact with each other?

Study Sheet 3.1   Neural Firing

Polarized membrane

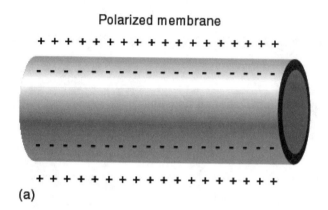

(a)

Depolarization
(sodium ions flow in)

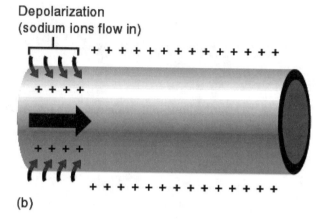

(b)

Sodium ions pumped
out of neuron   Depolarization

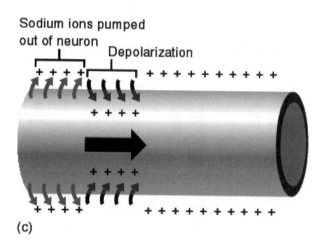

(c)

Flow of depolarization

Direction of
depolarization
wave

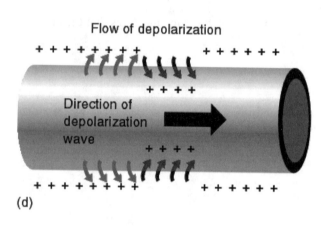

(d)

Study Sheet 3.2   Parts of the Neuron

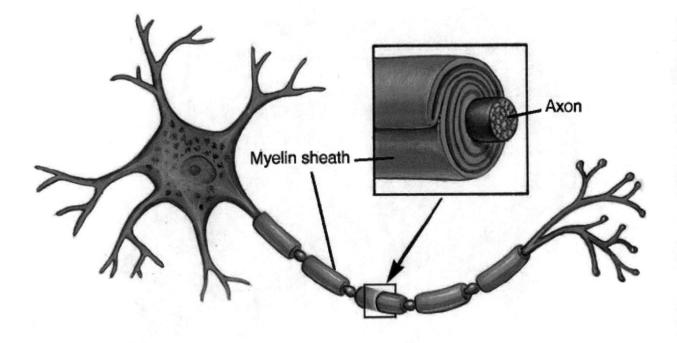

Study Sheet 3.3 Parts of the Brain

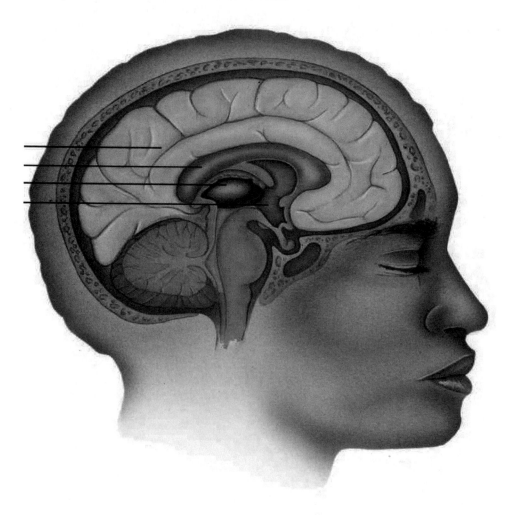

Answer Keys

Answer Key for Key Terms

The Neural Bases of Behavior

1. c
2. a
3. n
4. o
5. q
6. l
7. d
8. f
9. e
10. s
11. t
12. i
13. l
14. b
15. h
16. k
17. m
18. j
19. p
20. g
21. r
22. u

The Nervous System

1. t
2. x
3. ll
4. mm
5. l
6. ee
7. c
8. m
9. w
10. h
11. nn
12. jj
13. p
14. b
15. u
16. cc
17. k
18. gg
19. f
20. z
21. i
22. o
23. dd
24. e
25. aa
26. oo
27. r
28. n
29. g
30. q
31. bb
32. v
33. pp
34. ii
35. j
36. y
37. s
38. a
39. d
40. hh
41. kk
42. ff

Nervous System Interactions with the Endocrine and Immune Systems

1. b
2. d
3. e
4. a
5. c
6. f

Genetic Influences on Behavior

1. g
2. f
3. c
4. a
5. b
6. d
7. e
8. h

Answer Key for Review at a Glance

1. neurons
2. cell body
3. dendrites
4. axon
5. glial cells
6. action potential
7. depolarization
8. graded potential

9. action potential threshold

10. all-or-none law

11. ion channels
12. refractory
13. myelin sheath
14. neurotransmitters
15. receptor sites
16. reuptake
17. acetylcholine
18. dopamine
19. endorphins
20. sensory
21. motor
22. interneurons

23. central
24. peripheral
25. somatic

26. autonomic
27. sympathetic
28. parasympathetic
29. spinal reflexes
30. neuropsychological
31. destruction and stimulation
32. electroencephalogram
33. computerized axial tomography
34. positron emission tomography
35. magnetic resonance imaging
36. medulla
37. pons
38. midbrain
39. reticular formation
40. forebrain
41. thalamus
42. hypothalamus
43. limbic
44. hippocampus
45. amygdala
46. cerebral cortex
47. frontal

48. parietal
49. occipital
50. temporal

51. motor
52. somatic
53. Wernicke's
54. Broca's
55. association
56. agnosia
57. prefrontal
58. corpus callosum

59. lateralization

60. optic chiasma

61. neural plasticity
62. endocrine
63. hormones
64. adrenal
65. antigens
66. autoimmune
67. genotype
68. phenotype
69. dominant
70. recessive
71. polygenic transmission
72. recombinant DNA procedures
73. concordance
74. adoption
75. twin

Answer Key for Practice Test Multiple Choice Questions

1. c
2. d
3. c
4. a
5. c
6. a
7. a
8. c
9. d
10. b
11. b
12. c
13. d
14. c
15. c
16. b
17. c
18. a
19. d
20. b
21. c
22. a
23. b
24. a
25. b
26. c
27. d
28. c
29. c
30. b

Answer Key for Practice Test True/False Questions

1.	F		6.	T
2.	T		7.	F
3.	T		8.	T
4.	F		9.	T
5.	F		10.	F

Answer Key for Practice Test Short Answer Questions

1. The neuron has three main parts: the axon, dendrites, and a cell body. The cell body contains the biochemical structures needed to keep the neuron alive. Its nucleus contains the genetic information that determines how the cell develops. The dendrites collect messages from neighboring neurons and send the messages to the cell body. The axon conducts electrical impulses away from the cell body to other neurons, muscles, and glands.

2. The main divisions of the peripheral nervous system are the somatic and autonomic nervous systems. The somatic nervous system consists of the sensory neurons that are specialized to transmit messages from the body's sense organs and the motor neurons that send messages from the brain and spinal cord to the muscles. The autonomic nervous system controls the glands and smooth involuntary muscles of the heart and other organs and controls involuntary functions such as respiration and digestion. The autonomic nervous system is divided into two branches: the sympathetic and parasympathetic. The sympathetic activates or arouses behavior, while the parasympathetic branch slows down body processes. The interaction between the two branches generally creates a state of homeostasis, a balanced internal state.

3. Neuropsychological tests measure verbal and nonverbal behaviors that are known to be affected by brain damage. Destruction and stimulation techniques are used to destroy brain structures and stimulate them via electrical or chemical measures respectively to determine the functions of the structures. Electrical recordings such as EEGs are used to measure the activity of large groups of neurons. Finally, brain imaging techniques such as CT and PET scans as well as MRIs are used to study both the structure and activities of the brain.

4. Broca's area in the frontal lobe is involved in the production of speech through its connections with the motor cortex areas that control the muscles used in speech. Wernicke's area in the temporal lobe is involved in speech comprehension.

5. If a gene in the pair received from the mother and father is dominant, the particular characteristic that it controls will be displayed. However, if the gene is recessive, the characteristic will not show up unless the gene inherited from the other parent is also recessive.

Answer Key for Practice Test Essay Questions

1. An action potential is a sudden shift in the neuron's membrane voltage from –70mv to +40mv, a shift called depolarization. When the dendrites of one neuron are stimulated, small shifts in the cells's electrical potential called graded potentials occur. If the graded potential is large enough to reach the action potential threshold, the neuron fires according to the all-or-none law. The depolarization of the membrane is due to an influx of sodium ions through the ion channels when the neuron is stimulated. The influx of sodium ions creates a state of partial depolarization, which can generally reach the action potential threshold of –55mv.

2. Neurons communicate with each other via synaptic transmission. Neurotransmitters such as serotonin and dopamine formed inside the neuron are stored in synaptic vesicles in the axon terminals. When an action potential comes down an axon, neurotransmitters are released into the synapse. They then bind with postsynaptic receptors on the next neuron and either excite or inhibit the postsynaptic neuron.

3. The motor cortex controls 600 or more muscles involved in voluntary body movements. The somatic sensory cortex receives sensory input that gives rise to sensations of heat, touch, cold, and our senses of balance and body movement. The association cortex is involved in higher level mental functions such as perception, language, and thought.

4. Lateralization referes to the relatively greater localization of a function in one hemisphere or the other. Split-brain studies involve studying patients whose corpus callosum has been severed. Because the corpus callosum has been cut, visual information can be restricted to either side of the brain (right visual field to left hemisphere and left visual field to right hemisphere). The patient's perceptions and behavior are then measured to determine the functions of the hemispheres.

5. The immune, endocrine, and nervous systems are all part of a communication network. Studies of interactions between the immune and nervous systems have shown that stimulation or destruction of the hypothalamus and cerebral cortex affect immune system functioning. Activation of the immune system results in increased brain activity. Additionally, the action of immune system cells are influenced by neurotransmitters. Studies of the interaction of the immune and endocrine systems have found that immune cells can produce hormones, allowing them to directly influence glands.

Chapter 4
SENSATION AND PERCEPTION

Learning Objectives: *These questions, with a few additions (indicated with an asterisk), are taken from the directed questions found in the margins of the chapter. After reading the chapter, you should be able to answer these questions.*

1. Describe the five stages that comprise the process of sensory processing and perception of information.

2. How do psychologists differentiate between sensation and perception?

3. What two kinds of sensory capabilities are studied by psychophysics researchers?

4. What is the absolute threshold, and how is it technically defined and measured?

5. Why do signal detection theorists view stimulus detection as a decision? What are the four possible outcomes of such a decision?

6. What kinds of personal and situational factors influence signal detection decision criteria?

7. According to research results, what effects do subliminal stimuli have on consumer behavior, attitudes, and self-improvement outcomes?

8. What is the technical definition of a difference threshold? How does Weber's law help us compare jnd sensitivities in the various senses?

9. What accounts for sensory adaptation? Of what survival value is adaptation?

10 How does the lens affect visual acuity, and how does its dysfunction cause the visual problems of myopia and hyperopia?

11. How are the rods and cones distributed in the retina, and how do they contribute to brightness perception, color vision, and visual acuity?

11.1* By what route do rods and cones send neural messages to the brain?

12. What is transduction, and how does this process occur in the photoreceptors of the eye?

13. How is brightness sensitivity in rods and cones affected by the color spectrum?

14. What is the physiological basis for dark adaptation? What are the two components of the dark adaptation curve?

15. Describe the Young-Helmholtz trichromatic theory of color vision. What kinds of evidence support this theory, and what two phenomena challenge it?

16. Describe the opponent process theory. What evidence supports it?

17. How does the dual-process theory of color vision combine the trichromatic and opponent-process theories?

18. What are the two major types of color blindness? How are they tested?

19. What kinds of feature detectors exist in the visual system? What is meant by parallel processing of sensory information?

20. What are the two physical characteristics of sound waves, and which sensory qualities do these characteristics produce?

21. Describe how the middle and inner ear structures are involved in the auditory transduction process.

22. Describe the frequency and place theories of pitch perception. In what sense are both theories correct?

23. How does the structure of the auditory system permit humans to localize sounds? What sensory information is used by the brain in localization?

24. What are the two varieties of deafness, and how do they differ in their physical bases and in possible treatment?

25. Describe the sensory principles that are applied to create sensory prosthetics for visually and hearing impaired people.

26. Describe the stimuli and the receptors involved in gustation and olfaction. Why do researchers sometimes refer to a "common chemical sense?"

27. What is menstrual synchrony, and what evidence is there that pheromones are involved?

28. What four tactile sensations are humans sensitive to? How are these sensations localized, and how are phantom limb sensations produced?

29. Differentiate between bottom-up and top-down processing of sensory information.

30. What two complementary processes occur in attention? What are their adaptive benefits?

31. Describe the results of shadowing experiments in relation to attentional capabilities.

32. What stimulus and personal characteristics influence attention?

33. How does our tendency to separate figure and ground contribute to perception?

34. Define and give examples of the four Gestalt laws of perceptual organization.

35. In what sense is perception a kind of hypothesis testing? What is the role of perceptual schemas in this process?

36. What is a perceptual set? What factors can create such sets? How did the Vincennes incident illustrate this concept? How is it involved in social stereotypes?

37. What is the nature and adaptive value of perceptual constancies? What are the bases for shape, brightness, and size constancy in the visual sense?

38. Identify seven monocular cues for distance and depth.

39. Describe two binocular depth cues and how they function.

40. What is the primary cue for motion perception? How is stroboscopic movement used in motion pictures and television?

41. In what sense is an illusion a false perceptual hypothesis? In what ways are constancies and context involved in producing visual illusions?

42. How do endorphins exert their effects on pain perception?

43. How do researchers determine whether endorphins underlie the analgesic effects of a procedure, such as acupuncture or hypnosis?

44. What is stress-induced analgesia, and what is its adaptive value? How do we know if endorphins play a role in it?

45. Can endorphins have negative effects on the body?

46. What evidence is there that cultural learning, beliefs, and personality factors influence pain perception?

47. What evidence is there that cultural factors can influence picture interpretations, constancies, and susceptibility to illusions?

48. How do animal studies of restricted stimulation and human studies of restored vision illustrate the important role of critical periods for perceptual development?

Chapter Overview

This chapter covers the basic processes of sensation and perception and is divided into sections on sensory processes, the sensory systems, perception, illusions, pain, and critical periods. The scientific area that studies relations between the physical characteristics of stimuli and sensory capabilities is called psychophysics. Psychophysicists are interested in studying both the absolute limits of sensitivity and the sensitivity to distinguish between different stimuli. The lowest intensity at which a stimulus can be detected fifty percent of the time is called the absolute threshold of the stimulus. Signal detection theorists study the factors that influence such sensory judgments. There has been a lot of study of subliminal stimuli, stimuli so weak or brief that it cannot be perceived consciously, since the 1950's. Such studies have indicated that behavior cannot be controlled subliminally, but subliminal stimuli can affect attitudes, at least in the laboratory. The difference threshold (also known as the just noticeable difference or jnd) is defined as the smallest difference between two stimuli that can be perceived fifty percent of the time. Weber's law states that the jnd is directly proportional to the magnitude of the stimulus with which the comparison is being made. For instance, the jnd for weight is 1/50, so if one object weighs 50g, then a second object would have to weight at least 51g for you to notice a difference in weight (or if one object weighs 100g, then a second object would have to weigh 102g for you to notice it). People must be attuned to changes in their environmental stimulation. Diminishing sensitivity to an unchanging stimulus is called sensory adaptation.

Psychologists study a number of sensory systems. For example, psychologists study the processes of vision, audition, gustation, olfaction, and the tactile senses. The eye consists of several important structures such as the lens and retina. Nearsightedness, or myopia, occurs when the lens focuses the visual image in front of the retina, while farsightedness, or hyperopia, occurs when the image is focused behind the retina. Rods are black-and-white brightness receptors in the eye, while cones are color receptors. Bipolar cells have synaptic connections with rods and cones and also connect to ganglion cells, whose axons bundle to form the optic nerve, which sends visual information to the thalamus, which in turn sends information to the primary visual cortex in the brain. Groups of neurons within the primary visual cortex called feature detectors are organized to receive and translate nerve impulses coming from the retina. Visual association cortex is where the final processes of constructing a visual representation occur. Transduction is the process by which the characteristics of a stimulus are converted into nerve impulses. People must adapt to both bright and dark conditions. The progressive improvement in brightness sensitivity that occurs over time under conditions of low illumination (like in a movie theatre) is called dark adaptation. There are several theories of color vision. The trichromatic theory developed by Young and Helmholtz suggests that there are three types of color receptors in the retina that are sensitive to blue, green, or red. The opponent-process theory suggests that each of the three different cone types responds to *two* different wavelengths: one to red or green, a second to blue or yellow, and a third to black or white. Dual-process theory combines both theories, as evidence has been found for both. Some people are color blind. Dichromats are color blind in only one of the systems, while monochromats are sensitive only to black and white.

The stimuli for hearing are sound waves, which are measured in terms of their frequency (measured in hertz [Hz]) and amplitude (measured in decibels [db]). The transduction system for audition occurs in the inner ear. Vibrating activity of inner ear bones amplifies sound waves. When sound waves strike the eardrum, pressure created by the inner ear bones sets the fluid inside the cochlea into motion. The fluid waves that result vibrate the basilar membrane causing a bending of the hair cells in the organ of Corti. This bending triggers a release of neurotransmitters into the synapse between the hair cells and neurons of the auditory nerve, and nerve impulses are then sent to the brain. To use sound, we must code both pitch and loudness. Loudness is coded by a greater bend by the hair cells, resulting in the release of more neurotransmitters and a higher rate of firing in the auditory nerve. The frequency theory of pitch suggests that nerve impulses sent to the brain match the frequency of the sound wave, while the place theory of pitch suggests that the specific point in the cochlea where the fluid wave peaks and most strongly bends the hair cells serves as a frequency coding cue. Sounds are localized because we have two ears (thus we have binaural ability). Sounds arrive first and loudest at the ear closest to the sound, allowing us to figure out where it is coming from. More than 20 million people in the U.S. suffer from hearing loss. Conduction deafness occurs when there is a problem in the system that sends sound waves to the cochlea while nerve deafness occurs when there are damaged receptors in the inner ear or damage to the auditory nerve.

Gustation refers to our sense of taste. The four types of taste receptors found along the tongue create a "taste," which results from neural activity. Olfaction refers to our sense of smell. Humans have about 40 million olfactory receptors. Pheromones, chemical signals found in natural body scents, may affect human behavior. For instance, some studies show that women who live together or are close friends develop similar menstrual cycles, a phenomenon called menstrual synchrony.

The tactile senses are important to us too. Humans are sensitive to at least touch, pain, warmth, and cold. The sense of kinesthesis provides us with feedback about the positions of our muscles and joints, allowing us to coordinate body movements. Our vestibular sense is the sense of body orientation or equilibrium.

Perception also affects the way that we experience the world. Perception is an active, creative process, which can cause different people to experience exactly the same stimulus in very different ways. To create perceptions the brain uses both bottom-up and top-down processing. In bottom-up processing, a stimulus is broken down into its constituent parts and then combined and interpreted as a whole. In top-down processing, expectations and existing knowledge are used to interpret new information. Because there are so many stimuli impinging on our senses, we can only pay attention to a small fraction of them. These processes are studied experimentally through a technique called shadowing. Attention is affected by both the nature of the stimulus and by personal factors. People are especially attentive to stimuli that might represent a threat to their well-being. People tend to organize the world to make it simpler to understand. Gestalt theorists suggested that people use top-down processing to organize their worlds. For instance, we tend to organize stimuli into both a foreground and background, a process called figure-ground relations. People group and interpret stimuli according to the four Gestalt laws of perceptual organization: similarity, proximity, closure, and continuity. Recognizing an image requires that we have a perceptual schema (a representation of the image in memory) to compare it with. We make interpretations of stimulus input and sensory information based on our knowledge and experience. For instance, you can recognize what you're sitting on right now as a chair or sofa based on your experience with such objects in the past. Perceptual sets are sets of expectations that affect our perceptions. Perceptual constancies allow us to recognize familiar stimuli under varying conditions, allowing us to enter into different environments and be able to function. Without perceptual constancies, we would have to relearn what stimuli are in each environment we enter.

We perceive depth through both monocular (one-eye) and binocular (two-eye) cues. For instance, light and shadow (a monocular cue) helps us to see "depth" in paintings. Each eye sees a slightly different image (binocular disparity), and the resulting disparity is analyzed by feature detectors in the brain, which allow us to see depth. The perception of movement requires the brain to perceive various movement cues. Illusions are incorrect perceptions that often result from the inaccurate perception of both monocular and binocular depth cues.

Psychologists also study how pain is perceived by individuals. Endorphins, natural opiates in the body, inhibit the release of neurotransmitters involved in the synaptic transmission of pain impulses. Endorphins are also involved in stress-induced analgesia, a reduction in pain during stressful conditions. Pain is also perceived differently in different cultures, suggesting that psychological factors affect the perception of pain.

Finally, for some kinds of perception, critical periods during which certain kinds of experiences must occur if perceptual abilities and the brain mechanisms that underlie them are to develop suggest that environmental factors also influence the development of sensation and perception.

Chapter Outline

Sensory Processes
> Stimulus Detection: The Absolute Threshold
> Signal Detection Theory
> Subliminal Stimuli: Can They Affect Behavior?
> The Difference Threshold
> Sensory Adaptation

The Sensory Systems
> Vision
>> The Human Eye
>> Photoreceptors: The Rods and the Cones
>> Visual Transduction: From Light to Nerve Impulses
>> Brightness Vision and Dark Adaptation
>> Color Vision
>>> *The trichromatic theory*
>>> *Opponent-process theory*
>>> *Dual processes in color transduction*
>>> *Color-deficient vision*
>> Analysis and Reconstruction of Visual Scenes
>>> *Feature detectors*
>>> *Visual association processes*
> Audition
>> Auditory Transduction: From Pressure Waves to Nerve Impulses
>> Coding of Pitch and Loudness
>> Sound Localization
>> Hearing Loss
>> Applications of Psychological Science: Sensory Prosthetics: "Eyes" for the Blind, "Ears" for the Hearing Impaired
> Taste and Smell: The Chemical Senses
>> Gustation: The Sense of Taste
>> Olfaction: The Sense of Smell
> The Skin and Body Senses
>> The Tactile Senses
>> The Body Senses

Perception: The Creation of Experience
> Perception is Selective: The Role of Attention
>> Environmental and Personal Factors in Attention

Perceptions Have Organization and Structure
    Gestalt Principles of Perceptual Organization
Perception is Influenced by Expectations: Perceptual Sets
Stimuli Are Recognizable Under Changing Conditions: Perceptual Constancies

Perception of Depth, Distance, and Movement
    Depth and Distance Perception
        Monocular Depth Cues
        Binocular Disparity
    Perception of Movement

Illusions: False Perceptual Hypotheses
    Research Closeup: Stalking a Deadly Illusion

Perception as a Psychobiological Process: Understanding Pain
    Biological Mechanisms of Pain
        Natural Opiates Within the Body
        Endorphins and Pain Reduction
    Psychological Frontiers: Cultural and Psychological Influences on Pain

Experience, Critical Periods, and Perceptual Development
    Cross-Cultural Research on Perception
    Critical Periods: The Role of Early Experience
    Restored Sensory Capacity

Key Terms: *Write the letter of the definition next to the term in the space provided.*

Sensory Processes

1.	___ absolute threshold	a.	a "mixing of the senses"
2.	___ decision criterion	b.	the stimulus-detection process by which sense organs respond to and translate environmental stimuli into nerve impulses sent to the brain
3.	___ difference threshold	c.	the active process of recognizing stimulus input and giving it meaning
4.	___ perception	d.	the lowest intensity at which a stimulus can be detected 50% of the time
5.	___ psychophysics	e.	a standard of how certain a person must be that a stimulus is present before they will say they detect it
6.	___ sensation	f.	concerned with the factors that influence sensory judgments
7.	___ sensory adaptation	g.	a stimulus that is so weak or brief that it cannot be perceived consciously
8.	___ signal detection theory	h.	the smallest difference between two stimuli that people can detect 50% of the time
9.	___ subliminal stimuli	i.	the difference threshold is directly proportional to the magnitude of the stimulus with which the comparison is being made

10. ___ synesthesia   j.   diminishing sensitivity to an unchanging stimulus

11. ___ Weber's Law   k.   the study of the relationships between physical characteristics of stimuli and sensory capabilities

The Sensory Systems

1. ___ amplitude   a.   nearsightedness

2. ___ basilar membrane   b.   farsightedness

3. ___ bipolar cells   c.   color receptors

4. ___ cochlea   d.   cells with synaptic connections to the rods, cones, and ganglion cells

5. ___ conduction deafness   e.   cells whose axons are bundled to form the optic nerve

6. ___ cones   f.   black-and-white brightness receptors

7. ___ dark adaptation   g.   a small area in the center of the retina that contains only cones

8. ___ decibels   h.   the process by which the characteristics of a stimulus are converted into nerve impulses

9. ___ dual-process theory   i.   protein molecules that aid rods and cones in translating light waves into nerve impulses

10. ___ feature detectors   j.   the progressive improvement in brightness sensitivity that occurs over time under conditions of low illumination

11. ___ fovea   k.   theory that there are three types of color receptors in the retina

12. ___ frequency   l.   theory that each of the three cone types respond to two different wavelengths

13. ___ frequency theory   m.   theory that combines trichromatic and opponent-process theory

14. ___ ganglion cells   n.   part of the brain that receives visual information from the thalamus

15. ___ gustation   o.   cells that receive and integrate sensory nerve impulses originating in the retina

16. ___ hertz   p.   a process by which separate but overlapping modules within the brain are simultaneously analyzed

17. ___ hyperopia   q.   the number of sound waves per second

18. ___ kinesthesis   r.   place in the brain where successively more complex features of the visual scene are combined and interpreted

19. ___ lens   s.   the technical measure of cycles per second

20. ___ menstrual synchrony   t.   the vertical size of the sound wave

21. ___ myopia   u.   a measure of the physical pressure that occurs at the eardrum

22. ___ nerve deafness   v.   a coiled, snail-shaped tube filled with fluid in the inner ear

23. ___ olfaction   w.   a sheet of tissue within the cochlea that runs its length

24. ___ opponent-process theory   x.   contains thousands of hair cells

25. ___ optic nerve   y.   theory of pitch perception that states that nerve impulses sent to the brain match the frequency of the sound wave

26. ___ organ of Corti   z.   theory of pitch perception that states that the specific point in the cochlea where the fluid wave peaks and most strongly bends the hair cells serves as a frequency coding cue

27. ___ parallel processing

aa. a type of deafness caused by problems involving the mechanical system that transmits sound waves to the cochlea

28. ___ pheromones

bb. a type of deafness that is caused by damaged receptors within the inner ear or damage to the auditory nerve

29. ___ photopigments

cc. the taste sense

30. ___ place theory

dd. the smell sense

31. ___ primary visual cortex

ee. receptors concentrated along the edges and back surface of the tongue

32. ___ retina

33. ___ rods

ff. chemical signals found in natural body scents

gg. the tendency of women who live together or are close friends to become more similar in their menstrual cycles

34. ___ taste buds

hh. sense that provides us with feedback about our muscles' and joints' positions and movements

35. ___ transduction

ii. an elastic structure that becomes thinner to focus on distant objects and thicker to focus on nearby objects

36. ___ trichromatic theory

jj. a multilayered tissue at the rear of the eyeball

37. ___ visual acuity

kk. bundle of ganglion cells

38. ___ visual association cortex

ll. ability to see fine detail

Illusions, Pain, and Perceptual Development

1. ___ binocular cues

a. a processing function by which the brain takes in individual elements of the stimulus and combines them into a unified perception

2. ___ binocular disparity

b. a process by which sensory information is interpreted in the light of existing knowledge, ideas, and expectations

3. ___ bottom-up processing

c. a technique in which participants are asked to repeat one message while listening simultaneously to two messages sent through headphones

4. ___ convergence

d. the tendency to organize stimuli into a foreground and background

5. ___ critical periods

e. a mental representation of perceptual phenomenon that we use to compare new stimuli to in the process of recognition

6. ___ endorphins

f. a readiness to perceive stimuli in a particular way

7. ___ figure-ground relations

g. depth cues that require only one eye

8. ___ monocular cues

h. depth cues that require both eyes

9. ___ perceptual constancies

i. illusory movement produced when a light is flashed and another light is flashed nearby milliseconds later

10. ___ perceptual schema

j. natural opiates that act as pain-killers

11. ___ perceptual set

k. a reduction in perceived pain that occurs under stressful conditions

12. ___ shadowing

l. periods during which certain kinds of experiences must occur if perceptual abilities and the brain mechanisms that underlie them are to develop normally

13. ___ stress-induced analgesia

m. process by which each eye sees a slightly different image

14. ___ stroboscopic movement
    n. a binocular distance cue produced by feedback from the muscles that turn your eyes inward to view a near object

15. ___ top-down processing
    o. allow us to perceive familiar objects under varying conditions

Review at a Glance: *Write the term that best fits the blank to review what you learned in this chapter.*

Sensory Processes

We experience the world through our senses. However, some people suffering from (1) _____ experience sounds as colors or tastes as touch. The study of the relationships between physical characteristics of stimuli and sensory capabilities is called (2) _____. One thing that psychophysicists study is the intensity need to detect a stimulus. The minimal intensity needed to detect a stimulus 50% of the time is called the (3) _____ _____. People are sometimes uncertain about whether they have detected a stimulus and set their own (4) _____ _____ to decide whether they have detected it or not. The theory that is concerned with the factors that influence sensory judgment is called (5) _____ _____ theory. A stimulus so weak or brief that it cannot be perceived consciously is called a (6) _____ stimulus. People must also be able to distinguish between stimuli. The smallest difference between two stimuli that people can perceive 50% of the time is called the (7) _____ threshold or the (8) _____ _____ _____. (9) _____ _____ states that the jnd is directly proportional to the magnitude of the stimulus with which the comparison is made. Sensory systems are attuned to changes in stimulation. The diminishing sensitivity to an unchanging stimulus is called (10) _____ _____.

The Sensory Systems

(11) _____ _____ results when the (12) _____ focuses an image in front of the (13) _____ while (14) _____ occurs when the lens focuses the image behind the retina. The cells in the eye that detect color are called (15) _____, while the cells that detect black-and-white and brightness are called (16) _____. Rods and cones translate light waves into nerve impulses with the action of protein molecules called (17) _____ in the process of (18) _____. Rods and cones have synaptic connections with (19) _____ _____, which in turn have synaptic connections with ganglion cells, the axons of which form the (20) _____ _____. A small area of the retina containing only cones is called the (21) _____, where the cones have individual connections to bipolar cells. Our ability to see fine detail, or our (22) _____ _____, is greatest when the visual image projects directly onto the fovea. We must adapt to different levels of illumination. The progressive improvement in brightness sensitivity that occurs over time in conditions of low illumination like in a movie theatre is called (23) _____ _____. Several theories suggest how we sense color. According to the (24) _____ theory, there are three types of color receptors in the retina, while according to the (25) _____ _____ theory, each type of color receptor is sensitive to two different wavelengths. The (26) _____ _____ theory is a more modern theory, combining both theories. Feature detectors in the (27) _____ _____ _____ receive and integrate

various sensory nerve impulses originating in the retina. Visual information is finally analyzed and recombined in the (28) _____ _____ _____.

Psychologists also study how we detect sound. Sound waves are measured both in the number of sounds waves, or cycles, per second, which is the (29) _____ of the sound waves, and in their vertical size, or (30) _____. Sound waves travel into the auditory canal of the ear and stimulate the three tiny bones of the middle ear, which amplify the sound wave. The pressure created sets the fluid in the (31) _____ _____ into motion. The fluid waves that result vibrate the (32) _____ membrane and set the (33) _____ cells into motion. Neurotransmitters are then released and nerve impulses are sent to the brain. There are two theories of how we code pitch. The (34) _____ theory suggests that nerve impulses sent to the brain match the frequency of the sound wave, while the (35) _____ theory suggests that specific point in the cochlea where the fluid wave peaks and most strongly bends the hair cells serves as a frequency coding cue. A type of hearing loss called (36) _____ deafness occurs when the system sending sound waves to the cochlea is damaged, while (37) _____ deafness occurs when inner ear receptors or the auditory nerve is damaged. (38) _____ is the sense of taste, while (39) _____ refers to our sense of smell. Receptors called (40) _____ _____ concentrated on the tongue allow us to taste things. Some researchers believe that (41) _____, chemical signals found in natural body scents, may affect human and animal behavior. Humans are sensitive to at least four tactile senses: touch, pain, warmth, and cold. The body senses include (42) _____, which provides us with feedback about the positions of our muscles and joints and the (43) _____ sense, which is the sense of body orientation or equilibrium.

Perception: The Creation of Experience

Perception is an active, creative process. To create perceptions, the brain uses both (44) _____ - _____ processing, which involves taking in individual elements of a stimulus and then combining them into a unified perception, and (45) _____ - _____ processing, which is when the brain uses existing knowledge and expectations to perceive a stimulus. Perceptions have organization and structure. Gestalt theorists discovered many of the basic principles of organization. For example, we tend to organize stimuli into foreground figures and backgrounds, a process called (46) _____ - _____ relations. The four Gestalt principles of organization are (47) _____, (48) _____, (49) _____, and (50) _____. Perception involves hypothesis testing. Recognizing a new stimulus, for example a flying animal with feathers, wings, and a beak as a bird, requires use of a perceptual (51) _____. Readiness to perceive certain stimuli in a certain way is called a perceptual (52) _____. We can recognize familiar stimuli under different environmental conditions because of perceptual (53) _____.

Perception of Depth, Distance, and Movement

To judge depth, the brain relies on both (54) _____ cues, which require one eye, and (55) _____ cues, which require two eyes. Depth cues rely on (56) _____ _____, in which each eye sees a slightly different image. A second binocular distance cue called (57) _____ is produced by feedback from the muscles that turn our eyes inward to view a near object.

Perception as a Psychobiological Process: Understanding Pain

Pain involves a complex set of sensations and perceptions. To help us deal with pain, the brain has its own built-in analgesics called (58) _____. A phenomenon attributed to endorphins is (59) _____ - _____ _____, a reduction in perceived pain during stressful episodes. Culture and early experience can both influence the perception of pain. For some aspects of perception, there are (60) _____ _____, during which certain kinds of experiences must occur if perceptual abilities and the brain mechanisms that underlie them are to develop. If no experience stimulating the development during this time occurs, then it is too late to undo the deficit.

Apply What You Know

1. Describe how visual stimuli are projected to the two hemispheres by referring to the diagram on Study Sheet 4.1.

2. Describe the process shown in the diagram on Study Sheet 4.2.

3. Draw a figure using each of the four Gestalt principles of perceptual organization. Use Study Sheet 4.3.

Stretching Your Geographies

1. If perception is a subjective phenomenon, we would expect that people of different cultures would perceive the same objects or events in quite different ways. Using the PsycInfo database or Psychological Abstracts (available in your college library), find two studies that examine such cultural differences and report their findings.

Study #1:

Study #2:

Practice Test

Multiple Choice Items: *Please write the letter corresponding to your answer in the space to the left of each item.*

_____ 1. The lowest intensity at which a stimulus can be detected 50% of the time is known as the ____.

   a. difference threshold
   b. absolute threshold
   c. signal detection
   d. just noticeable difference

_____ 2. A participant in a signal detection study has the tendency to be bolder in her decisions regarding the presence of a target stimulus. As a result, she has more hits but also has more false alarms. This example demonstrates how ____ can affect ____.

   a. situational factors; participant characteristics
   b. situational factors; decision criterion
   c. participant characteristics; situational factors
   d. participant characteristics; decision criterion

_____ 3. Regarding the impact of subliminal messages on attitudes and behavior, research has found that subliminal messages have ____.

   a. no impact on attitudes and behaviors
   b. an equal impact on attitudes and behaviors
   c. a stronger impact on behaviors than on attitudes
   d. a stronger impact on attitudes than on behaviors

_____ 4. The ____ threshold is defined as the smallest difference between two stimuli that can be perceived 50% of the time.

   a. absolute
   b. sensation
   c. difference
   d. perceptual

_____ 5. According to a Weber fraction, the jnd for weight is 1/50. Therefore, if an object weighed 1kg (1000g), a second object would have to minimally weigh ____ for you to notice a difference between the two objects.

   a. 2kg
   b. 1020g
   c. 1050g
   d. 50g

_____ 6. You have just prepared a bath for yourself and as you are getting in, the water feels very hot, almost too hot. However, you continue to ease yourself into the tub and pretty soon, even though it has remained the same temperature, the water no longer feels so hot. The characteristic of sensory neurons that is responsible for this phenomenon is known as ____.

a. sensory adaptation
b. the refractory period
c. the all-or-none law
d. signal detection

_____ 7. The receptors for black-and-white and brightness are called ____, while the receptors for color are called ____.

a. rods; cones
b. cones; rods
c. ganglion cells; bipolar cells
d. bipolar cells; ganglion cells

_____ 8. The department of transportation contacts you and asks what color they should make their road signs so that they will be most visible at night. Given what you have learned in this class about the sensitivity of rods under conditions of low illumination, one color that you would **not** want to pick is ____.

a. yellow
b. blue
c. green
d. red

_____ 9. The progressive improvement in brightness sensitivity that occurs over time under conditions of low illumination is called ____.

a. transduction
b. dark adaptation
c. visual acuity
d. opponent-process

_____ 10. The current modern theory of color sensation uses the ____ theory to explain the behavior of the cones in color vision while a modified version of the ____ theory that emphasizes the role of ganglion cells is used to explain the presence of afterimages and certain types of color blindness.

a. trichromatic; additive color mixture
b. dual process; trichromatic
c. opponent process; dual process
d. trichromatic; opponent process

_____ 11. Groups of neurons within the primary visual cortex that are organized to receive and integrate sensory nerve impulses originating in specific regions of the retina are called _____.

   a. ganglion cells
   b. bipolar cells
   c. feature detectors
   d. opponent procesors

_____ 12. You are standing on the sidewalk and a bus drives past you with a billboard on the side. With seemingly no effort, your visual system is able to simultaneously process information about the words on the billboard, the color and speed of the bus, and how far away from you the bus is. This simultaneous analyzing of information related to different visual characteristics is called _____.

   a. parallel processing
   b. hierarchical processing
   c. transduction
   d. habituation

_____ 13. Fluid waves from inside the _____ vibrate the basilar membrane and the membrane above it, causing a bending in the _____ in the organ of Corti.

   a. tiny bones of the inner ear; eardrum
   b. hair cells; cochlea
   c. cochlea; hair cells
   d. tiny bones of the inner ear; hair cells

_____ 14. The place theory of pitch perception states that pitch is determined by _____.

   a. neurons that fire at the same frequency as the incoming stimulus
   b. neurons that fire at the same amplitude as the incoming stimulus
   c. the specific place in the cochlea where the fluid wave peaks more
   d. the way that the eardrum resonates in response to different frequencies

_____ 15. While cleaning his ear a little too vigorously, Steve accidentally punctures the eardrum in his right ear and is unable to hear out of this ear. Steve's injury would be classified as an example of _____.

   a. conduction deafness
   b. temporal lobe deafness
   c. nerve deafness
   d. localized deafness

_____ 16. The chemical sense of taste is called _____, while the chemical sense of smell is called _____.

   a. the vestibular sense; olfaction
   b. gustation; olfaction
   c. olfaction; the vestibular sense
   d. olfaction; kinesthesis

92

_____ 17. The four qualities that our sense of taste responds to are ___.

a. sweet, sour, salty, bitter
b. sweet, sour, salty, tart
c. sour, salty, biting, tart
d. sweet, sour, salty, sugary

_____ 18. Chemical signals found in natural body scents that may affect human and animal behavior are called ____.

a. olfactors
b. buds
c. gustators
d. pheromones

_____ 19. Of the following, the one which is <u>not</u> classified as a tactile sensation is ____.

a. pressure
b. touch
c. warmth
d. gustation

_____ 20. Our sense of body orientation or equilibrium is called ____.

a. kinesthesis
b. the vestibular sense
c. olfaction
d. balance

_____ 21. As you are reading this question, feature detectors in you visual system are analyzing the various stimulus components and recombining them into your perception of letters and words. This is an example of ____ processing.

a. figure-ground
b. top-down
c. parallel
d. bottom-up

_____ 22. Perceptual set is an example of ____ processing.

a. figure-ground
b. top-down
c. parallel
d. bottom-up

_____ 23. A new commercial presents its product in a rather novel and intense way, making use of a lot of movement and special effects. If this ad were to capture your attention, it would **best** be viewed as an example of how _____ can affect attention.

a. personal motives
b. sensory adaptation
c. internal factors
d. environmental factors

_____ 24. You would likely recognize the following set of stimuli as the word "cat" due to the Gestalt principle of _____.

C /-\ T

a. similarity
b. figure-ground
c. proximity
d. continuity

_____ 25. In 1950, psychologist Harold Kelley invited a guest lecturer to his class. Half of his students were led to believe that the guest lecturer was a warm person while the other half was told that he was rather cold. When rating the guest lecturer afterwards, students tended to rate him in way that was consistent with the expectations they had been given ahead of time. This example was presented to demonstrate how _____ can affect _____.

a. perceptual schemas; perceptual sets
b. perceptual schemas; bottom-up processing
c. perceptual sets; social perceptions
d. sensory adaptation; sensory habituation

_____ 26. A binocular distance cue produced by feedback from the muscles that turn your eyes inward to view a near object is called _____.

a. stroboscopic movement
b. convergence
c. monocularism
d. perceptual constancy

_____ 27. Stroboscopic movement refers to _____.

a. the movement of a visual image to an area outside of the fovea
b. instances where a light appears to move between two adjacent flashing lights
c. illusory movements that are due to binocular depth cues
d. illusory movements that are due to perceptual constancies

_____ 28. Compelling but incorrect perceptions of stimuli are called _____.

    a. illusions
    b. perceptual schemas
    c. perceptual sets
    d. stroboscopic movements

_____ 29. Endorphins are thought to exert their painkilling effects by _____.

    a. enhancing the release of neurotransmitters involved in pain impulses
    b. deadening or numbing the part of the frontal cortex that processes pain
    c. inhibiting the release of neurotransmitters involved in pain impulses
    d. facilitating the process of sensory adaptation

_____ 30. A possible adaptive function of stress induced analgesia is that _____.

    a. when it occurs long enough, it enhances the functioning of the immune system
    b. it allows defensive behavior to be given priority over normal responses to pain
    c. it allows the normal response to pain to be given priority over defensive behavior
    d. it allows the immune system to be given priority over endocrine system

True/False Items: _Write T or F in the space provided to the left of each item._

_____ 1. People who experience sounds as colors or tastes suffer from synesthesia.

_____ 2. A standard of how certain people must be that a stimulus is present before they will say they detect it is called the absolute threshold of the stimulus.

_____ 3. For people who suffer from myopia, the lens focuses the visual image behind the retina.

_____ 4. Transduction is the process whereby the characteristics of a stimulus are converted into nerve impulses.

_____ 5. Opponent-process theory proposed that each of the three cone types responds to two different wavelengths.

_____ 6. Amplitude is a measure of the loudness of sound and is measured in decibels.

_____ 7. There is no evidence for the hypothesis of menstrual synchrony.

_____ 8. Perceptual constancies allow us to recognize familiar objects under varying conditions.

_____ 9. People of all cultures perceive pain in the same way, suggesting that it is purely a biological function.

_____ 10. If particular patterns of perception do not develop during critical periods, they never will.

Short Answer Questions

1. What is sensory adaptation?

2. Describe the differences between the Young-Helmholtz trichromatic theory and the opponent-process theory.

3. What is the difference between frequency and amplitude?

4. What is the difference between bottom-up and top-down processing?

5. How do perceptual schemas and perceptual set affect perception?

Essay Questions

1. Describe how the absolute threshold, decision criteria, the difference threshold, and Weber's Law affect the process of stimulus detection.

2. Describe how rods and cones send their messages to the brain.

3. Describe the process of auditory transduction.

4. Describe the four Gestalt laws of perceptual organization.

5. How do we perceive depth and distance?

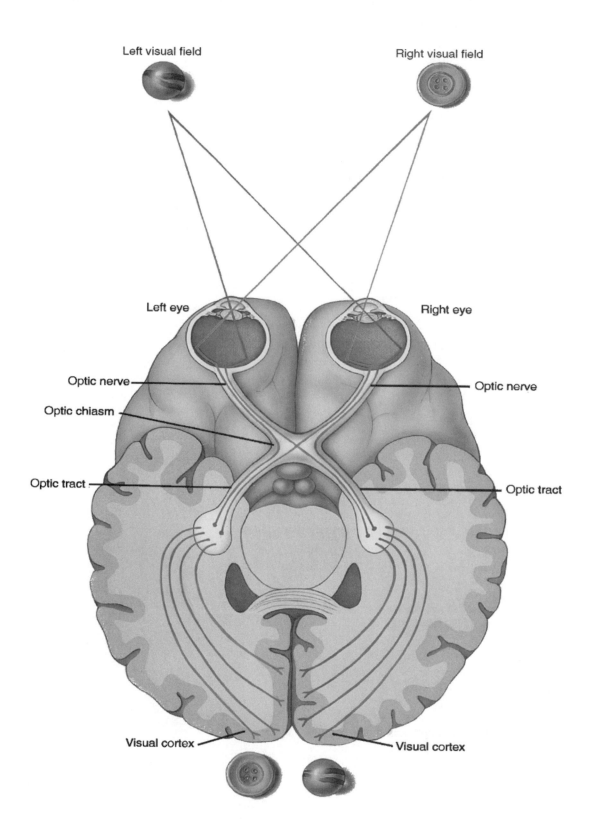

Left visual field

Right visual field

Left eye

Right eye

Optic nerve

Optic nerve

Optic chiasm

Optic tract

Optic tract

Visual cortex

Visual cortex

Study Sheet 4.2 Theories of Color Vision

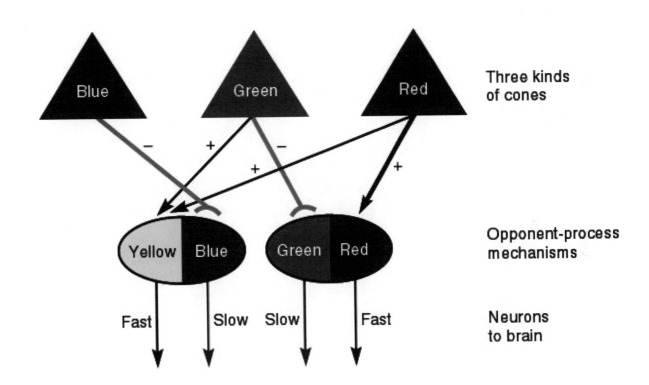

Three kinds of cones

Opponent-process mechanisms

Neurons to brain

Study Sheet 4.3 Gestalt Principles of Perceptual Organization

1. Similarity

2. Proximity

3. Closure

4. Continuity

Answer Keys

Answer Key for Key Terms

Sensory Processes

1. d
2. e
3. h
4. c
5. k
6. b

7. j
8. f
9. g
10. a
11. i

The Sensory Systems

1. t
2. w
3. d
4. v
5. aa
6. c
7. j
8. u
9. m
10. o
11. g
12. q
13. y
14. e
15. cc
16. s
17. b
18. hh
19. ii

20. gg
21. a
22. bb
23. dd
24. l
25. kk
26. x
27. p
28. ff
29. I
30. z
31. n
32. jj
33. f
34. ee
35. h
36. k
37. ll
38. r

Perception and Illusions

1. h
2. m
3. s
4. n
5. l
6. j
7. d
8. g

9. o
10. e
11. f
12. c
13. k
14. i
15. b

Answer Key for Review at a Glance

1. synesthesia
2. psychophysics
3. absolute threshold
4. decision criterion
5. sensory detection
6. subliminal
7. difference
8. just noticeable difference (jnd)
9. Weber's Law
10. Sensory adaptation
11. myopia
12. lens
13. retina
14. hyperopia
15. cones
16. rods
17. photopigments
18. transduction
19. bipolar cells
20. optic nerve
21. fovea
22. visual acuity
23. dark adaptation
24. trichromatic
25. opponent process
26. dual process
27. primary visual cortex
28. visual association cortex
29. frequency
30. amplitude
31. cochlea
32. basilar
33. hair
34. frequency
35. place
36. conduction
37. nerve
38. Gustation
39. olfaction
40. taste buds
41. pheromones
42. kinesthesis
43. vestibular
44. bottom-up
45. top-down
46. figure-ground
47. similarity
48. proximity
49. closure
50. continuity
51. schema
52. set
53. constancies
54. monocular
55. binocular
56. binocular disparity
57. convergence
58. endorphins
59. stress-induced analgesia
60. critical periods

Answer Key for Practice Test Multiple Choice Questions

1.	b		16.	b
2.	d		17.	a
3.	d		18.	d
4.	c		19.	d
5.	b		20.	b
6.	a		21.	d
7.	a		22.	b
8.	d		23.	d
9.	b		24.	d
10.	d		25.	c
11.	c		26.	b
12.	a		27.	b
13.	c		28.	a
14.	c		29.	c
15.	a		30.	b

Answer Key for Practice Test True/False Questions

1.	T		6.	T
2.	F		7.	F
3.	F		8.	T
4.	T		9.	F
5.	T		10.	T

Answer Key for Practice Test Short Answer Questions

1. Sensory adaptation refers to the diminishing sensitivity to an unchanging stimulus. This type of adaptation is sometimes called habituation. Sensory adaptation helps us to get used to stimuli.

2. Trichromatic theory argued that there are three types of color receptors, one sensitive to wavelengths that correspond to blue, another to green, and the third to red. Opponent-process theory argued that each of the three cone types correspond to two wavelengths: the first type to red or green, the second type to blue or yellow, and the third type to black or white.

3. Frequency is the number of sound waves, or cycles, per second and is measured in hertz (Hz). Frequency is a measure of the sound's pitch. Amplitude refers to the vertical size of the sound wave and is measured in decibels (db). Amplitude is a measure of the sound's loudness.

4. In bottom-up processing, feature detectors break down stimuli into their constituent parts, and the system then combines them into a unified perception. In top-down processing, existing knowledge and expectations guide the process of the perception of a stimulus.

5. Perceptual schemas are mental representations by which we compare new stimuli in order to recognize them. Perceptual sets are sets of expectancies that influence our perceptions of new stimuli.

Answer Key for Practice Test Essay Questions

1. The absolute threshold is the lowest intensity at which a stimulus can be detected 50% of the time. An example is a candle flame seen at 30 miles on a clear, dark night. People's level of sensitivity is different. Each person sets their decision criterion, which is a standard of how sure they must be that they have sensed a stimulus before they will report sensing it. The difference threshold refers to the smallest <u>difference</u> between two stimuli that people can perceive 50% of the time. The difference threshold is also known as the just noticeable difference (jnd). Weber's Law states that the jnd is directly <u>proportional</u> to the magnitude of a stimulus with which the comparison is being made.

2. Rods, black-and-white and brightness receptors, and cones, color receptors, are in the retina. Both have synaptic connections with bipolar cells. Bipolar cells, in turn, have synaptic connections with ganglion cells, whose axons collect into a bundle to form the optic nerve. The optic nerve sends the messages to the brain. Rods and cones translate light waves into nerve impulses through the action of protein molecules called photopigments. The absorption of light by these photopigments affects the rate of neurotransmitter release at the receptor's synapse with the bipolar cells.

3. Sound waves travel into an auditory canal leading to the eardrum. Beyond the eardrum, in the middle ear, in which three tiny bones, the hammer, anvil, and stirrup, amplify the sound waves. The pressure created sets the fluid inside the cochlea into motion, resulting in the vibration of the basilar membrane and the membrane above it. This vibration causes the bending of the hair cells in the organ of Corti, triggering a release of neurotransmitters into the synaptic space between the hair cells and the neurons of the auditory nerve, resulting in nerve impulses sent to the brain.

4. The law of similarity says that when parts of a configuration are perceived as similar, they will be perceived as belonging together. The law of proximity says that elements that are near each other are likely to be perceived as part of the same configuration. The law of closure states that people tend to close the open edges of a figure or fill in gaps in an incomplete figure. The law of continuity states that people link individual elements together so they form a continuous line or pattern that makes sense.

5. Depth and distance are perceived through both monocular and binocular depth cues. One monocular (one eye) cue is light and shadow. Linear perspective refers to the perception that parallel lines converge as they recede into the distance. An object's height in the horizontal plane, clarity, relative size, and motion parallax are also monocular cues. Binocular cues rely on the brain's feature detectors, which are attuned to depth cues. A second binocular distance cue, convergence, is produced by muscles that turn your eyes inward to view a near object.

Chapter 5
STATES OF CONSCIOUSNESS

Learning Objectives: *These questions, with a few additions (indicated with an asterisk), are taken from the directed questions found in the margins of the chapter. After reading the chapter, you should be able to answer these questions.*

1.   Describe some basic characteristics of consciousness.

2.   How do psychologists measure states of consciousness?

3.   Explain Freud's three-level system of consciousness?

4.   How do cognitive psychologists view the unconscious?

5.   What is automatic processing and why is it important?

6.   Can nonconscious processes influence emotional responses?

7.   Base on the modular model of the mind, how does consciousness arise?

8.   How do the brain and environment regulate circadian rhythms?

9.   What are free-running circadian rhythms?

10.   Explain how DAD, jet lag, and night-shift work involve circadian disruptions.

11.   How is exposure to light used to treat circadian disruptions?

11.1*   Besides exposure to light, what other methods are used to treat circadian disruptions?

12.   What brain wave patterns distinguish the first four stages of sleep?

13.   Describe the major characteristics of REM sleep.

14.   What brain areas help regulate sleep onset and REM sleep?

15.   How do sleep patterns change with age?

16.   What evidence indicates that genetic factors partly account for differences in people's sleep behaviors?

17.   How do different types of sleep deprivation affect mood and performance?

18.   Explain the restoration and evolutionary theories of sleep.

19.   What evidence supports and contradicts the hypothesis that REM sleep serves a special function?

20.   What is insomnia and how is it treated?

21.   Describe the major symptoms of narcolepsy and REM-BD.

21.1* Describe the major symptoms of sleep apnea and sleepwalking.

22.   Identify the major differences between nightmares and night terrors.

23.   When do we dream most? Why?

24.   According to the Freudian and activation-synthesis theories, why do we dream?

25.   Describe the main assumption of the cognitive-process dream theory. What evidence supports it?

26.   Does daydreaming serve any function? How similar are daydreams and night dreams?

27.   How do drugs increase and decrease synaptic transmission?

28.   What is the relation between tolerance, compensatory responses, and withdrawal?

29.   Describe some myths about drug dependence.

30.   Explain how alcohol affects the brain.

31.   How does being intoxicated affect decisions about drinking and driving?

32.   How do stimulants affect brain functioning? Why does heavy use lead to a "crash?"

33.   Describe the two main effects of opiates.

34.   What is the greatest danger of hallucinogens?

35.   Explain three myths about marijuana.

36.   What evidence supports the hypothesis that genetic factors influence drug reactions?

37.   Describe how environmental and psychological factors influence drug reactions.

38.   In what sense is hypnotic behavior "involuntary?" Does hypnosis have a unique power to coerce people against their will?

39.   Can non-hypnotized people produce the physiological reactions and feats displayed by hypnotized people?

40.   Does hypnosis produce pain relief? Is this a placebo effect?

41.   Explain the two major scientific concerns about the use of forensic hypnosis.

42.   According to the dissociation theory of hypnosis, why do hypnotic behaviors seem involuntary?

43.   According to the social-cognitive theory of hypnosis, why do hypnotic behaviors seem involuntary?

Chapter Overview

This chapter covers various aspects of consciousness, including what consciousness is thought to be, circadian rhythms, and states of altered consciousness that includesleep and dreaming, drugs, and hypnosis.

Consciousness is defined as our moment-to-moment awareness of ourselves and our environment. It is subjective, meaning that everyone's sense of reality is different (you might remember the term 'subjective reality' from previous chapters). It is also private. Other people don't have direct access to your consciousness. It is dynamic or changing in that we go through different states of awareness at different times. Finally, it is self-reflective. The mind is aware of itself. Thus, consciousness is central to how we define our "selves." Freud was one of the first psychologists to study consciousness, suggesting that we have a conscious mind, which contains everything that we are currently aware of, a preconscious mind, which contains things that can be brought into consciousness, and an unconscious mind, which contains things that ordinarily cannot be brought into conscious awareness. Some modern psychodynamic views suggest that emotional and motivational processes may operate unconsciously. States of consciousness are typically measured via self-report, physiological measures, and behavioral measures. Current cognitive psychologists view conscious and unconscious processes as complementary forms of information processing. People use both voluntary conscious effort, or controlled processing, and little or no conscious effort, or automatic processing, to perform various tasks. Automatic processing facilitates divided attention, enabling us to do several things at once, like watching TV, talking on the phone, and doing homework at the same time. The modular mind approach suggests that various "modules," or information processing subsystems within the brain, interact to help us perform various behavioral tasks.

Circadian rhythms are our daily biological clocks and are controlled by the suprachiasmatic nuclei of the hypothalamus. These rhythmic changes in body temperature, certain hormonal secretions, and other bodily functions like sleep and waking states are on an approximately 24 hour cycle. Various environmental changes such as seasons, jet lag, and night-shift work can alter our circadian rhythms. For example, seasonal affective disorder (SAD) is a cyclic tendency to become psychologically depressed during certain months of the year (particularly fall or winter). Some people's circadian rhythms adjust better to such environmental events than do those of others.

Psychologists have been very interested in the nature of the sleep cycle. EEG recordings of brain waves show that beta waves, which have a high frequency but a low amplitude, occur during active waking states, while alpha waves occur during feelings of relaxation or drowsiness. We go through several stages of sleep. Stage 1 is a stage of light sleep from which we can easily be awakened. As sleep becomes deeper in Stage 2, sleep spindles, periodic bursts of brain wave activity, occur in the EEG patterns. Very slow and large delta waves occur in Stage 3 and in Stage 4 sleep, and then the EEG pattern changes as we go back into Stage 3 and 2 patterns. At this point in the sleep cycle, people enter REM sleep, or rapid-eye-movement sleep. During REM sleep, physiological arousal increases to daytime levels for many people, and dreaming often occurs (although dreaming also occurs in non-REM stages).

Sleep is biologically regulated, but the environment plays a role as well. As we age, we sleep less and the time spent in Stages 3 and 4 declines. REM sleep declines during infancy and early childhood and then remains fairly stable. People have different sleep needs and don't necessarily need eight hours a night. The number of hours of sleep we need seems to be affected by both genetic and various environmental factors. Studies of sleep deprivation have generally showed deficits in mood, and in cognitive and physical performance. It is somewhat unclear exactly <u>why</u> we sleep. The restoration model argues that sleep recharges our rundown bodies. Experimental evidence has been only modestly supportive of this model, though. Evolutionary/circadian sleep models suggest that sleep has developed through evolutionary processes. Early members of the human species may have performed tasks like hunting and food gathering during the day and were more likely to survive predators if they stayed in shelter at night. Thus, the typical human today sleeps at night. There are several types of sleep disorders. Insomnia refers to chronic difficulty in falling or staying asleep. Narcoleptics suffer from extreme daytime sleepiness and sudden, uncontrollable sleep attacks. People with REM-sleep behavior disorder (REM-BD) don't experience normal REM sleep paralysis and may kick violently or throw punches while asleep! People with sleep apnea repeatedly stop and restart breathing during sleep. Sleepwalkers typically walk during Stage 3 or 4 sleep and seem vaguely aware of their environment, though they are typically unresponsive to other people. Most people have nightmares, and some, typically children, have night terrors.

Dreams are a source of endless curiosity for people, including psychologists, who study when and why we dream. We tend to dream more during REM states and during the last few hours of sleep. We typically dream about familiar people and places. Our cultural backgrounds, life experiences, and current concerns influence the content of our dreams. Freud's psychoanalytic theory argued that dreams serve "wish fulfillment," the gratification of unconscious urges. According to activation-synthesis theory, dreams occur because the cortex is trying to make sense of random neural activity. Problem-solving models suggest that dreams help us find creative solutions to problems. Cognitive-process dream theories argue that both dreaming and waking thought are produced via the same neural processes.

Psychologists study the effects of various drugs on the brain and on behavior. Agonists are drugs that increase neurotransmitter activity, while antagonists are drugs that decrease neurotransmitter activity. When a drug is used repeatedly, people may develop a tolerance to it and suffer compensatory responses, which are opposite of the drug effects. Discontinued drug use produces withdrawal symptoms, during which more compensatory processes occur. Depressants such as alcohol, barbituates, and tranquilizers depress nervous system activity. Stimulants such as amphetamines and cocaine increase neural firing, while opiates produce pain relief and a sense of euphoria. Hallucinogens like LSD produce hallucinations. Both genes and culture seem to determine drug effects.

Hypnosis is a state of heightened suggestibility. Hypnotized people subjectively experience their actions to be involuntary, but hypnosis does not seem to involve any unique power that would get people to act against their wills. People under hypnosis sometimes perform what seem to be fantastic physical feats, but the effects may simply be placebo effects. On the other hand, hypnosis seems to increase pain tolerance and is not a placebo effect. Researchers seem to agree that hypnosis can affect amnesia, but they dispute the causes. Whether hypnosis can <u>improve</u> memory is highly debatable. Dissociation theories of memory suggest that hypnosis literally involves a dissociation of consciousness such that a person simultaneously experiences two streams of consciousness. Social-cognitive theories suggest that people are acting out the <u>role</u> of being hypnotized when under a hypnotic trance and thus act in ways that conform to the role of what they believe a hypnotized person can do.

Chapter Outline

The Puzzle of Consciousness
    Measuring States of Consciousness
    Levels of Consciousness: Psychodynamic and Cognitive Perspectives
        The Cognitive Unconscious
            Controlled versus automatic processing
            Divided attention
        The Emotional Unconscious
        The Modular Mind

Circadian Rhythms: Our Daily Biological Clocks
    Keeping Time: Brain and Environment
        Early Birds and Night Owls
    Environmental Disruptions of Circadian Rhythms
        Applications of Psychological Science: Combating Winter Depression, Jet Lag, and Night Shift Disruptions

Sleep and Dreaming
    Stages of Sleep
        Stage 1 through Stage 4
        REM sleep
    Getting a Night's Sleep: Brain and Environment
    How Much Do We Sleep?
        Short- and Long-Sleepers
        From Genes to Lifestyles
    Sleep Deprivation
    Why Do We Sleep?
    Sleep Disorders
        Insomnia
        Narcolepsy
        REM-Sleep Behavior Disorder
        Sleep Apnea
        Sleepwalking
        Nightmares and Night Terrors
    The Nature of Dreams
        When Do We Dream?
        What Do We Dream About?
        Why Do We Dream?
            Freud's psychoanalytic theory
            Activation-synthesis theory
            Cognitive approaches
            Toward integration

Key Terms: *Write the letter of the definition next to the term in the space provided.*

1. ____ activation-synthesis theory
2. ____ alcohol myopia
3. ____ alpha waves

4. ____ amphetamine psychosis
5. ____ automatic processing
6. ____ beta waves
7. ____ blood-brain barrier

8. ____ circadian rhythms

9. ____ cognitive-process dream theory

10. ____ consciousness

a. our moment-to-moment awareness of ourselves and our environment
b. the voluntary use of attention and conscious effort
c. the ability to perform more than one activity at the same time
d. daily biological cycles
e. located in the hypothalamus, regulate circadian rhythms
f. a hormone that has a relaxing effect on the body
g. a cyclic tendency to become psychologically depressed during certain months of the year
h. large waves that regularly appear in Stage 3 and Stage 4 sleep
i. Stages 3 and 4 of sleep together
j. the sleep stage that includes rapid eye movements

11. ___ controlled effortful processing

k. theory that sleep recharges our run-down bodies and allows us to recover from physical and mental fatigue

12. ___ delta waves

l. theories that suggest that sleep's main purpose is to increase a species' chances of survival

13. ___ depressants

m. chronic difficulty in falling asleep, staying asleep, or getting restful sleep

14. ___ dissociation theory (of hypnosis)

n. extreme daytime sleepiness and sudden, uncontrollable sleep attacks

15. ___ divided attention

o. a sleep disorder in which the loss of muscle tone that causes normal REM sleep paralysis is absent

16. ___ evolutionary/circadian sleep models

p. breathing repeatedly stops and restarts during sleep

17. ___ fantasy-prone personalities

q. frightening dreams that are more intense than nightmares

18. ___ hallucinogens

r. the gratification of our unconscious desires and needs during dreams

19. ___ hypnosis

s. theory that during REM sleep the brain stem bombards the higher brain centers with random neural activity, causing the cortex to try to interpret the activity and resulting in dreams

t. theory that dreams can help us find creative solutions to problems

20. ___ hypnotic suggestibility scale

u. theory that proposes that dreaming and waking thought are produced by the same mental systems in the brain

21. ___ insomnia

v. people with these types of personality live in a fantasy world that they control

22. ___ melatonin

w. a special lining of tightly packed cells that lets vital nutrients pass so that neurons can function

23. ___ narcolepsy

x. decreasing responsivity to a drug

24. ___ night terrors

25. ___ opiates

y. occurrence of compensatory responses after discontinued drug use

26. ___ problem-solving dream model

z. formal name for drug addiction

27. ___ REM sleep

aa. drugs that decrease nervous system activity

28. ___ REM sleep behavior disorder

bb. a "shortsightedness" in thinking suffered by intoxicated people

29. ___ restoration model

cc. drugs that increase neural firing and arouse the nervous system

30. ___ seasonal affective disorder

dd. powerful mind-altering drugs that produce hallucinations

31. ___ sleep apnea

ee. a state of heightened suggestibility

32. ___ slow-wave sleep

ff. contains a standard series of pass/fail suggestions that are read to a subject after hypnotic induction

33. ___ social-cognitive theory (of hypnosis)

gg. theory that suggests that hypnosis creates a division of consciousness

34. ___ stimulants

hh. theory that suggests that hypnotic experiences result from expectations of people who are motivated to take on the role of being "hypnotized"

35. ___ substance dependence		ii.	brain waves that are indicative of feeling relaxed or drowsy
36. ___ suprachiasmatic nuclei		jj.	schizophrenia-like hallucinations and delusions due to drug-induced high levels of dopamine activity
37. ___ THC (tetrahydrocannabinol)		kk.	processing that involves little or no conscious effort
38. ___ tolerance		ll.	brain waves that occur when you are awake and alert
39. ___ wish fulfillment		mm.	effective pain killers
40. ___ withdrawal		nn.	marijuana's active ingredient

Review at a Glance: *Write the term that best fits the blank to review what you learned in this chapter.*

The Puzzle of Consciousness

(1) _____ is defined as our moment-to-moment awareness of ourselves and our environment. It is subjective, private, dynamic, and central to our sense of self. One of the earliest theorists about consciousness was (2) _____, who believed that the mind contains three levels of awareness, the conscious mind, the preconscious mind, and the unconscious. Today, cognitive psychologists believe that both conscious and unconscious thought are complementary forms of information processing. People use both voluntary attention and conscious effort, or (3) _____ processing, and (4) _____ processing, which is performed with little or no conscious effort. Automatic processing facilitates (5) _____ _____, which allows us to do more than one thing simultaneously.

Circadian Rhythms: Our Daily Biological Clocks

The daily biological cycles that we are all subject to are called (6) _____ rhythms. These daily cycles are regulated by the (7) _____ _____ of the hypothalamus. Environmental disruptions such as jet lag, night-shift work, and changes of season can affect circadian rhythms. A disorder called (8) _____ _____ _____ is a cyclic tendency to become psychologically depressed during certain months, which may result from a circadian rhythm disruption.

Sleep and Dreaming

When we are awake and alert, our brains show an EEG pattern of (9) _____ waves, while (10) _____ waves typically occur when we are relaxed or drowsy. Approximately every 90 minutes of sleep, we cycle through different stages of sleep. Stage 1 is a stage of light sleep, while Stage 2 is characterized by (11) _____ _____ in the EEG pattern. Stages 3 and 4 are characterized by (12) _____ waves in the EEG pattern, and, together, they are called (13) _____ - _____ sleep. Rapid eye movements and relaxation of the muscles due to lost muscle tone occur during (14) _____ sleep. It is not exactly clear <u>why</u> we sleep. The (15) _____ model argues that we sleep in order to recover from physical and mental fatigue. (16) _____ / _____ models argue that the main purpose of sleep is to increase a species' chances of survival. Many people suffer from sleep disorders. A chronic difficulty in falling asleep is called (17) _____. Extreme daytime sleepiness and sudden, uncontrollable sleep attacks are characteristic of (18) _____. When the loss of muscle tone that causes normal REM sleep "paralysis" fails to occur, a person experiences (19) _____ - _____ _____ _____. People who repeatedly stop and restart breathing during sleep suffer from (20) _____ _____. Dreams more intense than nightmares often suffered by children are called (21) _____ _____. Freud believed that main function of dreaming is (22) _____ _____, and distinguished between a dream's manifest content (the surface story) and the (23) _____ content, the disguised psychological meaning of the dream. A more modern theory argues that dreams are the result of the action of the cortex as it tries to make sense of random nerve impulses. This theory is called (24) _____ - _____ theory. According to (25) _____ - _____ models, dreams can help us find creative solutions to problems. Theories that focus on the process of how we dream and argue that dreams and waking states are governed by the same mental systems in the brain are called (26) _____ - _____ _____ theories. Sometimes people daydream a lot and live in a vivid fantasy world that they control. Such people are said to have a (27) _____ - _____ personality.

Drugs and Altered Consciousness

A special lining of tightly packed cells that screens out many foreign substances but lets vital nutrients and many drugs through is called the (28) _____ - _____ _____. When a drug is used repeatedly the intensity of effects the drug produces tends to decrease over time, a process called (29) _____. Because drugs affect homeostasis, the brain tries to adjust for the imbalance by producing (30) _____ responses. The occurrence of compensatory responses after discontinued drug use is called (31) _____. Drugs that decrease nervous system activity are called (32) _____, while drugs that increase neural firing are called (33) _____. Excessive use of alcohol, a depressant, may result in a "shortsightedness" in thinking that may cause people not to monitor their own actions or think about the long-term consequences of their behavior, a phenomenon called (34) _____ _____. Powerful mind-altering drugs that produce hallucinations are called (35) _____ .

Hypnosis

Hypnosis is a state of heightened suggestibility in which some people are able to experience test suggestions as if they were real. A standard series of pass/fail questions to determine the degree to which a person is subject to hypnotic induction is called a (36) _____ _____ _____. (37) _____ theory proposes that hypnosis involves a division of awareness such that a person simultaneously experiences two streams of consciousness. A second set of theories of hypnosis called (38) _____ - _____ theories suggest that people under hypnosis are simply acting out social roles.

Apply What You Know

1. Keep track of your dreams for one week. The best way to do this is to write down whatever you can remember about your dreams immediately after you wake up. Then, at the end of the week, look back at the content our your dreams and indicate whether you think that the content of your dreams best supports activation-synthesis theory or problem-solving theories. Use Study Sheet 5.1.

2. Not everyone sleeps eight hours per night. Design a survey to examine the mean numbers of hours people sleep per night. Graph your results. What do they show about the average sleeping habits of people at your school? Use Study Sheet 5.2.

Stretching Your Geographies

1. Not every culture in the world has similar sleep patterns to those that typically occur in the United States (7-8 hours per night). Do some library research to discover how people in other cultures deal with the universal need for sleep. Describe the research findings.

Practice Test

<u>Multiple Choice Items</u>: *Please write the letter corresponding to your answer in the space to the left of each item.*

_____ 1. Consciousness is _____ .

    a. subjective
    b. public
    c. static
    d. not central to our sense of self

_____ 2. Looking at a map and deciding what route to take to a new destination would be considered an example of _____ .

    a. compensatory processing
    b. controlled processing
    c. automatic processing
    d. preconscious processing

_____ 3. When a person is learning how to type, their behavior usually involves _____ processing, but someone who can type quickly, efficiently, and accurately is probably utilizing more _____ processing.

    a. automatic; controlled
    b. controlled; automatic
    c. automatic; effortful
    d. effortful; controlled

_____ 4. Most circadian rhythms are regulated by the brain's _____ .

    a. thalamus
    b. suprachiasmatic nuclei
    c. biological clock
    d. sleep waves

_____ 5. Some modern psychodynamic views that incoporate information processing perspectives from cognitive psychology also suggest that _____ .

    a. the mind is modular
    b. unconscious emotional and motivational urges influence our behavior
    c. divided attention is the source of all of our abilities
    d. the manifest content of dreams is the source of unconscious desires

_____ 6. The model that suggests that the mind is made up of information-processing subsystems within the brain that perform tasks related to sensation, perception, memory etc. is known as the ____ model.

a. activation-synthesis
b. emotional unconscious
c. circadian rhythm
d. modular

_____ 7. A really jolly old guy just before and during Christmas Eve, Santa Claus becomes regularly psychologically depressed during the dreary winter months at the North Pole and doesn't want to do anything. This really ticks off Mrs. Claus, who wants to hit the hot beaches of Rio during February. Santa's mood does improve after the winter months. His wife convinces Santa to visit Dr. Jack Frost, who believes that Santa likely suffers from a cyclic condition called ____.

a. REM
b. apnea
c. REM-sleep behavior disorder
d. SAD

_____ 8. One reason that shiftwork has a detrimental effect on circadian rhythms is that ____.

a. there isn't enough variability in the sleep schedules of shift workers
b. the nature of shiftwork is more physically taxing that other types of work typically done during the day
c. shift workers often get too much sleep
d. shift workers often go home in the morning daylight, which makes it difficult to reset their circadian clocks

_____ 9. EEG recordings of the brain's electrical activity show ____ waves during alert waking states, ____ waves during relaxation and drowsy states, and ____ waves during deep sleep states.

a. alpha; beta; delta
b. alpha; delta; beta
c. beta; alpha; delta
d. delta; alpha; beta

_____ 10. REM is a period of sleep when ____.

a. dreaming does not occur
b. physiological arousal increases to daytime levels
c. dreams are shorter than in non-REM sleep
d. legs and arms typically flail away

_____ 11. Studies examining the sleep habits of identical and fraternal twins have revealed that ____.

    a. while genetic factors are significant, environmental factors also account for important sleep differences
    b. environmental factors don't really account for any of the sleep differences
    c. genetic factors account for essentially all of the sleep differences
    d. environmental factors account for essentially all of the sleep differences

_____ 12. The fact that antidepressants suppress REM sleep yet people who take these medications do not show any obvious cognitive impairments was taken as evidence that ____.

    a. supported the assumption that dreaming can occur during NREM sleep stages
    b. supported the evolutionary/circadian rhythm models of REM sleep
    c. contradicted the argument that REM sleep serves a special psychological function
    d. contradicted the restoration model of sleep

_____ 13. You awaken in the middle of the night to find your roommate standing in the corner of your room with an aggressive look on his face, punching a pillow, and running in place. Despite this strange behavior, you realize that your roommate is still asleep and when you wake him he shares with you that he was having this bizarre dream about having been involved in a fight while running on a treadmill. Given what you have learned in introductory psychology, it is **most likely** that your roommate ____.

    a. may have narcolepsy
    b. was sleep waking
    c. experienced the REM rebound effect
    d. may have REM behavior disorder

_____ 14. A wife is awoken many times during the night by her husband's apparent difficulty breathing. Every few minutes, the husband's airway becomes momentarily obstructed until he gasps and then starts breathing again. It is **most likely** that the husband is suffering from _____.

    a. sleep apnea
    b. airway cataplexy
    c. side effects from the REM rebound effect
    d. nightmares related to drowning

_____ 15. Waking up after who knows how long, Rip Van Winkle decides to experience the new world he has found and runs off to Las Vegas to gamble, see the Strip, and take in a few shows. After 72 straight hours of gambling and boozing, he feels a great deal of physical and mental fatigue and goes back to his hotel suite for another snooze. The model that explains Rip's renewed need to sleep at this point is ____.

    a. evolutionary/circadian theory
    b. the REM sleep model
    c. the restoration model
    d. REM-sleep behavior disorder

_____ 16. Because of censorship codes in the early years of motion pictures, directors could not show sexual activity on screen. They thus sometimes used metaphors for such activity such as picturing a train going into a tunnel. Freud would argue that if such content appeared in a dream that the content would by symptomatic of ____.

a. problem-solving
b. activation-synthesis
c. the brain's attempt to understand random neural content
d. wish fulfillment

_____ 17. Criticism of the activation-synthesis theory of dreaming has suggested that it overestimates____ and fails to consider the fact that ____.

a. the role of unconscious desires; dreams occur during REM sleep
b. the problem-solving ability of dreams; dream occur during REM sleep
c. the bizarreness of dreams; dreams also occur during NREM sleep
d. the interpretive capacity of the higher brain; dreams also occur during NREM sleep

_____ 18. The theories that suggest that dreaming and waking thought are produced by the same mental systems in the brain are called ____ theories.

a. problem-solving
b. activation-synthesis
c. wish fulfillment
d. cognitive-process

_____ 19. Beth has a very vivid imagination. Though she has a very ordinary job, she often imagines that she is working on top-secret projects with national security implications. When at home by herself, she is easily able to visualize herself in many exciting and exotic places that she has in fact never actually visited. According to the text, Beth would **best** be classified as having ____.

a. high hypnotic susceptibility
b. a fantasy-prone personality
c. divided attention
d. an hallucinatory personality

_____ 20. Drugs that inhibit or decrease the actions of a neurotransmitter are called ____.

a. stimulants
b. antagonists
c. agonists
d. blood-brain barriers

_____ 21. Opiates such as morphine and codeine both contain molecules that are similar to endorphins, the body's natural painkillers. Opiates like these bind to receptor sites that are keyed to endorphins and trigger similar pain reducing responses. Given these characteristics, both morphine and codeine would be classified as ____.

a. antagonists
b. hallucinogens
c. antigens
d. agonists

_____ 22. In order to stay up late to study for exams, Sara starts drinking sodas with caffeine in them in order to better stay awake. After continuing this practice for several months, Sara notices that she needs to consume more caffeine to achieve the same effect. This decrease in her response to caffeine is **best viewed** as example of what is called ____.

a. withdrawal
b. tolerance
c. placebo effect
d. dependence

_____ 23. If a drug is introduced into the nervous system, the body attempts to maintain its state of optimal physiological balance called _____ by adjusting for this imbalance by producing ____, which are reactions opposite to the effect of the drug.

a. tolerance; compensatory responses
b. withdrawal symptoms; homeostasis
c. compensatory responses; withdrawal symptoms
d. homeostasis; compensatory responses

_____ 24. Alcohol is a(n) ____.

a. depressant
b. stimulant
c. hallucinogen
d. agonist

_____ 25. Drugs such as Angel Dust and Ecstasy are called _____ and usually distort or intensify sensory experience and can blur the boundary between reality and fantasy.

a. depressants
b. hallucinogens
c. opiates
d. stimulants

_____ 26. All of the following demonstrate how environmental factors affect reactions to drugs **except** ____.

a. compensatory responses can be triggered by familiar external stimuli
b. the reactions of people sharing a drug experience can effect an individual's response
c. in some cultures, drinking does not lead to aggressive behavior
d. people may behave "drunk" if they think they have consumed alcohol but actually haven't

_____ 27. Research in the area of forensic psychology has found that hypnosis _____ a reliable way to enhance memory and that hypnotized participants typically remember information _____ than nonhypnotized participants who are asked to use imagery or other memory tricks to facilitate recall.

a. is not; no better
b. is; no better
c. is not; better
d. is; better

_____ 28. A state of heightened suggestibility in which some people are able to experience imagined test suggestions as if they were real is called ____.

a. mesmerism
b. animal magnetism
c. hypnosis
d. hypnotic amnesia

_____ 29. Studies of hypnosis have shown that ____.

a. hypnosis can increase pain tolerance
b. hypnosis usually improves one's memory
c. those people under hypnotic induction perform physiological feats significantly greater than those in placebo control groups
d. hypnotized people do not subjectively experience their actions to be involuntary

_____ 30. The theory that argues that hypnotic effects occur because people are acting out a social role is called ____ theory.

a. dissociation
b. divided consciousness
c. social cognitive
d. forensic hypnosis

True/False Items: *Write T or F in the space provided to the left of each item.*

_____ 1. The voluntary use of attention and conscious effort in the performance of tasks is called automatic processing.

_____ 2. Most circadian rhythms are regulated by the brain's suprachiasmatic nuclei.

_____ 3. A pattern of beta waves occur in stage 1 sleep.

_____ 4. Dreams occur only in REM sleep.

_____ 5. It is imperative that all of us get at least eight hours of sleep per night.

_____ 6. People who suffer from narcolepsy have sudden, uncontrollable sleep attacks.

_____ 7. There is a single, agreed-upon model of dreaming.

_____ 8. Decreasing responsivity to a drug is called withdrawal.

_____ 9. Alcohol is a depressant.

_____ 10. Hypnosis can increase one's pain tolerance.

Short Answer Questions

1. Distinguish between controlled and automatic processing.

2. What are circadian rhythms, and how are they controlled by the brain?

3. Describe three different sleep disorders.

4. What is the relationship between drug tolerance, compensatory responses, and withdrawal symptoms?

5. Describe the difference between the dissociation and social cognition theories of hypnosis.

Essay Questions

1. Describe how environmental factors can affect circadian rhythms.

2. Describe the EEG patterns that occur during the various stages of sleep.

3. Describe three theories of dreams.

4. Describe how both genes and culture influence drug effects.

5. What do the studies that compare people under hypnotic induction with those in placebo control groups indicate about the effectiveness of hypnosis?

Study Sheet 5.1 Keeping Track of Dreams

Sunday:

Monday:

Tuesday:

Wednesday:

Thursday:

Friday:

Saturday:

Which theory (or theories) do the content of your dreams support? Explain why!

Study Sheet 5.2 Different Sleep Patterns

N (sample size):

Mean Number Hrs. Sleep:

Graph of Results (Don't forget to label your axes!)

Answer Keys

Answer Key for Key Terms

1.	s	11.	b	21.	m	31.	p
2.	bb	12.	h	22.	f	32.	i
3.	ii	13.	aa	23.	n	33.	hh
4.	jj	14.	gg	24.	q	34.	cc
5.	kk	15.	c	25.	mm	35.	z
6.	ll	16.	l	26.	t	36.	e
7.	w	17.	v	27.	j	37.	nn
8.	d	18.	dd	28.	o	38.	x
9.	u	19.	ee	29.	k	39.	r
10.	a	20.	ff	30.	g	40.	y

Answer Key for Review at a Glance

1. consciousness
2. Freud
3. controlled
4. automatic
5. divided attention
6. circadian
7. suprachiasmatic nuclei
8. seasonal affective disorder
9. beta
10. alpha
11. sleep spindles
12. delta
13. slow-wave
14. REM
15. restoration
16. Evolutionary/circadian
17. insomnia
18. narcolepsy
19. REM-sleep behavior disorder
20. sleep apnea
21. night terrors
22. wish fulfillment
23. latent
24. activation-synthesis
25. problem-solving
26. cognitive-process dream
27. fantasy-prone
28. blood-brain barrier
29. tolerance
30. compensatory
31. withdrawal
32. depressants
33. stimulants
34. alcohol myopia
35. hallucinogens
36. hypnotic suggestibility scale
37. Dissociation
38. social-cognitive

Answer Key for Practice Test Multiple Choice Questions

1. a
2. b
3. b
4. b
5. b
6. d
7. d
8. d
9. c
10. b
16. d
17. c
18. d
19. b
20. b
21. d
22. b
23. d
24. a
25. b

11.	a	26.	d
12.	c	27.	a
13.	d	28.	c
14.	a	29.	a
15.	c	30.	c

Answer Key for Practice Test True/False Questions

1.	F	6.	T
2.	T	7.	F
3.	F	8.	F
4.	F	9.	T
5.	F	10.	T

Answer Key for Practice Test Short Answer Questions

1. Controlled processing involves the voluntary use of attention and conscious effort. Automatic processing occurs when we carry out routine actions or well-learned tasks with little or no conscious effort.

2. Circadian rhythms are daily biological cycles of body temperature, certain hormonal secretions, and other bodily functions. Most circadian rhythms are regulated by the brain's suprachiasmatic nuclei, which are located in the hypothalamus.

3. Insomnia is difficulty in falling asleep, staying asleep, or getting restful sleep. Narcolepsy involves extreme daytime sleepiness and sudden sleep attacks. In REM-sleep behavior disorder, the normal REM-sleep paralysis is absent. People with sleep apnea stop and restart breathing during sleep. Some people sleepwalk. Some sleepers, particularly children, suffer from night terrors, which are more intense than nightmares.

4. Tolerance stems from the body's attempt to maintain homeostasis. The body will produce compensatory responses as a way of doing this. Withdrawal occurs when compensatory responses continue after drug use is discontinued.

5. According to dissociation theory, hypnosis involves a division of consciousness such that the person experiences two streams of consciousness simultaneously. Social-cognitive theories suggest that hypnotic experiences result from expectations of people who are taking on the "hypnotic" role.

Answer Key for Practice Test Essay Questions

1. Seasonal affective disorder is a cyclic tendency to become depressed during certain times of the year and may be a result of circadian disruptions caused by changes in exposure to daylight. Jet lag is a circadian disruption caused by flying across several time zones in one day. Night shiftwork also causes circadian shifts due to the necessity of different sleeping patterns.

2. Beta waves occur during alert waking states. As sleep begins, theta waves increase. Sleep spindles, which indicate bursts of rapid brain-wave activity, occur in Stage 2. As Stage 3 begins, large delta waves appear, and, in Stage 4, they dominate the EEG pattern. After 20-30 minutes of Stage 4 sleep, the EEG pattern changes as we go back through Stage 3 and Stage 2 sleep and then enter REM sleep.

3. Freud believed that the main purpose of dreams was wish fulfillment, the gratification of our unconscious desires and needs. Activation-synthesis theory suggests that the cortex creates a dream to best fit the pattern of neural activation during sleep. According to problem-solving models, dreams help us to find creative solutions to problems. Cognitive-process dream theories suggest that dreaming and waking thought are produced by the same mental systems in the brain.

4. Genetic factors influence sensitivity and tolerance to drug effects. Both the physical and the social setting in which a drug is taken can influence a user's reaction. Cultural factors can affect how people respond to a drug as well as drug consumption. People's beliefs and expectancies, which are influenced by culture, also affect drug reactions.

5. Most well-controlled studies of hypnosis show that nonhypnotized subjects show the same physiological effects. There is some evidence that hypnosis can increase pain tolerance and cause amnesia beyond placebo effects.

Chapter 6
LEARNING AND ADAPTATION: THE ROLE OF EXPERIENCE

Learning Objectives: *These questions, with a few additions (indicated with an asterisk), are taken from the directed questions found in the margins of the chapter. After reading the chapter, you should be able to answer these questions.*

1.   Historically, how have behaviorists and ethologists differed in their study of learning?

2.   How is the concept of adaptive significance tied to evolutionary theory?

2.1*   What is a fixed action pattern?

3.   What role does the environment play in <u>personal</u> and <u>species</u> adaptation?

4.   What is habituation, and what is its adaptive significance?

5.   How do you create a conditioned response (CR)?

6.   Under what circumstances are CRs typically acquired most quickly?

7.   Explain the key factor in producing the extinction of a CR.

8.   Explain the adaptive significance of stimulus generalization and discrimination.

9.   How does higher-order conditioning create attraction toward neutral stimuli?

10.   How does classical conditioning explain fear acquisition?

11.   How is classical conditioning used in society to increase and decrease our arousal/attraction to stimuli?

12.   What is ANV and how does it develop?

13.   How can classical conditioning boost immune system functioning?

14.   What evidence led Thorndike to propose the "law of effect?"

14.1* What is operant conditioning? What is the difference between reinforcement and punishment?

15.   Identify two key differences between classical and operant conditioning.

16.   Why are antecedent stimuli important in operant conditioning?

17.   How do secondary reinforcers become "reinforcers?"

18. How does negative reinforcement differ from positive reinforcement and punishment?

19. Explain how operant extinction, aversive punishment, and response cost differ.

20. Describe some disadvantages of using aversive punishment to control behavior.

20.1* Define what is meant by the term "delay of gratification."

21. How might you shape a child who never cleans up his room to do so?

22. What are some examples of discriminative stimuli in your own life?

23. Describe four major schedules of partial reinforcement and their effects on behavior.

24. Are variable or fixed schedules more resistant to extinction? Why?

25. Describe the role of negative reinforcement in escape and avoidance conditioning.

26. How has operant animal training helped humans?

27. In what broad ways has operant conditioning directly enhanced human welfare?

28. What is the purpose of each of the five major steps in a self-regulation program?

29. How do learned taste aversions illustrate the concept of preparedness?

30. How has knowledge of learned taste aversions been used to help animals?

31. What evidence led the Brelands to propose the concepts of instinctual drift?

32. How do biology and learning influence one another?

33. How do the concepts of "insight" and "cognitive maps" challenge the behavioral view of learning?

34. Explain some evidence that supports the "expectancy model" of classical conditioning.

35. What role does awareness play in operant conditioning?

36. How does latent learning challenge the behavioral view of learning?

37. What is the adaptive significance of observational learning?

38. Explain how Bandura's experiment illustrates the distinction between learning and performance.

39. Evaluate the internal and external validity of the *Lassie* experiment.

40. How does language make learning more efficient?

Chapter Overview

This chapter covers the basic processes of learning, which include habituation, classical conditioning, operant conditioning, and modeling. Psychologists have focused both on how we learn and why we learn. Ethologists focused on the functions of behavior, particularly its adaptive significance; its influence on an organisms' chances of survival and reproduction. Research has suggested that the environment shapes behavior through both personal and species adaptation. When we enter into environments, the environment shapes our personal behavior. Similarly, the biology of a species is shaped through the natural selection of behaviors that help members of the species adapt to the environment. The human brain has acquired the capacity to perform psychological functions that historically have helped members of our species to survive and reproduce, according to evolutionary psychologists.

There are several types of learning processes. The simplest type may be habituation, the decrease in response strength to a repeated stimulus. By learning not to respond to familiar stimuli, an organism may conserve resources to pay attention to important stimuli. Classical conditioning, in which an organism learns to associate two stimuli such that one stimulus comes to produce a response that only the other previously did, was made famous through the work of the Russian physiologist Ivan Pavlov with the salivary response of dogs. A stimulus that reflexively produces a response is called an unconditioned stimulus (UCS), and the response is called an unconditioned response (UCR). The stimulus repeatedly paired with the UCS that comes to produce the response is called the conditioned stimulus (CS), and the response is then known as the conditioned response (CR). This entire process is known as acquisition. Forward, short-delay conditioning appears to work best. The CS is presented first and is still present when the UCS appears in this procedure. Extinction occurs when the CS is repeatedly presented without the UCS, such that the response strength diminishes significantly. For example, if a dog has been conditioned to salivate in response to a bell (CS) paired with food (UCS), but the bell is then repeatedly sounded without the food being given to the dog, the dog will stop salivating. Occasionally, a response that has been extinguished will reappear after some time in response to the old CS, a process called spontaneous recovery. Once a CR is acquired, an organism may respond to similar stimuli in the same way, a process called stimulus generalization. The ability to discriminate between stimuli occurs when an organism responds differently to stimuli. When a neutral stimulus comes to produce a response through pairing with an already established CS, higher-order conditioning has occurred. Many examples of this can be seen in everyday life. For example, politicians who appear in front of large American flags are using higher-order conditioning to influence the development of attitudes toward them. Classical conditioning has other applied aspects. The process can be used to both influence the acquisition and elimination of fear. Attraction and aversion to other people and objects are likely also influenced through classical conditioning processes.

Operantly conditioned responses are emitted (voluntarily) rather than elicited like classically conditioned responses are, and they are influenced through their consequences. E.L. Thorndike's Law of Effect says that in a given situation, a response followed by a satisfying consequence will become more likely to occur while a response followed by an unsatisfying consequence will become less likely to occur. The term operant conditioning was coined by B.F. Skinner to describe how an organism operates on its environment to get what it wants and to avoid what it doesn't want. Reinforcement strengthens a response that precedes it, while punishment decreases the strength of a response that precedes it. Skinner's analysis of operant behavior involved studying the antecedents (A) of the behavior, the behavior emitted (B), and the consequences (C) of the behavior. In operant conditioning, the organism learns an association between the behavior and its consequences. The antecedent conditions come to signal that a certain consequence will occur if a certain behavior is emitted. Reinforcement and punishment are the consequences that affect the likelihood of a response under the antecedent conditions. Responses are strengthened by positive reinforcement. Primary reinforcers, such as food and water, are stimuli that satisfy biological needs. Secondary reinforcers, such as money, are conditioned reinforcers because they become associated with primary reinforcers. For example, you can use money to buy food. Negative reinforcement is not the same thing as punishment. Negative reinforcement occurs when a response is strengthened through the removal or avoidance of a stimulus. For example, people use umbrellas because they prevent us from getting wet. Through aversive punishment, a response is weakened by the presentation of a stimulus, such as a slap or a spanking. In response cost, a response is weakened by the removal of a stimulus. For example, taking away TV privileges or car keys is a way that some parents have of punishing their children for undesirable behavior. Operant conditioning can be used to shape behavior by rewarding successive approximations of the behavior. Similarly, chaining is used to condition complex behaviors. The last step of the behavior chain is trained first, and the prior step is reinforced by the ability to perform the next one until the entire chain of behavior is performed. Generalization and discrimination work with operant conditioning much like they work with classical conditioning. Operant generalization occurs when an operant response occurs to a new antecedent stimulus similar to an old one. Operant discrimination occurs when an operant response will occur to one antecedent stimulus but not to another. Schedules of reinforcement influence much of operant behavior. On a continuous schedule, every response is reinforced, while on a partial schedule, only some responses are reinforced. There are both fixed and interval schedules as well as both ratio and interval schedules. On a fixed-ratio schedule, reinforcement is given after a certain number of responses. On a variable-ratio schedule (e.g. VR-6), reinforcement is given after an average number of responses (e.g. sometimes after 3, sometimes after 6, sometimes after 9). On a fixed-interval schedule, the first response that occurs after a certain amount of time is reinforced. Finally, on a variable-interval schedule, the first response after a variable amount of time is reinforced. Ratio schedules tend to produce the highest rate of responding. Following reinforcement, there is typically a pause in responding, which is referred to as a "scallop" on graphs of response rates. Like with classical conditioning, there are many applications of operant conditioning. Skinner's work gave rise to the field of applied behavior analysis, which combines the behavioral approach with the scientific method in an attempt to solve individual and societal problems through the use of operant conditioning techniques.

Biology asserts certain limits on learning. Martin Seligman's concept of preparedness suggests that animals are biologically "prewired" to easily learn behaviors related to their survival as a species. For example, animals develop conditioned taste aversions to learn to avoid foods and liquids that are bad for them. Similarly, animals may be prepared to fear certain stimuli. This fear then helps them to avoid or escape the stimuli, thus increasing their chances of survival and reproduction. Some responses are difficult to operantly condition because of instinctive drift, the tendency of animals to engage in instinctive behavior regardless of their training. Biology also affects animals' ability to learn through the action of brain structures like the hypothalamus and through neurotransmitters like dopamine.

Cognition also affects learning. Such models are known as S-O-R models, suggesting that an organism's cognitions influence the relationship between stimulus and response. The expectancy model, for instance, argues that in classical conditioning the CS produces an expectancy (cognition) that the UCS will occur. Cognition is also present in operant conditioning. Cognitive theorists emphasize that organisms develop expectations of the relationships between their behavior and its consequences.

Much of what we learn is through observation of others. Albert Bandura suggests that observational learning, or modeling, involves four basic steps: attention, retention, reproduction, and motivation. Language frees us from trial-and-error learning and plays a role in teaching us how to perform certain behaviors.

Chapter Outline

Adapting to the Environment
       How Do We Learn? The Search for Mechanisms
       Why Do We Learn? The Search for Functions
       Crossroads of Learning: Biology, Cognition, and Culture

Habituation

Classical Conditioning: Associating One Stimulus With Another
       Pavlov's Pioneering Research
       Basic Principles
              Acquisition
              Extinction and Spontaneous Recovery
              Generalization and Discrimination
              Higher-Order Conditioning
       Applications of Classical Conditioning
               Acquiring and Overcoming Fear
              Conditioned Attraction and Aversion
              Psychological Frontiers: Can Classical Conditioning Make Us Ill – and Healthy Again?

Operant Conditioning: Learning Through Consequences
       Thorndike's Law of Effect
       Skinner's Analysis of Operant Conditioning
              ABC's of Operant Conditioning
       Antecedent Conditions: Identifying When to Respond
       Consequences: Determining How to Respond
               Positive Reinforcement
                    Primary and secondary reinforcers
              Negative Reinforcement
              Operant Extinction
              Aversive Punishment
              Response Cost
              Immediate Versus Delayed Consequences
       Shaping and Chaining: Taking One Step at a Time
       Generalization and Discrimination

Key Terms: *Write the letter of the definition next to the term in the space provided.*

Adapting to the Environment, Habituation, and Classical Conditioning

1. ____ adaptive significance

2. ____ anticipatory nausea and vomiting

3. ____ aversion therapy

4. ____ classical conditioning

5. ____ conditioned response

6. ____ conditioned stimulus

7. ____ discrimination (classical conditioning)

8. ____ exposure therapies

9. ____ extinction

10. ____ habituation

11. ____ higher order conditioning

12. ____ learning

13. ____ spontaneous recovery

14. ____ stimulus generalization

15. ____ unconditioned response

16. ____ unconditioned stimulus

a. a process by which experience produces a relatively enduring change in an organism's behavior or capabilities

b. how a behavior influences an organism's chances of survival and reproduction

c. a decrease in the strength of response to a repeated stimulus

d. stimulus that produces a UCR without learning

e. a response that occurs without learning and is elicited by a UCS

f. a stimulus that produces a CR

g. a learned response elicited by a CS

h. stimuli similar to the initial CS elicit a CR

i. a CR occurs to one stimulus but not to others

j. a neutral stimulus becomes a CS after being paired with an already established CS

k. basic goal is to expose a phobic patient to the CS without the UCS

l. when a CS is presented without the UCS, the response gradually weakens

m. the reappearance of a previously extinguished CR after a rest period

n. an organism learns to associate two stimuli such that one stimulus comes to produce a response originally produced only by the other stimulus

o. attempts to condition a repulsion to a stimulus that triggers unwanted behavior by pairing it with a noxious UCS

p. people become nauseous and vomit before cancer therapy

Operant Conditioning

1. ____ applied behavior analysis

2. ____ aversive punishment

3. ____ avoidance conditioning

4. ____ chaining

5. ____ continuous reinforcement schedule

a. a response followed by a satisfying consequence will become more likely to occur and a response followed by an unsatisfying consequence will become less likely to occur

b. a type of learning in which behavior is influenced by its consequences

c. a special chamber to study operant conditioning experimentally

d. a consequence that strengthens an outcome that it follows

e. a signal that a particular response will produce certain consequences

6. ___ delay of gratification

7. ___ discrimination (operant conditioning)

8. ___ discriminative stimulus

9. ___ escape conditioning

10. ___ extinction (operant conditioning)

11. ___ fixed interval schedule

12. ___ fixed ratio schedule

13. ___ law of effect

14. ___ negative reinforcement
15. ___ operant conditioning

16. ___ operant generalization

17. ___ partial reinforcement schedule
18. ___ positive reinforcement
19. ___ primary reinforcer

20. ___ punishment

21. ___ reinforcement

22. ___ response cost

23. ___ secondary reinforcer

24. ___ shaping

25. ___ Skinner box

26. ___ target behavior

27. ___ token economy
28. ___ two-factor theory of avoidance learning
29. ___ variable interval schedule

30. ___ variable ratio schedule

f. a response is strengthened by the subsequent presentation of a stimulus

g. stimulus that an organism finds reinforcing because it satisfies biological needs

h. stimulus that through association with primary reinforcers becomes a reinforcer itself

i. a response is strengthened by the removal or avoidance of a stimulus

j. the weakening and disappearance of a response because it is no longer reinforced

k. a response is weakened by the presentation of a stimulus

l. a response is weakened by the removal of a stimulus

m. the ability to forego an immediate but smaller reward for a delayed but more satisfying outcome

n. used to develop a sequence of responses

o. an operant response occurs to a new antecedent stimulus that is similar to the original one

p. an operant response will occur to one antecedent stimulus but not to another

q. every response of a particular type is reinforced

r. only some responses are reinforced

s. reinforcement is given after a fixed number of responses

t. reinforcement is given after an average number of responses

u. the first correct response that occurs after a time interval is reinforced

v. reinforcement occurs after the first response that occurs after a variable time interval

w. organisms learn a response to escape from an aversive stimulus

x. organisms learn a response to avoid an aversive stimulus

y. both classical and operant conditioning are involved in avoidance learning

z. combines a behavioral approach with the scientific method to solve individual and societal problems

aa. the specific goal to be changed

bb. desirable behaviors are reinforced with tokens that can be exchanged for tangible rewards

cc. reinforcing successive approximations toward a desired response

dd. weakens a certain response

Biology and Learning, Cognition and Learning, Observational Learning, and the Role of Language

1. ___ cognitive map
2. ___ conditioned taste aversion
3. ___ insight
4. ___ instinctive drift
5. ___ latent learning
6. ___ observational learning
7. ___ preparedness

a. produced by pairing a taste with stomach illness
b. a conditioned response "drifts back" toward instinctive behavior
c. the sudden perception of a useful relationship that helps to solve a problem
d. a mental representation of a spatial layout
e. learning that occurs but is not demonstrated until there is an incentive to do so
f. learning that occurs by observing the behavior of a model
g. species are biologically prewired to easily learn behaviors related to their survival

Review at a Glance: *Write the term that best fits the blank to review what you learned in this chapter.*

Adapting to the Environment

(1) _____ is a process by which experiences produces a relatively enduring change in an organism's behavior or capabilities. Our capacity for learning increases our likelihood of surviving and reproducing in our environment. Thus, behaviors that help us to so adapt are said to have (2) _____ _____. The environment thus shapes behavior through (3) _____ _____. Over time, through the process of evolution, certain behaviors in a species are likely to be selected because of their aid in survival and reproduction, a process called (4) _____ _____. There are several types of learning. One of the simplest is (5) _____, a decrease in the strength of a response to a repeated stimulus.

Classical Conditioning: Associating One Stimulus With Another

An organism learns to associate two stimuli, with the result that one of the stimuli comes to produce a response previously produced only by the other one in the learning process called (6) _____ _____, a phenomenon studied in dogs by (7) _____. During the period of (8) _____, a response is being learned. Initially a stimulus known as the (9) _____ stimulus produces a response, the (10) _____ response, without learning. A second stimulus is repeatedly paired with the UCS, after several learning trials the second stimulus is presented by itself, and the animal will then respond in a similar way to the second stimulus as it had originally done to the UCS. This second stimulus is then known as the (11) _____ stimulus, and the response is known as the (12) _____ response. Classically conditioned responses can be eliminated through the use of (13) _____ procedures, during which the CS is presented repeatedly without the UCS also being present. Sometimes, extinguished responses will appear weeks, months, or even years later, a phenomenon called (14) _____ _____. Another phenomenon of classical conditioning, called (15) _____ _____, occurs when stimuli similar to the initial CS elicit a CR. Stimulus (16) _____ is the ability to distinguish between stimuli. Finally, a process of pairing a neutral stimulus with an already established CS is known as (17) _____-_____ conditioning.

Operant Conditioning: Learning Through Consequences

While Pavlov was studying classical conditioning, Edward L. Thorndike was formulating his (18) _____ ___ _____, which states that responses that are followed by "satisfying" consequences will become more likely to occur, while those responses followed by "unsatisfying" consequences will become less likely to occur. B. F. Skinner studied (19) _____ conditioning, a type of learning in which behavior is influenced by its consequences. Skinner studied operant conditioning experimentally by designing a special chamber called a (20) _____ _____. Through his work, Skinner identified several important types of consequences. (21) _____ strengthens a response that precedes it, while (22) _____ weakens a response that precedes it. Skinner identified the ABC's of operant conditioning, or the (23) _____, (24) _____, and (25)_____. An antecedent condition that signifies that a particular response will now produce a consequence is called a (26) _____ stimulus. Consequences determine how we respond to a stimulus. A response is strengthened by the subsequent presentation of a stimulus in the procedure called (27) _____ _____. There are two types of positive reinforcers. (28) _____ reinforcers are stimuli that an organism finds reinforcing because they satisfy biological needs, while (29) _____ reinforcers become reinforcers through their association with primary reinforcers. A response is strengthened by the removal or avoidance of an aversive stimulus through (30) _____ _____. The weakening and eventual disappearance of a response, called operant (31) _____, occurs because the response is no longer being reinforced. In the procedure called (32) _____ _____, a response is weakened by the subsequent presentation of a stimulus. In (33) _____ _____, a response is weakened by the subsequent removal of a stimulus. In general, reinforcement or punishment occurs immediately after a response. Sometimes, people are asked to forego immediate reinforcement to wait for a better, later reinforcement. The ability to do this is called (34) _____ _____ _____. Operant conditioning can be used to create new responses and sequences of behaviors. (35) _____ is a procedure by which new behaviors or sequences of behaviors are created through reinforcements of successive approximations of the target behavior. (36) _____ creates a sequence of responses by reinforcing each response with the opportunity to perform the next behavior in the sequence. Reinforcement typically occurs on schedules of reinforcement. On a (37) _____ schedule, every response is reinforced, while on (38) _____ schedules, only some responses are reinforced. On (39) _____ _____ schedules, reinforcement is given after a fixed number of responses, while on (40) _____ _____ schedules, reinforcement is given for the first response after a certain amount of time. On a (41) _____ _____ schedule, reinforcement is given after a variable number of responses, while on a (42) _____ _____ schedule, reinforcement is given for the first response after an average amount of time. (43) _____ schedules tend to produce the highest rate of response.

Biology and Learning

Pairing a taste with the experience of illness (such as stomach illness, nausea, and vomiting) produces a (44) _____ _____ _____. Martin Seligman has proposed that humans may be biologically prepared to acquire certain fears, a phenomenon also true of other animals and called (45) _____. The Brelands discovered that some animals could not be operantly conditioned because they fell back on behaviors that were part of their evolutionary history instead, a phenomenon called (46) _____ _____.

Cognition and Learning

Cognitive processes seem to play important roles in learning. German psychologist Wolfgang Köhler discovered that chimps were able to learn by (47) _____, the sudden perception of a useful relationship. Psychologist Edward Tolman discovered that rats seem to develop a mental representation or (48) _____ _____ of a maze. Tolman's experiments also supported the concept of (49) _____ learning, learning that occurs but is not demonstrated until there is an incentive to do so. Robert Rescorla found that animals learn to expect that a UCS will occur after the presentation of a CS, and his model of classical conditioning is known as the (50) _____ model.

Observational Learning: When Others Pave The Way

(51) _____ _____ helped pioneer the study of observational learning, which is also known as (52) _____.

Apply What You Know

1. Classical conditioning, operant conditioning, and modeling are used a great deal in advertising. Find one advertisement that uses classical conditioning to persuade us to buy the product, find one advertisement that uses operant conditioning, and find one that uses modeling. Photocopy the ad (or cut it from the newspaper or magazine if it belongs to you), and attach it in the appropriate space on Study Sheet 6.1. Write a brief explanation of how the ad exemplifies the use of that particular model of learning.

2. See Study Sheet 6.2. How might you use operant conditioning to condition this cute little creature to press a lever or stand on its hind legs?

Stretching Your Geographies

1. Much recent thought in education has suggested that males and females have different <u>learning styles</u>. Do some library research on this and present the basic arguments and research findings.

Practice Test

Multiple Choice Items: *Please write the letter corresponding to your answer in the space to the left of each item.*

_____ 1. The process that produces a relatively enduring change in an organism's behavior or capabilities is called ____.

    a. learning
    b. positive reinforcement
    c. negative reinforcement
    d. shaping

_____ 2. Assume that, through a process of natural selection, a particular species of tree squirrels develops a fur coloring that allows it to blend-in more effectively in their natural environment. As a result, they are more difficult to spot in the trees, are less likely to become prey for local predators, and are thus more likely to survive and reproduce. This **best demonstrates** the process of ____.

    a. classical conditioning
    b. personal adaptation
    c. operant conditioning
    d. species adaptation

_____ 3. You have just settled down to begin studying for your exam in this course when your roommate decides to turn on some music. At first, the music distracts you from your studying but after a short time, the music no longer bothers you even though it continues to play. This example **most clearly demonstrates** the process of ____.

    a. extinction
    b. negative reinforcement
    c. classical conditioning
    d. habituation

_____ 4. A stimulus that produces a response without learning is called a(n) ____ stimulus.

    a. conditioned
    b. reflexive
    c. unconditioned
    d. primary

_____ 5. The procedure that seems to work best in producing classically conditioned responses is ____ pairing.

    a. forward short-delay
    b. forward trace
    c. simultaneous
    d. backward

_____ 6. The best explanation for the success of the answer to question #5 is the _____ model.

    a. operant conditioning
    b. expectancy
    c. spontaneous recovery
    d. observational learning

_____ 7. You are conducting an experiment where you are trying to manipulate the immune response of rats by using the principles of classical conditioning. First, for several days of an experiment, you give rats artificially sweetened water with an immune system enhancing drug in it. You later remove the drug and notice that the immune systems of rats are boosted when they consume the sweetened water. In your experiment, the conditioned stimulus is _____.

    a. the sweetened water
    b. the drug
    c. enhanced immune system functioning in response to the drug
    d. enhanced immune system functioning in response to the sweetened water

_____ 8. A woman living in London during WWII learned to associate air-raid sirens with destruction created by bombs dropped from Nazi airplanes. After moving to the United States, sirens no longer predicted such destruction, so her fear responses to sirens subsided over time. In the language of classical conditioned, the fear response has become _____.

    a. discriminated
    b. generalized
    c. extinguished
    d. spontaneously recovered

_____ 9. On a trip back to London forty-four years after the war ended, the same woman hears a recording of an old air-raid siren and becomes very upset. Classical conditioning researchers would suggest that the woman is experiencing _____.

    a. discrimination
    b. generalization
    c. extinction
    d. spontaneous recovery

_____ 10. Stuart has a rather unusual fear. He is afraid of public speaking but only when he has to make speeches on the weekend. He is a professor and has no trouble speaking in front of large groups of students and he has made effective presentations at conferences, as long as he presents during a weekday. The specificity of Stuart's fear mostly clearly demonstrates the process of _____.

    a. escape conditioning
    b. avoidance conditioning
    c. stimulus generalization
    d. discrimination

_____ 11. The goal of exposure therapies is to expose a phobic person to the feared stimulus without the _____, so that the process of _____ can occur.

a. CS; habituation
b. CS; discrimination
c. UCS; generalization
d. UCS; extinction

_____ 12. A young child is hungry and wants a cookie but is too short to reach the table where the cookie jar is kept. She tries various things to get the jar, such as jumping or throwing her teddy bear at the jar in hopes of knocking it off the table, but to no avail. Eventually, almost by accident, she realizes that she can pull the tablecloth on which the jar rests and is thus able to reach the jar. In the future, she will be more likely to try this technique again since it was effective. This example **best demonstrates** _____.

a. Thorndike's law of effect
b. the principles of classical conditioning
c. shaping
d. partial reinforcement

_____ 13. Joey likes to watch wrestling matches on TV but his mother usually does not allow him to do this. However, Joey has noticed that when his mom has a bad day at work and gets very tired, she usually doesn't mind if he watches wrestling. As a result, Joey usually will only ask to watch wrestling if his mother has had a hard day at work. In this instance, the kind of day that Joey's mother has at work would be considered a(n) _____.

a. conditioned stimulus
b. discriminative stimulus
c. negative reinforcer
d. consequence

_____ 14. In operant conditioning, an organism learns an association between _____.

a. a CS and a UCS
b. an antecedent and a CS
c. an emitted behavior and an operant behavior
d. a behavior and a consequence

_____ 15. Suppose that Andy Warhol was right and in the future everybody will be famous for 15 minutes. Those 15 minutes of fame might be a secondary reinforcer for someone's behavior if the _____.

a. 15 minutes are positively reinforcing
b. 15 minutes are negatively reinforcing
c. famous person is given food, water, and other primary reinforcers because of their fame
d. process of operant extinction occurs

_____ 16. A mother has been continually nagging her daughter about how messy her room is. Finally, the daughter gets so tired of her mom's complaints that she cleans her room, thus stopping the nagging of her mother. Given the fact that the withdrawal of the mother's nagging served to strengthen the daughter's room-cleaning behavior, the mother's nagging would be considered a(n) _____.

    a. negative reinforcer
    b. positive reinforcer
    c. aversive punishment
    d. response cost punishment

_____ 17. Parents are interested in getting their son to play piano. In order to do this, they decide to reinforce him by paying him $1.00 for every hour that he practices. Shortly after this, the son decides that he also wants to learn how to play guitar and, since his parents are still paying him, he continues practicing both instruments. After a couple of months, the parents decide that the important thing is that their son is involved in music and so they quit paying him to practice the piano, whereupon the son gradually quits playing the piano and continues playing the guitar. The weakening and disappearance of the son's piano playing behavior would **best** be considered as an example of _____.

    a. operant extinction
    b. negative reinforcement
    c. positive reinforcement
    d. classical extinction

_____ 18. You are driving down the freeway rather quickly because you are late for a meeting but you notice a police car parked on the side of the freeway. You quickly apply the breaks and slow down to the speed limit. In this instance, the police car represents a _____.

    a. negative reinforcer
    b. primary stimulus
    c. discriminative stimulus
    d. positive reinforcer

_____ 19. You stay inside on very hot days because you don't want to expose yourself to the heat. By doing so, you don't subject yourself to such problems as sunburns or heatstroke. The learning that has taken place for you is **most similar** to _____.

    a. escape conditioning
    b. a variable ratio schedule of reinforcement
    c. avoidance conditioning
    d. a fixed interval schedule of reinforcement

_____ 20. After exactly 187 battles, Klingons get a Klingon Homeworld mandated vacation from their constant battling with the Cardassians, Romulans, Borg, and Dominion and go relaxing at Club Med. Klingons would appear to be on a(n) _____ schedule of reinforcement.

   a. FR
   b. VR
   c. FI
   d. VI

_____ 21. A continuous schedule of reinforcement is actually a(n) _____ schedule.

   a. FR
   b. VR
   c. FI
   d. VI

_____ 22. Skinner's work gave rise to a field called _____, which combines a behavioral approach with the scientific method to solve individual and societal problems.

   a. shaping
   b. applied behavior analysis
   c. chaining
   d. operant conditioning

_____ 23. Through evolution, animals seem to be biologically prewired to more easily learn behaviors that are related to their survival as a species. Seligman has termed this _____.

   a. conditioned taste aversion
   b. preparedness
   c. instinctive drift
   d. biological learning

_____ 24. When a conditioned response "drifts back" to more instinctive behavior, _____ has occurred.

   a. conditioned taste aversion
   b. preparedness
   c. instinctive drift
   d. evolution

_____ 25. Studies of brain effects on learning have shown that _____.

   a. the hypothalamus is the only part of the brain that controls learning
   b. neurotransmitters are not involved in learning
   c. the cerebellum, but not the cerebral cortex, is involved in learning
   d. no single part of the brain "controls" learning

_____ 26. The _____ model asserts that the key factor in classical conditioning in **not** how often the CS is paired with the UCS but how well the CS predicts the appearance of the UCS.

a. insight
b. expectancy
c. latent learning
d. cognitive

_____ 27. A researcher conducts an experiment where rats in one group (Group 1) receive ten learning trials where they receive a shock after a light is lit. Another group of rats (Group 2) receives the same ten trials where the shock is paired with the light but they also receive ten additional random trials where the light is not followed by a shock. According to the expectancy model of classical conditioning, we would expect that the light to become a CS for fear for the rats _____.

a. only in Group 1
b. only in Group 2
c. in both Group1 and Group 2
d. in neither Group 1 nor Group 2.

_____ 28. Learning that occurs but is not shown until there is an incentive to do so is called _____ learning.

a. backward
b. operant
c. classically conditioned
d. latent

_____ 29. Bamm-Bamm Rubble learns to hit other kids over the head with his club by watching his wrestling favorites like "The Rock" on stone-age TV. Bandura would argue that Bamm-Bamm has learned his behavior through _____.

a. latent learning
b. observational learning
c. classical conditioning
d. operant conditioning

_____ 30. Studies of the role of language in learning have shown that _____.

a. people learn better in English than in any other language
b. language abilities do not affect learning
c. language plays a critical role in teaching us how to perform various actions
d. spoken but not signed languages facilitate learning

True/False Items: *Write T or F in the space provided to the left of each item.*

_____ 1. Research shows that biology plays no role in learning.

_____ 2. An initially neutral stimulus that through association with an unconditioned stimulus comes to produce a response initially produced only by the unconditioned stimulus is called the conditioned response.

_____ 3. Extinction occurs when a CS is presented repeatedly without the UCS also being present.

_____ 4. When stimuli similar to the initial CS come to produce the same response, the phenomenon is called stimulus discrimination.

_____ 5. Exposure therapies are used to treat phobias.

_____ 6. Operant responses are emitted.

_____ 7. Secondary reinforcers like money become reinforcers through their association with primary reinforcers.

_____ 8. An example of negative reinforcement is spanking a child for bad behavior.

_____ 9. Interval schedules of reinforcement produce the highest rates of response.

_____ 10. Studies of conditioned taste aversions support the idea that biology constrains learning.

Short Answer Questions

1. What is habituation and why is it important for human behavior?

2. Describe the process of the acquisition of a classically conditioned response.

3. What does the Law of Effect say?

4. What is the difference between shaping and chaining?

5. How do insight and cognitive maps show that cognition is important in the learning process?

Essay Questions

1. Describe what the function of learning is thought to be.

2. Describe how classical conditioning can be used to both acquire and overcome fear.

3. Describe how the ABC's of operant conditioning interact to produce operant behaviors.

4. Describe the differences between the different types of reinforcement schedules.

5. What are the differences between negative reinforcement, aversive punishment, and response cost?

Study Sheet 6.1 Use of Learning Models in Advertising

Classical Conditioning

Explanation:

Study Sheet 6.1 Use of Learning Models in Advertising

Operant Conditioning

Explanation:

Study Sheet 6.1 Use of Learning Models in Advertising

Modeling

Explanation:

Study Sheet 6.2   Operant Conditioning

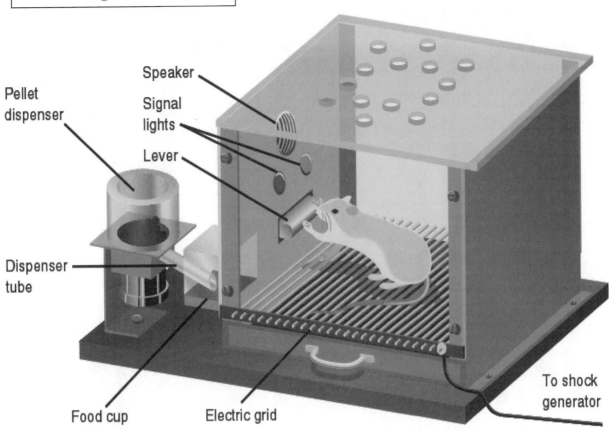

Pellet dispenser

Speaker

Signal lights

Lever

Dispenser tube

Food cup

Electric grid

To shock generator

Answer Keys

Answer Key for Key Terms

Adapting to the Environment, Habituation, and Classical Conditioning

1.	b	9.	l	
2.	p	10.	c	
3.	o	11.	j	
4.	n	12.	a	
5.	g	13.	m	
6.	f	14.	h	
7.	i	15.	e	
8.	k	16.	d	

Operant Conditioning

1.	z	16.	o	
2.	k	17.	r	
3.	x	18.	f	
4.	n	19.	g	
5.	q	20.	dd	
6.	m	21.	d	
7.	p	22.	l	
8.	e	23.	h	
9.	w	24.	cc	
10.	j	25.	c	
11.	u	26.	aa	
12.	s	27.	bb	
13.	a	28.	y	
14.	i	29.	v	
15.	b	30.	t	

Biology and Learning, Cognition and Learning, Observational Learning, and the Role of Language

1.	d	5.	e	
2.	a	6.	f	
3.	c	7.	g	
4.	b			

Answer Key for Review at a Glance

1.	learning	27.	positive reinforcement
2.	adaptive significance	28.	Primary
3.	personal adaptation	29.	secondary
4.	species adaptation	30.	negative reinforcement
5.	habituation	31.	extinction
6.	classical conditioning	32.	aversive punishment
7.	Pavlov	33.	response cost

8. acquisition
9. unconditioned
10. unconditioned
11. conditioned
12. conditioned
13. extinction
14. spontaneous recovery
15. stimulus generalization
16. discrimination
17. higher-order
18. Law of Effect
19. operant
20. Skinner box
21. reinforcement
22. punishment
23. antecedents
24. behavior
25. consequences
26. discriminative
34. delay of gratification
35. Shaping
36. Chaining
37. continuous
38. partial
39. fixed ratio
40. fixed interval
41. variable ratio
42. variable interval
43. Ratio
44. conditioned taste aversion
45. preparedness
46. instinctive drift
47. insight
48. cognitive map
49. latent
50. expectancy
51. Albert Bandura
52. modeling

Answer Key for Practice Test Multiple Choice Questions

1. a
2. d
3. d
4. c
5. a
6. b
7. a
8. c
9. d
10. d
11. d
12. a
13. b
14. d
15. c
16. a
17. a
18. c
19. c
20. a
21. a
22. b
23. b
24. c
25. d
26. b
27. a
28. d
29. b
30. c

Answer Key for Practice Test True/False Questions

1. F
2. F
3. T
4. F
5. T
6. T
7. T
8. F
9. F
10. T

Answer Key for Practice Test Short Answer Questions

1. Habituation refers to a decrease in the strength of a response to a stimulus that is repeated. If we paid attention to every stimulus in our environment, we would quickly become overwhelmed. Thus, through habituation, we learn to pay attention to only those stimuli that are important, and we filter out stimuli that do not provide us with important information.

2. Acquisition refers to the period during which a response is being learned. Initially a stimulus called the unconditioned stimulus will elicit a response, called the unconditioned response, without learning. This is called a natural, unlearned reflex. Learning trials then occur in which a new stimulus, called a conditioned stimulus, is repeatedly paired with the unconditioned stimulus. After a number of such learning trials, the CS is presented alone, and, if the animal or human has been classically conditioned, the response that originally was elicited only by the UCS will now occur in the presence of the CS.

3. Edward L. Thorndike's Law of Effect says that any behavior that is followed by a satisfying consequence will become more likely to occur in the future and any behavior that is followed by an unsatisfying consequence will become less likely to occur in the future.

4. Shaping and chaining are used to condition new behaviors and complex sequences of behavior. When shaping is used, successive approximations toward the final goal are reinforced. For example, to shape a child to study one hour per night, you could reinforce her for studying ten minutes a night. Next, you would only reinforce her for studying twenty minutes a night, and so on. Chaining involves reinforcing the last step of the chain first and working backwards. Each step then is reinforced by the opportunity to perform the next step in the chain.

5. At one time, most psychologists believed in S-R, or stimulus-response learning. That is, stimulus produced a response without any thought. Today, many psychologists believe in S-O-R models, which argue that cognition is important in behavior. German psychologist Wolfgang Kohler discovered that chimpanzees could learn to perform tasks through insight, the sudden perception of useful relationships, rather than just through the trial-and-error learning of the conditioning process. Similarly, Edward Tolman discovered that rats being trained through conditioning procedures in a maze were learning a mental representation, or cognitive map, of the maze, and were using it to find food. Such findings challenged the traditional view that cognitive processes were not important in the learning process.

Answer Key for Practice Test Essay Questions

1. Learning has adaptive significance. That is, it helps us to adapt to and survive in our environment. The environment shapes behavior through both personal and species adaptation. Personal adaptation occurs through the laws of learning. Species adaptation occurs through the process of evolution.

2. Through the process of classical conditioning, some fears may be learned. People become afraid of stimuli paired with noxious stimuli such as pain or electric shock. Systematically exposing a person to the feared stimulus while he or she practices muscular relaxation is a technique (systematic desensitization) used to reduce fear.

3. The antecedent conditions, if present, act as stimuli for emitted behaviors. Such conditions are discriminative stimuli, signals that a particular behavior will produce a desired consequence. Thus, the voluntary emitted behavior is performed to produce the desired consequence.

4. On a fixed-ratio schedule, reinforcement occurs after a certain number of responses. On a variable-ratio schedule, reinforcement occurs after an average number of responses. On a fixed-interval schedule, reinforcement occurs after the first response following a fixed time period. On a variable-interval schedule, reinforcement occurs for the first response following a variable time interval.

5. A response is strengthened by the removal or avoidance of a stimulus in negative reinforcement. A response is weakened by the presentation of a stimulus. In response cost, a response is weakened by the removal of a stimulus.

Chapter 7
MEMORY

Learning Objectives: *These questions, with a few additions, are taken from the directed questions found in the margins of the chapter. After reading the chapter, you should be able to answer these questions.*

1. How is memory likened to an information-processing system?

2. What is sensory memory? How did Sperling assess the duration of iconic memory?

3. Describe the limitations of short-term memory, and how they can be overcome.

4. Why do researchers refer to short-term memory as "working memory?"

5. Identify three components of working memory.

6. What is the serial position effect? Under what conditions do primacy and recency occur?

7. According to the three-component model, why do primacy and recency occur?

8. Provide some examples of effortful and automatic processing in your own life.

9. Explain the concept of "depth of processing."

10. How effectively do maintenance and elaborative rehearsal process information into long-term memory?

11. Why do hierarchies, chunking, mnemonic devices, and imagery enhance memory?

12. What is a schema? Explain how schemas influence encoding.

13. In what sense are schemas and expert knowledge related?

14. Explain the concepts of associative networks and priming.

15. How do neural network models differ from associative network models?

16. Use the concepts of declarative versus procedural memory, and explicit versus implicit memory, to explain the pattern of H. M.'s amnesia.

17. Describe some ways to measure explicit and implicit memory.

18. Why does having multiple, self-generated retrieval cues enhance recall?

19. Do flashbulb memories always provide an accurate picture? Describe some evidence.

20. Explain how context-dependent and state-dependent memory illustrate the encoding specificity principle.

21.   Identify practical principles of encoding and retrieval that can be used to enhance memory.

22.   Describe Ebbinghaus' "forgetting curve" and factors that contributed to his rapid, substantial forgetting.

23.   Identify encoding, storage, retrieval, and motivational processes that have been hypothesized to contribute to forgetting.

24.   Describe the nature and some possible causes of retrograde, anterograde, and infantile amnesia.

25.   How do Bartlett's research and studies of boundary extension illustrate memory construction?

26.   Explain how source confusion contributes to misinformation effects.

27.   Are younger and older children equally susceptible to misinformation effects, and equally accurate in recalling traumatic events? Describe some evidence.

28.   Do people ever forget traumatic personal events?   What are recovered memories and repression controversial topics?

29.   What major approaches do scientists use to study the brain regions involved in memory?

30.   What major roles do the hippocampus, cerebral cortex, thalamus, amygdala, and cerebellum play in memory?

31.   How has research with Aplysia aided our understanding of memory formation?

32.   What is long-term potentiation, and what role does it appear to play in memory?

33.   According to some researchers, what basic memory principles account for exceptional memory? Do you agree with this position?

34.   In what ways is "forgetting" adaptive? How might perfect memory be a burden?

Chapter Overview

Memory as Information Processing

The guiding metaphor used by most cognitive psychologists today to study the mind is that the mind is a processing system that encodes, stores, and retrieves information. Encoding refers to getting information into the system, storage involves retaining information, and retrieval involves getting the information out of memory. Cognitive psychologists also work with a three-component model of memory. Sensory memory holds sensory information, including both visual (or iconic) memory and auditory (or echoic) memory. Information that we pay attention to is passed into short-term, or working memory; other information is lost. The capacity of sensory memory is large, while the capacity of working memory is small, though the latter can be increased via chunking. Both maintenance and elaborative rehearsal techniques can keep information in short-term memory, but information is best transferred to long-term memory via elaborative techniques.

Encoding: Entering Information

The more effectively we encode information, the more likely it is that it can be retrieved. According to the levels of processing concept, the more deeply we process information, the better it will be remembered. Elaborative rehearsal techniques, including techniques like the use of mnemonic devices, increase the depth of processing. Prior knowledge shapes encoding through the use of schemas, which are organized patterns of thought about some aspect of the world.

Storage: Retaining Information

One prominent theory of memory is that it can be represented by an associative network. The idea is memory consists of associated ideas and concepts. Biologically, memory may occur through the firing of synaptically connected neurons. Long-term memory consists of all facts we have learned over time. Cognitive psychologists distinguish between different aspects of long-term memory such as declarative, episodic, semantic, and procedural memories.

Retrieval: Accessing Information

Memory is typically triggered via retrieval cues. The more retrieval cues we have, the more likely we are to remember information. Context, state, and mood can also influence retrieval. We typically remember information better if we are in the same context and state in which the information was originally encoded.

Forgetting

The Ebbinghaus forgetting curve shows that we rapidly lose much information, but the progress of loss levels off after a short period of time. We forget for a number of reasons. Decay theory argues that we forget things because the memory trace decays. Other theories suggest that encoding failures and interference, both proactive and retroactive, contribute to forgetting. We may also be motivated to forget undesirable experiences through repression of them. Amnesia also affects memory loss.

Memory as a Constructive Process

Schemas influence the memory process through providing expectancies about what one perceives or believes is likely to have happened in the past. As a result, sometimes our memories are shaped to fit our schemas. The misinformation effect says that distortion of memory occurs via misleading postevent information. A major controversy has emerged about the validity of children's memories. Some think that children's memories are particularly susceptible to suggestion and bias. The "recovered memory" syndrome is also controversial for the same reasons.

The Biology of Memory

Scientists rely on both naturally- and experimentally-induced lesions, as well as brain imaging to study the biology of memory. The hippocampus and its surrounding tissue have been found to play a major role in encoding long-term declarative memories. The cerebral cortex plays a role in encoding by processing information from the sensory registers and also by storing semantic memories. The frontal lobes of the cortex play a central role in working memory. The amygdala seems to encode emotionally arousing and disturbing aspects of events. The cerebellum plays an important role in the formation of procedural memories. Memories in general seem to be formed biologically through physical and chemical changes in the brain's neural circuitry. Long-term potentiation, which is an increase in synaptic strength between neurons, plays a key role in memory consolidation.

Chapter Outline

Memory As Information Processing
    A Three-Component Model
        Sensory Memory
        Short-Term/Working Memory
            Mental Representations
            Capacity and duration
            Putting short-term memory "to work"
        Long-Term Memory

Encoding: Entering Information
    Effortful and Automatic Processing
    Levels of Processing: When Deeper is Better
    Exposure and Rehearsal
    Organization and Imagery
        Hierarchies and Chunking
        Mnemonic Devices
        Visual Imagery
    How Prior Knowledge Shapes Encoding
        Schemas: Our Mental Organizers
        Schemas and Expert Knowledge

Storage: Retaining Information
    Memory as a Network
        Associative Networks
        Neural Networks
    Types of Long-Term Memory
        Declarative and Procedural Memory
        Explicit and Implicit Memory

Retrieval: Accessing Information
    The Value of Multiple and Self-Generated Cues
    The Value of Distinctiveness
        Flashbulb Memory: Fogging Up the Picture?
    Context, State, and Mood Effects on Memory
        Context-Dependent Memory: Returning to the Scene
        State-Dependent Memory: Arousal, Drugs, and Mood
    Applications of Psychological Science: Improving Memory and Academic Learning

Forgetting
    The Course of Forgetting
    Why Do We Forget?
        Encoding Failure
        Decay of the Memory Trace
        Interference, Retrieval Failure, and the Tip-of-the-tongue
        Motivated Forgetting
    Amnesia
    Forgetting to Do Things: Prospective Memory

Memory as a Constructive Process
    Memory Distortion and Schemas: On Ghosts, "Gargoils," and Scenes Beyond the Edge
    The Misinformation Effect and Eyewitness Testimony
        Confusing the Source
    Psychological Frontiers: How Accurate Are Young Children's Memories? The "Recovered
    Memory" Controversy: Repression or Reconstruction?

The Biology of Memory
    Where in the Brain are Memories Formed?
        The Hippocampus and Cerebral Cortex
        The Thalamus and Amygdala
        The Cerebellum
    How Are Memories Formed?

Exceptional Memory
    Research Close-Up: Is Exceptional Memory Really Exceptional?

A Final Thought: The "Curse" of Exceptional Memory

Key Terms: *Write the letter of the definition next to the term in the space provided.*

Memory as Information Processing
Encoding: Entering Information
Storage: Retaining Information
Retrieval: Accessing Information

1. ___ associative network	a.	the processes that allow us to record and later retrieve experiences and information
2. ___ chunking	b.	getting information into the system by translating it into a neural code that the brain processes
3. ___ context-dependent memory	c.	retaining information over time
4. ___ declarative memory	d.	pulling information out of storage
5. ___ dual-coding theory	e.	part of the memory system that holds sensory information just long enough for it to be recognized
6. ___ elaborative rehearsal	f.	holds the information that we are conscious of at any one time
7. ___ encoding	g.	another name for short-term memory
8. ___ encoding specificity principle	h.	combining individual items into larger units of meaning
9. ___ episodic memory	i.	simple repetition of information

163

10. ___ explicit memory

j. focuses on the meaning of information or relates new information to things we already know

11. ___ implicit memory

k. our vast library of durable stored memories

12. ___ levels of processing

l. a U-shaped graphical pattern that shows that recall is influenced by a word's position in a series of items

13. ___ long-term memory

m. concept that the more deeply we process information the better it will be remembered

14. ___ maintenance rehearsal

n. theory that suggests that if we encode information through both visual and verbal codes we will better remember it

15. ___ memory

o. an organized pattern of thought about some aspect of the world

16. ___ mood-congruent recall

p. a massive network of associated ideas and concepts

17. ___ neural network

q. the activation of one concept by another

18. ___ overlearning

r. a network in which each concept is represented by a particular pattern or set of nodes that become activated simultaneously

19. ___ priming

s. our store of factual knowledge concerning personal experiences

20. ___ procedural memory

t. represents general factual knowledge about the world and language

21. ___ retrieval

u. factual knowledge that includes two categories: episodic and semantic memories

22. ___ retrieval cue

v. memory for skills and actions

23. ___ schema

w. involves conscious or intentional memory retrieval

24. ___ semantic memory

x. memory that influences our behavior without conscious awareness

25. ___ sensory memory

y. any stimulus that activates information in long-term memory

26. ___ serial position effect

z. memory that is easier to recall in the same environment in which it was acquired

27. ___ short-term memory

aa. the principle that memory is enhanced when conditions present during retrieval match those present during encoding

28. ___ state-dependent memory

bb. theory that proposes that our ability to retrieve information is greater when our internal state at the time of retrieval matches that during learning

29. ___ storage

cc. tendency to recall information or events that are congruent with our current mood

30. ___ working memory

dd. continued rehearsal past the point of initial learning

Forgetting
Memory as a Constructive Process
The Biology of Memory
Exceptional Memory
A Final Thought: The "Curse" of Exceptional Memory

1. ___ anterograde amnesia

a. theory that proposes that with time and disuse the physical memory trace in the nervous system fades away

2. ___ decay theory

b. occurs when material learned in the past interferes with recall of newer material

3. ___ infantile amnesia

c. occurs when newly acquired information interferes with the ability to recall information learned at an earlier time

4. ___ long-term potentiation

d. psychodynamic theory that motivational processes may protect us by blocking the recall of anxiety-arousing memories

5. ___ memory consolidation

e. memory loss for events after the initial onset of amnesia

6. ___ misinformation effect

f. memory loss for early experiences

7. ___ proactive interference

g. memory loss for events that occurred prior to the onset of amnesia

8. ___ prospective memory

h. remembering to perform an activity in the future

9. ___ repression

i. the distortion of memory by misleading postevent information

10. ___ retroactive interference

j. our tendency to recall something or recognize it as familiar, but to forget where we encountered it

11. ___ retrograde amnesia

k. hypothetical "binding" of memory process that may occur in the hippocampus

12. ___ source confusion

l. enduring increase in synaptic strength

Review at a Glance: *Write the term that best fits the blank to review what you learned in this chapter.*

Memory As Information Processing

(1) _____ refers to the processes that allow us to record and later retrieve experiences and information. Today the mind is visualized as a processing system. It takes in information by translating it into a neural code that your brain processes, a process called (2) _____. The brain retains information over time through (3) _____ and pulls information out of long-term memory through (4) _____ processes. Most cognitive psychologists suggest a three-component model of memory. (5) _____ memory holds incoming sensory information just long enough for it to be recognized. Our visual sensory register is called the (6) _____ store, while the auditory sensory register is called the (7) _____ store. Most information in sensory memory quickly fades away, but information that we pay attention to enters (8) _____ memory, which is also called (9) _____ memory. The capacity of working memory is rather small, but it can be increased through (10) _____, which requires the combination of individual items into larger units of meaning. By rehearsing information, we can keep it in short-term memory longer. (11) _____ rehearsal involves the simple repetition of information, like repeating a phone number in order to remember it, while (12) _____ rehearsal involves focusing on the meaning of information or relating it to things we already know. Our vast library of stored information is called (13) _____ memory.

Encoding: Entering Information

According to the (14) _____ ___ _____ notion, the more deeply we process information, the better it will be remembered. Because of this, (15)_____ rehearsal is the best method of facilitating the transfer of information into long-term memory. Organizational devices such as using hierarchies, chunking, and mnemonic devices help us to remember information. Paivio discovered that we encode information in both verbal and visual codes, which is known as his (16) _____ theory. Prior knowledge also shapes encoding. A (17) _____ is an organized pattern of thought about some aspect of the world.

Storage: Retaining Information

After information is encoded, it is organized and stored in long-term memory. One group of theories suggests that memory is represented as a massive network of associated ideas and concepts, called an (18) _____ network. In such a network, when people think about one concept, it triggers thinking about related concepts throughout the network, through the process called (19) _____ _____. The term (20) _____ refers to the activation of one concept by another. In a (21) _____ network, each concept is represented by a particular pattern or set of nodes that becomes activated simultaneously. There are several types of long-term memory. (22) _____ memory involves factual knowledge and consists of two types. Our store of factual information about the world and language is called (23) _____ memory, while our store of factual memory about our personal experiences is called (24) _____ memory. (25) _____ memory is reflected in skills and actions we perform. Memory retrieval can involve both conscious and unconscious processes. (26) _____ memory involves conscious memory retrieval while (27) _____ memory influences our behavior without conscious awareness.

Retrieval: Accessing Information

A stimulus that activates of information stored in long-term memory is called a (28) _____ cue. Sometimes memories are so clear that we can picture them like a snapshot in time. Such memories are called (29) _____ memories. Context, state, and mood affect our ability to retrieve information. The principle that states that memory is enhanced when conditions present during retrieval match those that were present during encoding is called the (30) _____ _____ _____. Sometimes it is easier to remember information if we are in the same environment in which the information was first encoded, a phenomenon called (31) _____ _____ memory. Similarly, our ability to retrieve information is greater when our internal state at the time of retrieval matches our original state during learning, which is called (32) _____ _____ memory. We also tend to recall information or events that are congruent with our current mood, which is known as (33) _____ _____ recall.

Forgetting

Hermann Ebbinghaus pioneered the study of forgetting, discovering that memory declines rapidly and then levels off after initial learning. There are several theories of why we forget things. One theory is that we forget things because we fail to encode them well enough. Another theory, called (34) _____ theory, suggests that with time and disuse the physical memory trace in the nervous system just fades away. Yet another theory, interference theory, suggests that we forget because other items in long-term memory overwrite or impair our ability to retain information. (35) _____ interference occurs when material learned in the past interferes with the learning of new information. (36) _____ interference occurs when newly acquired information interferes with the ability to retrieve information stored at an earlier time. Psychodynamic theorists suggest that we may be motivated to forget particularly disturbing information through (37) _____. Amnesia involves a dramatic forgetting of basic information. (38) _____ amnesia refers to memory loss for events that occur after the initial onset of amnesia while (39) _____ amnesia represents memory loss for events that occurred prior to the amnesia. Most of us can't remember events of our early childhood due to (40) _____ amnesia.

Memory as a Constructive Process

The use of appropriate (41) _____ helps us to organize information as we encode and retrieve it. Sometimes, though, schemas can influence the distortion of information. The distortion of a memory by misleading postevent information is called the (42) _____ effect. Misinformation effects also occur because of (43) _____ _____, our tendency to recall something or recognize it without being able to remember where we encountered it.

The Biology of Memory

The (44) _____ and its adjacent tissues seem to play a key role in encoding long-term declarative memories. The cerebral cortex also seems to play an important role in encoding. One hypothetical process called (45) _____ _____ suggests that the diverse aspects of an experience are first processed by different parts of the cortex and are then consolidated or "bound" together in the hippocampus. Memory may involve the stimulation of synaptic connections. An enduring increase in synaptic strength between neurons is called (46) _____ _____.

Apply What You Know

1. Construct two lists of 20 words. Learn one list using maintenance rehearsal techniques. Learn the other list using elaborative rehearsal techniques, such as making up a story using the words or creating mental images of the concepts the words represent in your mind. Measure your immediate recall of the words right after you've learned them by recording the number of words you can recall from each list. Then measure your recall of both lists a day later. Do you find that you better remember words from one list as measured by immediate recall? If so, why? How about after one day? If so, why?

2. Suppose that you are an attorney and are interested in using the misinformation effect to sway the testimony of an eyewitness. Describe how you could do so.

Stretching Your Geographies

1. Research in education suggests that males and females may have different learning styles, suggesting that males and females should be taught in somewhat different ways. Using what you learned from your research in the "Stretching Your Geographies" exercise in Chapter 6, describe some differences in the ways that males and females might be taught.

Practice Test

Multiple Choice Items: *Please write the letter corresponding to your answer in the space to the left of each item.*

_____ 1. In the three stage memory model, iconic memory is part of _____ memory.

    a. sensory
    b. short-term
    c. long-term
    d. echoic

_____ 2. Both elaborative and maintenance rehearsal keep information active in _____ memory but ____ rehearsal is more effective in transferring information to long-term memory.

    a.   short-term; elaborative
    b.   sensory; maintenance
    c.   short-term; maintenance
    d.   sensory; elaborative

_____ 3. According to psychologist Alan Baddeley, working memory is divided into _____ components.

    a.   sensory, short-term, and long-term memory
    b.   episodic, procedural, and semantic memory
    c.   auditory, visual-spatial, and central executive
    d.   encoding, storage, and retrieval

_____ 4. New professor Cyko L. Gist is faced with the unenviable task of trying to memorize all of his new students' names, so he decides to employ elaborative rehearsal techniques to do this. To help his long-term recall of student Melody Balobalo, Gist should _____.

    a. repeat her name over and over again
    b. associate a mental image of her with a ball bouncing up and down over a song melody
    c. divide her name into chunks like Mel - O - Dy Bal - O - Bal - O
    d. use only short-term memory

_____ 5. Of the following, the one which is not one of the three basic memory processes is _____.

    a. encoding
    b. attention
    c. storage
    d. retrieval

_____ 6. The capacity of short-term, or working memory is thought to be about _____ units of information.

    a. an infinite
    b. ten
    c. seven ± two chunks
    d. seven

_____ 7. Words at the end of a list are typically remembered better than words presented in the middle, when recalled immediately. This is known as the _____ effect and it presumably happens because the last few words on the list remain in _____ memory.

    a. serial position; sensory
    b. recency; long-term
    c. primacy; short-term
    d. recency; short-term

_____ 8. Making a grocery list and taking notes for a class are both examples of _____, which is encoding that is initiated intentionally and requires conscious attention.

    a. effortful processing
    b. automatic processing
    c. maintenance rehearsal
    d. state-dependent memory

_____ 9. The method of loci is a memory enhancing technique based on _____ and is consistent with the predictions of _____ theory.

    a. imagery; dual-coding
    b. chunking; dual-coding theory
    c. hierarchies; encoding specificity
    d. acronyms; encoding specificity

_____ 10. If you go to a movie, you know that the movie isn't going to start as long as the lights are on. Once the movie starts, you also know that it is considered polite not to talk during the movie and that if you need to leave, it is best to try not to disturb others. This collection of thoughts is best considered to be an example of _____.

    a. overlearning
    b. a schema
    c. chunking
    d. implicit memory

_____ 11. If you think for a moment about the concept SCHOOL, it is likely that other concepts such as TEXTBOOKS, TEACHERS, and EXAMS may also come to mind. The fact these other words can be triggered by the word SCHOOL is best considered as an example of _____.

    a. elaborative rehearsal
    b. proactive interference
    c. dual encoding
    d. priming

_____ 12. A memory researcher claims that a concept such as "dog" is triggered by the simultaneous firing of nodes #8, #47, and #123 in a network but if node #8 is simultaneously triggered with nodes #9 and #301, an entirely different concept appears in the mind. The views of this researcher are most consistent with the _____ theory of memory.

    a. dual coding
    b. associative network
    c. state-dependence
    d. neural network

_____ 13. Research by Mantyla (1986) has revealed that having _____ that is/are _____ is the most effective way to improve recall memory.

    a. a single vivid retrieval cue; generated by an expert
    b. multiple retrieval cues; self-generated
    c. a single vivid retrieval cue; self-generated
    d. multiple retrieval cues; generated by an expert

_____ 14. According to the _____, memory is better when the conditions present during encoding match those that are present during retrieval.

    a. dual processing theory
    b. decay theory
    c. encoding specificity principle
    d. the principles of implicit memory

_____ 15. Imagine that you have studied for an exam in a quiet environment and your physiological arousal has been low while you were studying. If on the day of the exam, you were given the test in a quiet environment and your physiological arousal remained low, the concept of state-dependent memory would predict that your recall would _____ and the concept of context-dependent memory would predict that your recall would _____.

    a. be worse; also be worse
    b. be better; be worse
    c. be worse; be better
    d. be better; also be better

_____ 16. Jim has a hard time remembering to do things that he plans to do in the future, such as mailing letters or remembering to call someone. These memories are examples of what are called _____ memorics and the _____ is thought to be play an important role in their recreation.

    a. retroactive; parietal lobe
    b. prospective; frontal lobe
    c. anterograde; amygdala
    d. retrograde; hippocampus.

_____ 17. An eyewitness from a crime is asked to look through some mug shots to see if he can identify the person who committed a crime. After doing this, he sees a police line up of suspects and identifies one of the men as the person who committed the crime because he looks very familiar. Unfortunately, the man in the line up looks familiar not because the eyewitness saw him commit the crime but because he saw his face in the mug shot books a few hours ago and the eyewitness has forgotten this. This example best demonstrates the phenomenon of _____.

    a. proactive interference
    b. retrograde amnesia
    c. source confusion
    d. memory consolidation

_____ 18. The _____ appears to be an "encoding station" for long-term declarative memory.

    a. cerebral cortex
    b. thalamus
    c. hippocampus
    d. cerebellum

_____ 19. New horse racing sensation Dog Meat, about to win the Kentucky Derby by 47 lengths, suddenly pulls up just before the finish line because he spots the legendary Mr. Ed in the stands and demands an autograph. It seems that Dog Meat has lots of wonderful memories spent watching ancient reruns of Ed's TV show while engaged in "horse-play" with long-time steady flame Trashy Lady. These memories of the good-times are likely stored in Dog Meat's _____ memory.

    a. episodic
    b. iconic
    c. echoic
    d. prototype

_____ 20. Humpty Dumpty sat on a wall. Humpty Dumpty had a great fall. Fortunately due to modern technology, the king's horses and men were now able to put the giant cracked egg-guy back together again. Humpty would be able to remember how to sit on a wall again due to retention of his _____ knowledge.

    a. declarative
    b. procedural
    c. iconic
    d. echoic

_____ 21. The process of getting information into the brain by translating it into a neural code that the brain processes is called _____.

    a. retrieval
    b. recall
    c. storage
    d. encoding

_____ 22. Recognizing someone's voice when you hear it on the phone shows that you have a _____ for that person.

a. chunk
b. icon
c. mental representation
d. elaboration

_____ 23. According to the _____ concept, the more deeply we encode information, the better we will remember it.

a. dual-coding
b. levels of processing
c. maintenance rehearsal
d. chunking

_____ 24. An organized pattern of thought about some aspect of the world is called a _____.

a. chunk
b. code
c. proposition
d. schema

_____ 25. A massive network of associated ideas and concepts is called a(n) _____ network.

a. associative
b. schema
c. neural
d. priming

_____ 26. Studies of _____ show that it is generally easier to remember information in the same environment in which it was originally learned.

a. state-dependent learning
b. schemas
c. context-dependent learning
d. decay

_____ 27. When material learned in the past interferes with recall of newer material, _____ has occurred.

a. retroactive interference
b. motivated forgetting
c. the tip-of-the-tongue phenomenon
d. proactive interference

_____ 28. Memory loss for early life experiences is called _____.

a. infantile amnesia
b. anterograde amnesia
c. retroactive interference
d. Korsakoff's syndrome

_____ 29. The distortion of memory by misleading postevent information is called ____.

    a. anterograde amnesia
    b. Korsakoff's syndrome
    c. the misinformation effect
    d. priming

_____ 30. The ____ and its surrounding tissue seem to play key roles in encoding long-term declarative memories.

    a. hypothalamus
    b. hippocampus
    c. cerebellum
    d. amygdala

True/False Items: *Write T or F in the space provided to the left of each item.*

_____ 1. Combining individual items into larger units of meaning is called chunking.

_____ 2. The best technique for transferring information from short-term memory to long-term memory is maintenance rehearsal.

_____ 3. A U-shaped pattern that shows that recall is influenced by a word's position in a series of items is called the primacy effect.

_____ 4. According to Paivio's dual coding theory, memory is improved by encoding information using both verbal and visual cues.

_____ 5. An organized pattern of thought about some aspect of the world is called a schema.

_____ 6. Our store of factual knowledge concerning our own personal experiences is called declarative memory.

_____ 7. Studies of context dependent memory show that it is easier to remember something in a different environment from which it was first encoded.

_____ 8. Proactive interference occurs when newly acquired information interferes with the ability to recall information learned at an earlier time.

_____ 9. Studies of the biology of memory have shown that the hippocampus plays a major role in encoding long-term declarative memories.

_____ 10. Synaptic connections seem to become stronger as a result of stimulation.

Short Answer Questions

1. Describe the three-component model of memory.

2. Describe the two different types of rehearsal.

3. What are associative and neural networks?

4. What are the major types of amnesia?

5. What is the misinformation effect?

Essay Questions

1. Describe the process of encoding information.

2. Describe the various types of long-term memory.

3. Why do we forget?

4. What is meant when psychologists say that memory involves a "constructive process?"

5. Where in the brain are memories formed?

Answer Keys

Answer Key for Key Terms

Memory as Information Processing
Encoding: Entering Information
Storage: Retaining Information
Retrieval: Accessing Information

1. p	16. cc
2. h	17. r
3. z	18. dd
4. u	19. q
5. n	20. v
6. j	21. d
7. b	22. y
8. aa	23. o
9. s	24. t
10. w	25. e
11. x	26. l
12. m	27. f
13. k	28. bb
14. i	29. c
15. a	30. g

Forgetting
Memory as a Constructive Process
The Biology of Memory
Exceptional Memory
A Final Thought: The "Curse" of Exceptional Memory

1. e	7. b
2. a	8. h
3. f	9. d
4. l	10. c
5. k	11. g
6. i	12. j

Answer Key for Review at a Glance

1. memory	24. episodic
2. encoding	25. Procedural
3. storage	26. Explicit
4. retrieval	27. implicit
5. Sensory	28. retrieval
6. iconic	29. flashbulb
7. echoic	30. encoding specificity principle
8. short-term	31. context dependent
9. working	32. state dependent
10. chunking	33. mood congruent

11. Maintenance
12. elaborative
13. long-term
14. levels of processing
15. elaborative
16. dual-code
17. schema
18. associative
19. spreading activation
20. priming
21. neural
22. Declarative
23. semantic

34. decay
35. Proactive
36. Retroactive
37. repression
38. Anterograde
39. retrograde
40. infantile
41. schemas
42. misinformation
43. source confusion
44. hippocampus
45. memory consolidation
46. long-term potentiation

Answer Key for Practice Test Multiple Choice Questions

1. a
2. a
3. c
4. b
5. b
6. c
7. d
8. a
9. a
10. b
11. d
12. d
13. b
14. c
15. d

16. b
17. c
18. c
19. a
20. b
21. d
22. c
23. b
24. d
25. a
26. c
27. d
28. a
29. c
30. b

Answer Key for Practice Test True/False Questions

1. T
2. F
3. F
4. T
5. T

6. F
7. F
8. F
9. T
10. T

Answer Key for Practice Test Short Answer Questions

1. The three component model of memory consists of sensory memory, short-term, or working memory, and long-term memory. Sensory memory holds incoming sensory information just long enough for it to be recognized. Short-term memory holds the information that we are conscious of at any given time. Long-term memory is our vast store of more durable stored memories.

2. Maintenance rehearsal involves the simple repetition of information and is useful for retaining information in short-term memory. Elaborative rehearsal involves focusing on the meaning of information

or relating it to other things we already know. Elaborative rehearsal is a better technique than maintenance rehearsal for transferring information from short-term to long-term memory.

3. An associative network is a massive network of associated ideas and concepts. In a neural network, each concept is represented by a pattern or set of nodes that becomes activated simultaneously. There is no single node for a concept in a neural network, while there is in an associative network.

4. Retrograde amnesia represents memory loss for events that occurred prior to the onset of amnesia. Anterograde amnesia involves memory loss for events that occur after the initial onset of amnesia. Infantile amnesia refers to an inability to remember information from the first few years of life.

5. The misinformation effect is the distortion of memory by misleading postevent information.

Answer Key for Practice Test Essay Questions

1. Encoding refers to the process of getting information into the system by translating it into a neural code that your brain processes. Encoding may involve effortful processing, which is encoding that is initiated intentionally and requires conscious attention. This may involve maintenance and elaborative rehearsal, making lists, and taking notes. Much encoding is also done by automatic processing, which occurs without intention and requires minimal attention. The deeper that information is encoded the more likely it will be able to be retrieved.

2. Declarative memory involves factual knowledge and includes episodic memory, which is our store of factual knowledge about our life experiences, and semantic memory, which represents general factual knowledge about the world. Procedural memory is our memory for skills and actions.

3. There are several theories of forgetting. Failure to encode information in a useful fashion at the time of learning often leads to later forgetting. Decay theory says that with time and disuse the physical memory trace in the nervous system fades away. According to interference theory, we forget information because other items in long-term memory overwrite it or impair our ability to retain it. Proactive interference occurs when material learned in the past interferes with recall of newer information. Retroactive interference occurs when newly acquired information interferes with the ability to recall information learned at an earlier time. Psychodynamic theorists believe that some information is lost due to motivated forgetting. Such a process may keep us from remembering traumatic or other upsetting memories.

4. We may reconstruct a memory in a way that intuitively "makes sense" and therefore feels real and accurate. Schemas often help us to distort information because we try to shape information to fit our schemas, rather than the other way around. Postevent information can distort memory in this way, a process called the misinformation effect.

5. Studies show that the hippocampus and its adjacent tissue play a major role in encoding long-term declarative memories. The cerebral cortex plays a vital role in encoding by processing information from the sensory registers. Semantic memory also seems to be stored in the cerebral cortex. The frontal lobes seem to play a central role in carrying out the functions of working memory. The amygdala seems to encode emotionally arousing and disturbing aspects of events. The cerebellum may play an important role in the formation of procedural memories.

Chapter 8
INTELLIGENT THOUGHT AND BEHAVIOR

Learning Objectives: *These questions, with a few additions, are taken from the directed questions found in the margins of the chapter. After reading the chapter, you should be able to answer these questions.*

1.   What are mental representations? How are they involved in thinking and communicating?

2.   Name and define three properties common to any human language.

3.   Differentiate between surface structure and deep structure.

4.   What are phonemes and morphemes? Where do they fit in the hierarchy of language?

5.   What scientific evidence supports the notion that human language has a biological basis?

6.   How does learning interact with biology to affect language development?

6.1*   What is motherese? What is telegraphic speech?

7.   What two factors affect bilingual effects on quality and flexibility of thinking? How does age influence the learning of a second language?

8.   Define the linguistic relativity hypothesis and evaluate its validity. How does language influence thought?

9.   What are the three major modes of thought?

10.   What are propositions, and how are they formed?

11.   What are concepts, and what is the role of prototypes in their formation?

12.   What evidence supports the position that animals can exhibit true language? What evidence is used to dispute that position?

13.   Distinguish between deductive reasoning and inductive reasoning. Why is deductive reasoning seen as the stronger form of reasoning?

14.   How might a combination of inductive and deductive reasoning be involved in a medical diagnosis?

15.   Summarize three factors that can interfere with the correct application of deductive reasoning. What is meant by belief bias?

16.   Summarize the four stages of problem solving.

17.	How does the Crow and Trains problem demonstrate the importance of framing a problem?

18.	How did Luchins's water jars problems demonstrate the dangers of a mental set?

19.	What are problem-solving schemas? How do they enter into being an expert, and how do they relate to the strengths and weaknesses of human memory?

20.	Differentiate between an algorithm and a heuristic.

21.	Describe two commonly used problem solving heuristics.

22.	Describe the representativeness heuristic and indicate how it applies to people's response to the Linda problem.

23.	How does the availability heuristic influence judgments of likelihood or probability?

24.	What is meant by confirmation bias? Why does it tend to occur, and how can it interfere with problem solving?

25.	What is our working definition of intelligence?

26.	How was Sir Francis Galton's research influenced by Darwin? How did he attempt to measure intelligence?

27.	What two assumptions did Alfred Binet make in developing his measure of intelligence?

28.	What was Stern's original IQ ratio? Why do today's tests no longer use the mental age concept? How is IQ now defined?

29.	What is the distinction between achievement and aptitude tests? What controversy exists concerning their respective values for measuring mental skills?

30.	Define reliability and describe three different varieties of reliability that apply to psychological tests.

31.	Define validity and distinguish between construct, content, and predictive (criterion-related) validity.

32.	How well do intelligence tests predict academic and job performance?

33.	What are the two meanings of the term standardization?

34.	Differentiate between the psychometric and cognitive psychology approaches to intelligence.

35.	What kinds of evidence gave rise to the g-factor and specific mental abilities conceptions of intelligence?

36.	Differentiate between crystallized and fluid intelligence. How is their application related to age?

37.	Of what relevance do savants' abilities have to Gardner's theory of multiple intelligence?

38.	What is emotional intelligence? Describe the five abilities that comprise it.

39.	What are the three levels of psychological processes that underlie intelligence in Sternberg's triarchic theory? What are the three different kinds of "intelligence"?

40.	What evidence is there that intelligence might involve neural efficiency?

41.	What is the relation between genetic similarity and similarity in IQ? How much of the variation in IQ is accounted for by genetic variation?

42.	How does the concept of reaction range help account for the interaction between heredity and environment?

43.	What differences are found in average IQ between ethnic groups in the United States?

44.	How well do intelligence tests predict the performance of different ethnic groups?

45.	Are IQ differences between blacks and whites increasing or decreasing? What does this imply?

46.	What are the major differences between men and women in cognitive skills? What biological and environmental factors might be responsible for them?

47.	How do beliefs about self and others influence cognitive performance?

48.	What is stereotype threat, and how does it operate? How has it been shown to affect academic performance?

49.	What are the behavioral capabilities of mildly disabled people?

50.	What did Terman's longitudinal study of gifted children find regarding their success as adults?

Chapter Overview

Language

Language consists of a system of symbols and rules for combining these symbols in such a way that can produce an infinite number of possible messages or meanings. Language is symbolic and uses sounds, written signs, or gestures to refer to objects, events, ideas, and feelings. With language we can talk about not only the present but the past, future, and imaginary events, a feature of language called displacement. Language has both a surface and a deep structure. The surface structure is the way symbols are combined (through rules of grammar called syntax) while the deep structure refers to the underlying meaning. Phonemes are the smallest units of sound in a language while morphemes are the smallest units of meaning. The development of language seems to be both biological and psychological. All infants, regardless of culture or society, vocalize the entire range of phonemes found in the world's languages. Some linguists believe that there is a critical period during which language is most easily learned. Learning through imitation, rewards, and punishments, also seems to be important in the development of language, though it cannot completely explain the development of language skills. A second language is best learned and spoken most fluently when learned during the sensitive period of childhood. Language seems to affect thinking processes. Benjamin Lee Whorf, in fact, argued that language determines what we are capable of thinking, though most modern linguists disagree with that assertion. We do seem to think in propositions, statements that express fact. Propositions consist of concepts, basic units of semantic memory. Many concepts in turn are defined by prototypes, the most typical and familiar members of a category.

Reasoning and Problem Solving

We reason through both deductive (top-down) and inductive (bottom-up) reasoning. Sometimes, though, we run into stumbling blocks in reasoning. These stumbling blocks include being distracted by irrelevant information, failing to apply deductive rules, and belief bias, the tendency to abandon logical rules in favor of one's own personal beliefs. To solve a problem, we must first frame it. Following that, we generate potential solutions, test the solutions, and evaluate the results. Problem-solving schemas help us to select information and solve problems. Algorithms are formulas for solving problems, while heuristics are general problem-solving strategies that we employ to solve problems. Means-ends analysis, which can involve the generation of subgoals, is used to move us from an initial state to a desired goal state. The representativeness heuristic is used to determine whether a new stimulus is a member of a particular class or category, while the availability heuristic can bias our perceptions by focusing on what is available in our memories. Similar to belief bias is the confirmation bias, by which we search only for information that supports our beliefs. Yet another problem with problem solving is functional fixedness, which involves being unable to think about alternative uses for an object. On the other hand, divergent thinking and incubation can aid problem solving.

Intelligence

Intelligence is a concept that refers to individual differences in the ability to acquire knowledge, to think and reason effectively, and to deal adaptively with the environment. The measurement of mental abilities was begun by French psychologist Alfred Binet. He assumed that mental abilities developed with age and that the rate at which people gain mental competence is a characteristic of the person and is stable over time. German psychologist William Stern developed the idea of the intelligence quotient (IQ), which was originally expressed as the ratio mental age/chronological age x 100. In the United States, Lewis Terman and David Wechsler developed the most prominent IQ tests. Other tests that measure mental abilities are achievement tests, which measure learning, and aptitude tests, which measure potential for future learning and performance.

There are standards for psychological tests to be considered good tests. Reliability refers to the consistency of measurement while validity refers to whether a test is measuring what it is supposed to measure. Test-retest reliability, internal consistency, and interjudge reliability are ways of measuring reliability, while construct validity, content validity, and predictive validity are all measures of validity. A third requirement for good tests is standardization.

The nature of intelligence is a widely debated topic in psychology. Charles Spearman argued for one general factor that he called "g" which he argued underlies all mental abilities. Thurstone argued for seven distinct primary mental abilities. Cattell and Horn argued that intelligence is of two types, crystallized and fluid. Crystallized intelligence consists of the ability to apply existing knowledge while fluid intelligence consists of the ability to deal with novel situations. In that tradition, Robert Sternberg has developed a triarchic theory of intelligence. Sternberg suggests that intelligence consists of planning and regulating task behavior, executing behavioral strategies, and encoding and storing information. Finally, emotional intelligence refers to the abilities to read and respond to others' emotions appropriately, to motivate oneself, and to be aware of and to control one's own emotions.

Heredity and environment both influence intelligence. The reaction range for intelligence, or any trait for that matter, refers to the range of possibilities that the genetic code allows. Studies of ethnic group differences show that African-Americans score, on average, 12-15 IQ points below the White-American average, while Asian-Americans score, on average, above the White-American mean. Hispanic-Americans score, on average, roughly the same as White-Americans. Studies of African-Americans have shown that the mean differences with White-Americans have declined over the past 25 years as greater educational and vocational opportunities for African-Americans have emerged, suggesting an environmental component to group differences in intelligence. Sex differences in cognitive abilities have also been discovered. Males perform better on spatial tasks and tasks involving mathematical reasoning. Females perform better on tests of perceptual speed, verbal fluency, mathematical calculation, and precise manual tasks. Finally, about 3-5 percent of the U.S. population is disabled, requiring special help, while the intellectually gifted also need special educational opportunities.

Chapter Outline

Language
       The Nature and Structure of Language
              Surface and Deep Structure
              Language From the Bottom Up
       Acquiring a Language
              Biological Foundations
              Social Learning Processes
              Bilingualism: Learning a Second Language
       Linguistic Influences on Thinking
       Concepts and Propositions
       Psychological Frontiers: Can Animals Acquire Human Language?

Reasoning and Problem Solving
       Reasoning
              Stumbling Blocks in Reasoning
                  Distraction by irrelevant information
                  Failure to apply deductive rules
                  Belief bias

Key Terms: *Write the letter of the definition next to the term in the space provided.*

Language

1. ___ concepts
2. ___ deep structure
3. ___ displacement
4. ___ imaginal thought
5. ___ language
6. ___ linguistic relativity hypothesis
7. ___ mental representations
8. ___ morphemes
9. ___ motoric thought
10. ___ phonemes
11. ___ propositional thought
12. ___ propositions
13. ___ prototypes
14. ___ semantics
15. ___ surface structure
16. ___ syntax
17. ___ telegraphic speech

a. includes images, ideas, concepts, and principles
b. consists of a system of symbols and rules for combining symbols
c. consists of the way symbols are combined within a given language
d. rules of grammar
e. the underlying meaning of combined symbols
f. rules for connecting symbols to what they represent
g. the smallest units of sound that are recognized as separate in a given language
h. the smallest units of meaning in a language
i. two-word sentences uttered by two-year-old children
j. belief that language determines what we are capable of thinking
k. thought that expresses a statement
l. thought that consists of images
m. thought that relates to mental representations of movement
n. statements that express facts
o. basic units of semantic memory
p. the most typical and familiar member of a category
q. the feature of language that indicates that past, future, and imaginary events and objects that are not physically present can be symbolically represented

Reasoning and Problem Solving

1. ___ algorithms
2. ___ availability heuristic
3. ___ belief bias
4. ___ confirmation bias
5. ___ deductive reasoning
6. ___ divergent thinking
7. ___ functional fixedness
8. ___ heuristics
9. ___ incubation

a. reasoning from general principles to a conclusion about a specific case
b. reasoning involving developing a general principle from specific facts
c. the tendency to abandon logical rules in favor of our own personal beliefs
d. the tendency to stick to solutions that have worked in the past
e. mental blueprints for selecting information and solving specialized classes of problems
f. formulas or procedures that automatically generate correct solutions
g. general problem-solving strategies that we apply to certain classes of situations
h. a strategy by which we identify differences between the present situation and one's desired state and then make changes to reduce the difference
i. attacking a large problem by forming subgoals

187

10. ___ inductive reasoning	j. used to infer how closely something or someone is to a prototype
11. ___ means-ends analysis	k. leads us to pass judgments and decisions based on the availability of information in memory
12. ___ mental set	l. tendency to look only for information that will confirm our beliefs
13. ___ problem-solving schemas	m. the generation of novel ideas that depart from the norm
14. ___ representativeness heuristic	n. the tendency to be blind of new ways to use an object
15. ___ subgoal analysis	o. not working on a problem for a while, after which a flash of insight occurs

Intelligence

1. ___ achievement test	a. individual differences in the ability to acquire knowledge, think, reason effectively. and respond adaptively
2. ___ aptitude test	b. mental age/chronological age x 100
3. ___ cognitive process theories	c. a test designed to find out how much someone has learned
4. ___ construct validity	d. a method for measuring potential for future learning and performance
5. ___ content validity	e. a method for measuring individual differences related to a psychological concept based on a sample of relevant behavior in a scientifically designed and controlled condition
6. ___ crystallized intelligence	f. consistency of measurement
7. ___ emotional intelligence	g. consistency measured by giving a test twice to the same group of participants and correlating the scores
8. ___ factor analysis	h. consistency of measurement within a test itself
9. ___ fluid intelligence	i. how well a test measures what it is designed to measure
10. ___ intelligence	j. the degree to which a test is measuring discriminant validity
11. ___ intelligence quotient	k. whether the items on a test measure all the knowledge and skills that are assumed to comprise the construct of interest
12. ___ interjudge reliability	l. determined by how highly test scores correlate with a criterion
13. ___ internal consistency	m. creating a well-controlled environment for administering a test and determining norms
14. ___ knowledge acquisition components	n. provide a basis for comparing an individual's score with others' scores
15. ___ mental age	o. a bell-shaped curve of scores
16. ___ metacomponents	p. the statistical study of psychological tests
17. ___ normal distribution	q. a statistical tool that analyzes patterns of correlations between test scores to discover clusters of measures
18. ___ norms	r. Thurstone's seven distinct abilities
19. ___ performance components	s. the ability to apply previously acquired knowledge to current problems

188

20. ___ predictive validity
21. ___ primary mental abilities
22. ___ psychological test
23. ___ psychometrics
24. ___ reaction range
25. ___ reliability
26. ___ savants
27. ___ standardization
28. ___ test-retest reliability
29. ___ triarchic theory of intelligence
30. ___ validity

t. the ability to deal with novel problem-solving situations
u. involves abilities to read and respond to other's emotions appropriately, to motivate oneself, and to be aware of and to control one's emotions
v. people disabled in a general sense who have exceptional skills in some areas
w. theory addressing both the cognitive processes involved in intelligence and the forms that intelligence can take
x. higher-order processes used to plan and regulate task performance
y. mental processes used to perform a task
z. processes that help us encode and store information
aa. the range of possibilities that the genetic code allows for a trait
bb. theories that explain why people differ in cognitive skills
cc. consistency of measurement when different people score the same test
dd. the level of mental performance that is characteristic at a particular chronological age

Review at a Glance: *Write the term that best fits the blank to review what you learned in this chapter.*

Language

Humans have a remarkable ability to represent the world through symbols. (1) _____ _____ take a variety of forms, including images, ideas, concepts, and principles. (2) _____ consists of a system of symbols and rules for combining those symbols in ways that can produce an infinite number of possible messages or meanings. Language is symbolic and can represent the present as well as past, future, and imaginary events and objects, the latter of which is a feature of language called (3) _____. Language has both structure and rules. The (4) _____ structure of a language consists of the way symbols are combined within a given language. The rules for such combination are called the (5) _____ of a language. The underlying meaning of the combined symbols is called (6) _____ structure. Human languages have a hierarchical structure. The smallest units of sound that are recognized as separate in a given language are called (7) _____, while the smallest units of meaning in a language are called (8) _____. Language can influence how we think. Benjamin Lee Whorf, in his (9) _____ _____ hypotheses, argues that language actually <u>determines</u> what we are capable of thinking. Thinking may be considered to be the "internal language of the mind." Verbal sentences that we hear are called (10) _____ thought. Images that we can "see" in our minds are called (11) _____ thought, while (12) _____ thought relates to mental representations of motor movements. Much of our thinking, in fact, occurs in terms of statements that express facts, which are called (13) _____. We seem to understand the world, in part, by understanding concepts. According to Rosch (1977), concepts are defined by (14) _____, the most familiar and typical members of a category.

Reasoning and Problem Solving

Two types of reasoning affect our abilities to make decisions and solve problems. (15) _____ reasoning involves reasoning from general principles to a conclusion about a specific case, while (16) _____ reasoning involves starting with specific facts and developing a general principle from them. To solve problems, we often employ (17) _____ _____ _____, which are step-by-step scripts for selecting information and solving specialized classes of problems. Formulas that automatically generate correct solutions are called (18) _____. Shortcut problem-solving strategies that we often employ rather than algorithms to solve problems are called (19) _____. One type of heuristic is (20) _____ _____ _____, during which we identify differences between the desired state and our present state and make changes to reduce the differences. Often this strategy involves (21) _____ analysis, by which people form intermediate steps toward a problem solution. Another heuristic allows us to infer how closely something or someone fits our prototype for a particular class, or concept. This type of heuristic is called the (22) _____ heuristic. A heuristic that leads us to base judgments and decisions on the availability of information in memory is called the (23) _____ heuristic.

Intelligence

In the early days of mental testing, examiners like Alfred Binet tried to determine whether a child was performing at the correct mental level for children of that age. The result of the testing was a score called the (24) _____ age. German psychologist William Stern developed the (25) _____ _____, based on the ratio of mental age to chronological age. Psychologists today distinguish between tests that measure how much someone has learned, or (26) _____ tests, and tests that measure potential for future learning and performance, or (27) _____ tests. Good tests have both reliability and validity. The consistency of measurement of a test is called (28) _____. One way to measure reliability, known as (29) _____ _____ reliability, is to administer the same measure to the same group of participants on two different occasions and to correlate the scores. Determining the consistency of measurement within the test itself is known as (30) _____ _____. (31) _____ refers to how well a test actually measures what it is supposed to measure. (32) _____ validity refers to how well a measure can predict some other criterion, like a future behavior. Creating a standardized environment and (33) _____, helps to meet the third measurement requirement for a good test, (34) _____. There is great debate about the nature of intelligence. British psychologist Charles Spearman believed that there is a general factor known as (35) _____, in mental abilities. American psychologist L. L. Thurstone argued that there are seven distinct, or (36) _____ _____ abilities that underlmy human mental performance. Cattell and Horn suggest two types of intelligence. (37) _____ intelligence involves the ability to apply previously acquired knowledge to solve new problems while (38) _____ intelligence is used to deal with novel problem-solving situations. (39) _____ _____ has argued for multiple intelligences. One of the newer theories of intelligence is that it is not purely cognitive. An intelligence that involves the abilities to read and respond to others' emotions appropriately, to motivate oneself, and to be aware of and to control one's own emotions is called (40) _____ intelligence. Robert Sternberg has developed a (41) _____ theory of intelligence. He suggests that people use higher-order processes, or (42) _____, to plan and regulate task performance,

(43) _____ components to actually do the task, and (44) _____ _____ components to encode and store information.

Apply What You Know

1. Find an intelligence test on the WWW. Evaluate whether it meets the criteria for a sound psychological test. Use Study Sheet 8.1.

2. Examining the female-male differences in problem-solving you see on p. 354, use both evolutionary psychological theory and theories of socialization to explain why those differences exist. Use Study Sheet 8.2.

Stretching Your Geographies

1. Thinking about Sternberg's triarchic theory of intelligence, describe items on an intelligence test that should be free of cultural, ethnic, and sex bias.

2. Describe some hypotheses about why there is an IQ gap between whites and blacks while there is no apparent gap between whites and Hispanics.

Practice Test

<u>Multiple Choice Items:</u> *Please write the letter corresponding to your answer in the space to the left of each item.*

_____ 1. The three essential properties that define _____ are that it is symbolic, it has structure, and it is generative.

    a. language
    b. a prototype
    c. fluid intelligence
    d. a heuristic

_____ 2. Consider the statement, "Last night, I shot an elephant in my pajamas." Since this sentence has two different interpretations (the pajamas could be worn by the man OR they could be worn by the elephant), this means that this sentence has _____ and _____.

    a. two different deep structures; one surface structure
    b. two different surface structures; one deep structure
    c. two different surface structures; two different deep structures
    d. one surface structure; one deep structure

_____ 3. Prior to 6 months of age, infants around the world are able to vocalize _____ but at about 6 months of age they begin vocalizing _____.

    a. only 5-10 phonemes; only the phonemes associated with their native language
    b. only the phonemes associated with their native language; the phonemes of all languages
    c. only 5-10 phonemes; the phonemes of all languages
    d. the phonemes of all languages; only the phonemes associated with their native language

_____ 4. While at the park, 19-month-old Suzy points to the swing set and says, "Push swing!" After she has had enough and wants to leave, she turns to her father and says, "Go car." Utterances such as these are called _____.

    a. baby talk
    b. telegraphic speech
    c. motherese
    d. child-speak

_____ 5. Many _____ are difficult to describe in words but we often can define them using _____, which are typical and familiar members of a particular class.

    a. prototypes; concepts
    b. concepts; propositions
    c. concepts; prototypes
    d. phonemes; morphemes

_____ 6. One morning, John decides to have oatmeal for breakfast and he performs very well on a math test that he takes later that day. He doesn't think too much about this until a few weeks later when he does very well on an English test and recalls that he had oatmeal for breakfast before this test too. He concludes that eating oatmeal in the morning helps him to perform better on exams. This example **best demonstrates** the ____.

    a. use of the representativeness heuristic
    b. process of inductive reasoning
    c. use of problem-solving schemas
    d. process of deducting reason

_____ 7. You are hungry and would like something to eat. You decide to look through the pantry and see a box of macaroni and cheese that looks good. Without really thinking about it, you know how to do all the various steps involved in making this meal such as filling a pot with water, boiling the water, cooking the pasta, mixing in the cheese sauce, and finding a plate on which to put the finished meal. Based on the discussion in the text, this type of specialized knowledge is **best considered** as an example of ____.

    a. a problem solving schema
    b. a mental set
    c. deductive reasoning
    d. a norm

_____ 8. According to Tversky and Kanheman, the errors in logic that occur in response to the "Linda the feminist bank teller" problem (where participants think it is more likely that Linda is a feminist bank teller than simply a bank teller) are due to the fact that they confuse ____.

    a. representativeness with availability
    b. representativeness with probability
    c. availability with confirmation bias
    d. availability with probability

_____ 9. Shelley is attempting to solve a problem and at this point in time, she is trying to generate as many solutions as possible and trying to incorporate new and unusual ideas into her potential solutions. Shelley is engaged in ____ thinking.

    a. convergent
    b. propositional
    c. divergent
    d. confirmatory

_____ 10. Suppose you take a psychological test and receive a score of 82 (out of a possible 100) on it. Imagine that you take the same test again 2 days later and this time you receive a score of 46. Other people who have taken the test twice have also had similar positive and negative changes in scores. These results mean that this test has ____.

    a. high internal consistency
    b. low internal consistency
    c. low test-retest reliability
    d. high test-retest reliability

_____ 11. The ability to apply previously learned knowledge to current problems that heavily involves verbal reasoning and factual knowledge is called _____ intelligence.

a. crystallized
b. fluid
c. psychometric
d. deductive

_____ 12. Compared to other existing theories of intelligence, Gardner's theory of multiple intelligences is **most unique** in that he _____.

a. argues that additional abilities such as musical talents and interpersonal skills should also be considered part of intelligence
b. believes that intelligence consists of several distinct abilities
c. asserts that there are only 3 different types of intelligence: linguistic, mathematical, and visual-spatial
d. believes that a general "g" factor was largely responsible for intelligence

_____ 13. According to Sternberg's triarchic theory, the types of intelligence that can be demanded by the environment are _____.

a. mathematical, linguistic, and visual-spatial
b. musical, bodily-kinesthetic, and personal
c. crystallized and fluid
d. analytical, practical, and creative

_____ 14. Researchers who believe in the concept of a reaction range are **most likely** to argue that intelligence is _____.

a. a product of the interaction between genetics and the environment
b. the product of many separate but correlated individual mental abilities
c. completely determined by genetic factors
d. the result of a single underlying intelligence factor

_____ 15. The fact that IQ differences between black and white students has _____ in recent years is generally taken as evidence that this difference may largely be due to _____ factors.

a. decreased; unchangeable genetic
b. increased; unchangeable genetic
c. remained the same; changeable environmental
d. decreased; changeable environmental

_____ 16. According to Spearman, the type of intelligence that is common to all mental abilities is _____.

a. I.Q.
b. verbal intelligence
c. mathematical intelligence
d. g

_____ 17. Snoopy, dreaming once more of being a World War I flying ace, sits on top of his doghouse and flies once more into battle against the evil Red Baron. Snoopy's unique use of his doghouse suggests that he is **not** suffering from _____.

a. problem-solving set
b. functional fixedness
c. heuristics
d. deep structure

_____ 18. If Captain Picard leaves Deep Space Nine at 0900 hours and travels at Warp 4 in his shuttlecraft, he can rendezvous with the Starship Enterprise in 4.2 hours. However, in order to reach the ship so quickly, he would have to travel through the Neutral Zone, and his presence would undoubtedly be noticed by Romulan warships, which would attack and destroy his craft. Thus, Picard realizes that he will have to take another route to the ship and thus devises what comes to be known as the "Picard loop" to get around the neutral zone. The Captain has applied _____.

a. crystallized intelligence ability
b. an algorithm
c. deductive reasoning skill
d. means-ends analysis

_____ 19. A step-by-step problem strategy for solving a problem or achieving a goal is called a(n) _____.

a. algorithm
b. heuristic
c. exemplar
d. prototype

_____ 20. Having given up his bumbling ways to become a high school teacher at alma mater Riverdale High, the formerly bungling Jughead looks to former teacher Miss Grundy as his role model, believing that she is the ideal representative of the category "teacher." Jughead would be said to be employing the _____ model of categorization.

a. classical
b. prototype
c. exemplar
d. functional

_____ 21. Salovey & Mayer (1990) argue that "emotional intelligence" includes _____.

a. being able to recognize the emotions of others
b. a lack of self-control
c. not examining your feelings when making decisions
d. a need for power

_____ 22. _____ consists of a system of symbols and rules for combining those symbols in ways that can produce an infinite number of possible messages or meanings.

a. A proposition
b. A schema
c. Language
d. Deep structure

_____ 23. The smallest units of meaning in a language are called _____.

a. phonemes
b. morphemes
c. surface structures
d. deep structures

_____ 24. The fact that all adult languages throughout the world have a common underlying deep structure suggests that _____.

a. deep structure is more important than surface structure
b. phonemes are more important than morphemes
c. morphemes are more important than phonemes
d. language has a biological basis

_____ 25. Reasoning from the "top down" is called _____ reasoning.

a. deductive
b. inductive
c. schematic
d. propositional

_____ 26. Based on the fact that he has seen 10,776 murders on TV in the last week, LaWanda believes that she is far more likely to be murdered than to die of old age. LaWanda seems to be _____.

a. using the representativeness heuristic
b. applying an algorithm
c. using the availability heuristic
d. subject to the confirmation bias

_____ 27. According to Stern's work in Germany, _____ was originally defined as mental age/chronological age x 100.

a. aptitude
b. achievement
c. IQ
d. problem-solving ability

_____ 28. An _____ test is thought to measure an applicant's potential for future learning and performance.

    a. achievement
    b. aptitude
    c. intelligence
    d. psychological

_____ 29. The statistical study of psychological tests is called _____.

    a. psychometrics
    b. standardization
    c. the establishment of norms
    d. the "g" factor

_____ 30. Thurstone argued that human mental performance depends on _____.

    a. the "g" factor
    b. primary mental abilities
    c. triarchic intelligence
    d. emotional intelligence

True/False Items: _Write T or F in the space provided to the left of each item._

_____ 1. The surface structure of a language consists of the way symbols are combined within a given language.

_____ 2. Phonemes are the smallest units of sound that are recognized as separate in a given language.

_____ 3. The linguistic relativity hypothesis suggests that language determines how we think.

_____ 4. The most typical and familiar members of a concept are called prototypes.

_____ 5. Reasoning from general principles to a conclusion about a specific case is called inductive reasoning.

_____ 6. Using problem-solving schemas to solve problems is called a mental set.

_____ 7. The availability heuristic is involved in exaggerating the likelihood that something will occur because it easily comes to mind.

_____ 8. Content validity refers to how highly test scores correlate with criterion measures.

_____ 9. Fluid intelligence refers to the ability to deal with novel problem-solving situations for which personal experience does not provide a solution.

_____ 10. According to Sternberg's triarchic theory of intelligence, metacomponents are used to encode and store information.

Short Answer Questions

1. What is the difference between the surface and deep structure of a language?

2. What is a proposition?

3. What are algorithms and heuristics?

4. Describe the three scientific standards for sound psychological tests.

5. What abilities comprise emotional intelligence?

Essay Questions

1. What processes, both biological and environmental, are involved in learning a language?

2. Describe three major stumbling blocks in the reasoning process.

3. Describe the general process involved in problem-solving.

4. Describe Sternberg's triarchic theory of intelligence.

5. How do both heredity and environment seem to affect intelligence?

Study Sheet 8.1
WWW Intelligence Tests

URL (Web Address) of Test:

http://

Reliability:

Validity:

Standardization:

Study Sheet 8.2 Male-Female Differences in Problem-Solving

List of Problem-Solving Tasks Favoring Women	Evolutionary Explanation	Sociocultural Explanation

Study Sheet 8.2 Male-Female Differences in Problem-Solving

List of Problem-Solving Tasks Favoring Men	Evolutionary Explanation	Sociocultural Explanation

Answer Keys

Answer Key for Key Terms

Language

1. o
2. e
3. q
4. l
5. b
6. j
7. a
8. h
9. m
10. g
11. k
12. n
13. p
14. f
15. c
16. d
17. i

Reasoning and Problem Solving

1. f
2. k
3. c
4. l
5. a
6. m
7. n
8. g
9. o
10. b
11. h
12. d
13. e
14. j
15. i

Intelligence

1. c
2. d
3. bb
4. j
5. k
6. s
7. u
8. q
9. t
10. a
11. b
12. cc
13. h
14. z
15. dd
16. x
17. o
18. n
19. y
20. l
21. r
22. e
23. p
24. aa
25. f
26. v
27. m
28. g
29. w
30. i

Answer Key for Review at a Glance

1. Mental representations
2. Language
3. displacement
4. surface
5. syntax
6. deep
7. phonemes
8. morphemes
9. linguistic relativity
10. propositional
11. imaginal
12. motoric
13. propositions
14. prototypes
15. deductive
16. inductive
17. problem solving schemas
18. algorithms
19. heuristics
20. means ends analysis
21. subgoal
22. representativeness
23. availability
24. mental
25. intelligence quotient
26. achievement
27. aptitude
28. reliability
29. test retest
30. internal consistency
31. Validity
32. Predictive
33. norms
34. standardization
35. g
36. primary mental
37. Crystallized
38. fluid
39. Howard Gardner
40. emotional
41. triarchic
42. metacomponents
43. performance
44. knowledge acquisition

Answer Key for Practice Test Multiple Choice Questions

1. a
2. a
3. d
4. b
5. c
6. b
7. a
8. b
9. c
10. c
11. a
12. a
13. d
14. a
15. d
16. d
17. b
18. d
19. a
20. c
21. a
22. c
23. b
24. d
25. a
26. c
27. c
28. b
29. a
30. b

Answer Key for Practice Test True/False Questions

1. T
2. T
3. T
4. T
5. F
6. F
7. T
8. F
9. T
10. F

Answer Key for Practice Test Short Answer Questions

1. Surface structure consists of the way symbols are combined within a given language. Deep structure refers to the underlying meaning of the combined symbols.

2. A proposition is a statement that expresses a fact. All propositions consist of concepts that contain a subject and a predicate.

3. Algorithms are formulas or procedures that automatically generate correct solutions. Heuristics are general problem-solving strategies that we apply to certain classes of situations. They are mental shortcuts that may or may not provide correct solutions.

4. There are three major standards for sound psychological tests. Reliability refers to the consistency of measurement. Validity measures the extent to which a test measures what it is designed to measure. Standardization has two facets: creating a standardized environment for testing and the establishment of norms for comparison.

5. Emotional intelligence involves the abilities to read others' emotions accurately, to respond to them appropriately, to motivate oneself, to be aware of one's emotions, and to regulate and to control one's own emotional responses.

Answer Key for Practice Test Essay Questions

1. Some linguists believe that there is a sensitive period during which language is most easily learned, suggesting a biological foundation for the acquisition of language. This period typically extends from infancy to puberty or early adolescence. In terms of social learning, parents influence their children's acquisition of language in a variety of ways. Parents use *motherese* to maintain their children's interest and attract their attention. Rewarding of appropriate vocalizations and nonrewarding of inappropriate ones have been hypothesized to influence acquisition. Such rewards may focus more on deep structure than on grammar.

2. Sometimes we can be distracted by irrelevant information. The ability to pay attention only to relevant information is a key to effective problem-solving. A second problem in the reasoning process involves failure to apply deductive rules. The use of formal logic and algorithms such as mathematical formulas can help us solve problems more accurately. A third problem is called belief bias. Belief bias is the tendency to abandon logical rules in favor of our own personal beliefs.

3. The first step in problem-solving is understanding, or framing, the problem. If we frame a problem poorly at the beginning, incorrect problem-solving strategies are likely to be followed. The second step involves generating potential solutions. To do that, we might first determine what procedures will be considered and then use those procedures to test whether they are helpful in moving us toward solution. If a procedure is not useful, we move to another procedure and test it. The final stage of problem-solving involves evaluating the results.

4. Robert Sternberg's triarchic theory of intelligence addresses the psychological processes involved in intelligence and the different forms that intelligence takes. It is a three-component model. Metacomponents are higher-order cognitive processes used to plan and regulate performance on a task. Performance components are used to perform a task. Knowledge-acquisition components allow us to learn from experience, store information, and combine new

insights with previously acquired knowledge. Sternberg has stressed that we should look at analytical intelligence, which involves academically-oriented knowledge, practical intelligence, which refers to the skills needed to cope with everyday demands, and creative intelligence, which helps us to deal with novel problems. The three components of the triarchic model are likely involved in all three kinds of intelligence Sternberg proposes.

5. There is evidence that genetic factors play an important role in intelligence. For example, monozygotic twins seem to be more alike in intelligence than are dizygotic twins. The reaction range for intelligence, as well as that for other traits, provides upper and lower limits for the development of intelligence, meaning that intelligence is not fixed at birth and is influenced as well by environmental factors. Heredity and environmental factors such as culture, ethnicity, and parental influences interact in complex ways to influence intelligence.

Chapter 9
MOTIVATION

Learning Objectives: *These questions, with a few additions, are taken from the directed questions found in the margins of the chapter. After reading the chapter, you should be able to answer these questions.*

0.1*   Define the term motivation.

1.   According to evolutionary psychologists, how does the concept of adaptive significance help us understand human motivation?

2.   How are homeostatic and drive concepts of motivation related?

3.   According to expectancy x value theory, why might people respond differently to the same incentive?

3.1*   Distinguish between intrinsic and extrinsic motivation.

4.   Explain Maslow's concept of a need hierarchy. Do you agree with this model?

4.1*   To what does the term metabolism refer? How much energy goes to support the resting, continuous work of cells in the body?

5.   Describe some physiological signals that initiate hunger.

6.   What physiological signals cause us to stop eating?

7.   Explain how leptin regulates appetite. How did scientists learn about leptin's role?

8.   What evidence suggested that the LH and VMH were hunger "on" and "off" centers? What evidence suggests otherwise?

9.   Describe some factors that contribute to the pressure women feel to be thin.

9.1*   According to objectification theory, what does American culture teach women about their bodies?

10.   Identify several environmental and cultural factors that influence eating.

10.1*   What is known about the possible psychological causal factors associated with obesity?

11.   What evidence suggests a genetic role in obesity? How does obesity among the Pima Indians illustrate a gene-environment interaction?

12.   Why is it especially hard for obese people to lose weight? Are diets doomed to fail?

13.   Describes some symptoms and causes of anorexia and bulimia.

14.   What evidence suggests that sensation seeking has a biological basis?

209

14.1*   What noticeable trend regarding sexuality has emerged during the past 50 years? What is the current status of this trend?

15.   Explain the stages of the sexual response cycle.

16.   Describe the organizational and activational effects of sex hormones. How do the activational effects differ in humans versus nonhumans?

17.   What psychological factors stimulate and inhibit sexual functioning?

18.   How do cultural norms and environmental stimuli influence sexual behavior?

19.   According to social learning and catharsis principles, how should viewing pornography affect sexual aggression? What does research find?

20.   Do you believe that research findings should influence societal decisions about pornography? Why or why not?

21.   Why is the issue of defining sexual orientation complicated?

22.   What are your personal beliefs about the causes of sexual orientation? Do any of these correspond to scientific theories that have been rejected?

23.   What evidence suggests that sexual orientation has biological roots? Describe the limitations of this evidence.

24.   From evolutionary and social comparison viewpoints, why are humans such social creatures?

25.   How does fear influence affiliation?

26.   How and why does proximity influence affiliation and attraction?

27.   Do birds of a feather flock together or do opposites attract? Describe the evidence.

28.   Identify two factors that may underlie the desire to affiliate more with attractive people.

28.1*   What is the matching effect and what predictions does it make regarding dating preferences?

29.   Describe some gender differences in mate preferences.

30.   How do evolutionary and social structure models explain gender differences in mate preferences?

31.   How consistent are gender differences in mate preferences across cultures? How might this support both evolutionary and social structure views?

32.   According to social penetration and social exchange theories, what factors influence whether a relationship will deepen, be satisfying, and continue?

33.   How does Sternberg's model expand upon the passionate-companionate love distinction?

34. Explain how transfer of excitation can influence our feelings of love.

34.1* What percentage of marriages end in divorce? How well can marital researchers predict marriage outcomes?

35. Based on marital research, give some advice to a newlywed couple about behaviors that will help keep their relationship strong.

36. What types of achievement goals are associated with a high motive for success, and with a high fear of failure?

37. How do people with high versus low achievement needs differ in the difficulty of the tasks they select? Explain why this occurs.

38. How do cultural factors influence the expression of achievement needs?

39. In the workplace, are most people motivated primarily by money? Explain.

40. How strongly is job satisfaction related to job productivity? Do you have any ideas why this might be?

41. Describe three types of programs that psychologists have designed to enhance work motivation. What major perspectives do these programs rest upon?

42. Explain three types of motivational conflict. Can you think of examples from your own life?

Chapter Overview

Perspectives on Motivation

Motivation is a process that influences the direction, persistence, and vigor of goal-directed behavior. Instinct theories of motivation, prominent a century ago, soon gave way to other models. The body's biological systems are balanced to ensure survival. Homeostasis, a state of internal equilibrium, is important to maintain, and many behaviors may be motivated by the need to return to homeostasis. Drive theory assumed that physiological disruptions to homeostasis produces drives to reduce the tension caused by the disruptions. Incentive theories, on the other hand, focus attention on external stimuli as motivators of behavior. According to expectancy x value theory, goal-directed behavior is jointly determined by the person's expectation that a behavior will lead to a goal and the value that the person places on the goal. Many cognitive theorists also distinguish between extrinsic motivation, which is motivation produced by the desire to obtain rewards and to avoid punishments, and intrinsic motivation, which is performing an activity for its own sake. Psychodynamic theorists suggest that unconscious motives, thoughts, and inner tensions are an important motivator of behavior. Humanistic theorists such as Maslow stress need hierarchies, particularly the need to fulfill our potential, or self-actualization.

Hunger and Weight Regulation

The body monitors its energy supplies, and this information interacts with other signals to regulate food intake. Homeostatic mechanisms are designed to prevent us from running low on energy. Some researchers believe that there is a set point around which body weight is regulated.

Studies of humans and rats show a temporary drop-rise in glucose patterns prior to experiencing hunger. As we eat, stomach and intestinal distention act as satiety signals, and peptides such as cholecystokinin stimulate brain receptors to decrease eating. Fat cells regulate food intake and weight by secreting leptin. Many parts of the brain also influence eating. Early studies indicated that the lateral hypothalamus seemed to be a "hunger-on" center. The ventromedial hypothalamus seemed to be a "hunger-off" center. However, modern research indicates that it is not that simple. Various neural circuits within the hypothalamus regulate food intake. Many of these pathways involve the paraventricular nucleus. Eating is also affected by psychological factors. Eating is positively reinforced by good taste and is negatively reinforced by hunger reduction. Beliefs, attitudes, habits, and psychological needs also affect food intake. Studies of obesity have indicated a strong genetic component. Eating disorders such as anorexia nervosa, where people severely restrict their food intake because of a fear of being fat, and bulimia nervosa, where the fear of being fat causes binging and purging, pose serious health problems.

Sensation-Seeking

The motivation to seek out stimulation and novelty is called sensation-seeking. Those higher in sensation-seeking tend to enjoy activities involving higher risks, are less likely to become depressed, and engage in a wider variety of sexual activities with more partners. High sensation-seekers may have a less "reactive" nervous system.

Sexual Motivation

People engage in sex for a variety of reasons. Secretions of gonadotropins from the pituitary glands affect the rate at which the sex organs secrete androgens and estrogens. These sex hormones have both organizational effects that direct the development of sex organs and activational effects that stimulate sexual desire and behavior. Psychological factors like sexual fantasy can also trigger sexual arousal. The psychological meaning of sex depends strongly on cultural contexts and learning. Cultural norms influence what stimuli are sexually arousing and what sexual behaviors occur. Studies of pornography are controversial. Violent pornographic films seem to increase, at least temporarily, men's aggression toward women and may promote rape myths. Sexual orientation may have three dimensions: self-identity, sexual attraction, and actual sexual behavior. Many researchers believe in a genetic basis for sexual orientation. Altering prenatal sex hormones can also influence sexual orientation. These findings, for human, though, are correlational and controversial.

The Desire for Affiliation and Intimacy

We affiliate with others for a number of reasons. Social comparison allows us to compare our beliefs, feelings, and behaviors with others. Initial attraction often occurs through mere exposure and matching with others of similar physical attractiveness. Men and women have somewhat different mate preferences. Evolutionary theories such as parental investment theory argue that the difference is due to evolutionary forces, while theories such as social structure theory stress environmental forces. As relationships progress, interactions become both broader and deeper according to social penetration theory. Rewards and costs also influence the course of relationships, according to social exchange theory. Love, including both passionate and companionate love, is an important aspect of many human relationships. Sternberg's triangular theory of love stresses that different types of love are combinations of three components: intimacy, passion, and commitment. Gottman's "four horsemen of the apocalypse": criticism, contempt, defensiveness, and stonewalling, have been found to negatively influence relationships.

Achievement Motivation

Need for achievement is influenced by both motive for success and fear of failure. Individual perceptions, family influences, and cultural influences all influence achievement motivation.

Motivation in the Workplace

People work for a number of different reasons, including money, personal accomplishment, opportunities for mastery, growth, and satisfying interpersonal relationships. Job enrichment programs attempt to increase people's intrinsic motivation to work. Employee participation in programs like management by objectives (MBO) is increasingly being stressed by industrial-organizational psychologists as an important way to increase worker motivation.

Motivational Conflict

Approach-approach, avoidance-avoidance, and approach-avoidance conflicts influence motivation through having to choose between two attractive alternatives, two unattractive alternatives, and attractive and unattractive aspects of the same goal respectively.

Chapter Outline

Perspective on Motivation
    Instinct Theory and Modern Evolutionary Psychology
    Homeostasis and Drive Theory
    Incentive and Expectancy Theories
    Psychodynamic and Humanistic Theories

Hunger and Weight Regulation
    The Physiology of Hunger
        Signals That Start and Terminate a Meal
        Signals That Regulate General Appetite and Weight Brain Mechanisms
    Psychological Aspects of Hunger
    Environmental and Cultural Factors
    Obesity
        Genes and Environment
        Dieting and Weight Loss
    Psychological Frontiers: Eating Disorders: Anorexia and Bulimia

Sensation-Seeking

Sexual Motivation

    Sexual Behavior: Patterns and Changes
    The Physiology of Sex
        The Sexual Response Cycle
        Hormonal Influences
    The Psychology of Sex
        Sexual Fantasy

Key Terms: *Write the letter of the definition next to the term in the space provided.*

Perspectives on Motivation
Hunger and Weight Regulation
Sensation-Seeking

1. ___ anorexia nervosa	a.	a process that influences the direction, persistence, and vigor of goal-directed behavior
2. ___ bulimia nervosa	b.	an inherited characteristic that automatically produces a particular response when the organism is exposed to a particular stimulus
3. ___ CCK (cholecystokinin)	c.	a state of internal physiological equilibrium
4. ___ drive theory	d.	theory that physiological disruptions to homeostasis produce states of internal tensions that motivate organisms
5. ___ expectancy x value theory	e.	proposes that goal-directed behavior is produced by a person's strength of expectation that behavior will lead to a goal and the value the person places on the goal
6. ___ extrinsic motivation	f.	performing an activity to obtain an external reward or to avoid a punishment
7. ___ glucose	g.	performing an activity for its own sake
8. ___ homeostasis	h.	a progression of needs, with deficiency needs at the bottom and growth needs at the top
9. ___ incentives	i.	the need to fulfill our potential
10. ___ instinct	j.	the body's rate of energy utilization
11. ___ intrinsic motivation	k.	a simple sugar that is the body's major source of fuel
12. ___ leptin	l.	a peptide that stimulates brain receptors to terminate eating
13. ___ metabolism	m.	a hormone that decreases appetite
14. ___ motivation	n.	a cluster of neurons packed with receptor sites for transmitters that stimulate or reduce appetite
15. ___ need hierarchy	o.	disorder in which victims have an intense fear of being fat and thus severely restrict their food intake
16. ___ paraventricular nucleus (PVN)	p.	disorder in which victims binge eat and then purge the food
17. ___ self-actualization	q.	the motivation to seek out stimulation and novelty
18. ___ sensation-seeking	r.	environmental stimuli that "pull" an organism toward a goal

Sexual Motivation
The Desire for Affiliation and Intimacy
Achievement Motivation
Motivation in the Workplace
Motivational Conflict

1. ___ androgens	a.	"masculine" sex hormones
2. ___ approach-approach conflict	b.	"feminine" sex hormones
3. ___ approach-avoidance conflict	c.	one's emotional and erotic preference for partners of a particular sex

4. ___ avoidance-avoidance conflict

d. a four-stage pattern of sexual response

5. ___ cognitive-arousal model of love

e. comparing our beliefs, feelings, and behaviors with other people

6. ___ companionate love

f. repeated exposure to a stimulus typically increases our liking of it

7. ___ estrogens

g. we are most likely to have a dating partner or spouse whose physical attractiveness is similar to our own

8. ___ job enrichment

h. theory that the gender with a greater investment in producing offspring will be more selective in choosing a mate

9. ___ management by objectives

i. proposes that men and women display different mating preferences because society directs them into different social roles

10. ___ matching effect

j. theory that relationships progress as interactions become broader and deeper

11. ___ mere exposure effect

k. theory that the course of a relationship is guided by rewards and costs

12. ___ need for achievement

l. involves intense emotion, arousal, and yearning for the partner

13. ___ parental investment theory

m. involves affection and deep caring about a partner's well-being

14. ___ passionate love

n. theory that the passionate component of love has interacting cognitive and physiological components

15. ___ sexual motivation

o. arousal due to one source perceived as due to another source

16. ___ sexual response cycle

p. represents the desire to accomplish tasks and to attain standards of excellence

17. ___ social comparison

q. programs that attempt to increase intrinsic motivation

18. ___ social exchange theory

r. combines goal setting with employee participation and feedback

19. ___ social penetration theory

s. involves choosing between two attractive alternatives

20. ___ social structure theory

t. a person must choose between two undesirable alternatives

21. ___ transfer of excitation

u. involves being attracted to and repulsed by the same goal

22. ___ triangular theory of love

v. theory of love that focuses on intimacy, passion, and commitment

Review at a Glance: *Write the term that best fits the blank to review what you learned in this chapter.*

Perspectives on Motivation

(1) _____ is a process that influences the direction, persistence, and vigor of goal-directed behavior. An inherited characteristic, common to all members of a species, that automatically produces a particular response is called an (2) _____. According to Hull's (3) _____ theory, states of internal tension motivate people to behave in ways that return them to (4) _____. (5) _____ motivation involves external rewards to motivate

behavior, while (6) _____ motivation involves performing an activity for its own sake. Abraham Maslow proposed the concept of a (7) _____ _____, a progression of needs from deficiency needs at the bottom to (8) _____ _____, the need to fulfill our potential, at the top.

Hunger and Weight Reduction

The body's rate of energy (or caloric) utilization is called (9) _____. When we eat, digestive enzymes break food down into various nutrients, including (10) _____, a simple sugar that is the body's major source of fuel. Several hormones called peptides help to terminate a meal. For example, (11) _____ is released into the bloodstream by the small intestine as food arrives in the stomach, travels to the brain, and stimulates brain receptors. A hormone that decreases appetite is called (12) _____. Early studies of the brain indicated "hunger-on" and "hunger-off" centers. A proposed "hunger-on" center of the brain is called the (13) _____ _____. A proposed "hunger-off" center is called the (14) _____ hypothalamus. However, later research did not support the early ideas. A cluster of neurons that are packed with receptor sites for various transmitters that stimulate or reduce appetite is called the (15) _____ nucleus. Victims of (16) _____ _____ have an intense fear of being fat and severely restrict their food intake to the point of self-starvation. People who suffer from (17) _____ _____ are also overconcerned about being fat but binge eat and then purge the food.

Sensation-Seeking

The motivation to seek out stimulation and novelty is called (18) _____ _____.

Sexual Motivation

A four-stage pattern of sexual response is called the (19) _____ _____ _____. The "masculine" sex hormones, or (20) _____, and the "feminine" sex hormones, or (21) _____, affect sexual behavior. (22) _____ _____ refers to one's emotional and erotic preference for partners of a particular sex.

The Desire for Affiliation and Intimacy

Initial attraction is often influenced by both beauty and by a (23) _____ effect, by which we pair up with people of about the same level of physical attractiveness as ourselves. Attraction is also influenced by the (24) _____ _____ effect, through which repeated exposure to someone or something increases our liking for them or it. Men and women are attracted to some different characteristics. According to (25) _____ _____ theory, the gender with a greater investment in producing offspring will be more selective in choosing a mate. In contrast, (26) _____ _____ theory proposes that men and women display different mating preferences because they are socialized into different roles. As relationships grow, interactions between people become both broader and deeper, according to (27) _____ _____ theory. Additionally, according to (28) _____ _____ theory, the course of a relationship is governed by rewards and costs that the partners experience. Love is a widely researched topic in social psychology. (29) _____ love involves intense emotion, arousal, and yearning for a partner, while (30) _____ love involves affection and deep caring for another. Robert Sternberg's (31) _____ theory of love focuses on intimacy, passion, and commitment as components of love.

Achievement Motivation

(32) _____ _____ _____ represents the desire to accomplish tasks and attain standards of excellence. A negatively oriented motivation to avoid failure is called (33) _____ of failure.

Motivation in the Workplace

Reflecting Maslow's humanistic theory, (34) _____ _____ programs attempt to increase (35) _____ motivation by making jobs more fulfilling and providing workers with opportunities for growth. Another important development in the workplace is called (36) _____ _____ _____, which combines goal setting by management with employee participation and feedback.

Motivational Conflict

Motivational goals sometimes conflict with each other. An (37) _____ - _____ conflict involves opposition between two attractive alternatives, an (38) _____ - _____ conflict involves a choice between two undesirable alternatives, and an (39) _____ - _____ conflict involves being attracted to and repulsed by the same goal.

Apply What You Know

1. Describe your own behaviors that support both drive theories and sensation-seeking theories.

2. Interview members of couples to determine if they are indeed similar in values and attitudes, as the similarity hypothesis would suggest. What do you find?

3. Give examples of all three motivational conflicts from your own life.

Stretching Your Geographies

1. Survey both males and females in your classes to determine similarities and differences in what they are attracted to in other people. Do your results support evolutionary theory, social structural theory, or neither? How so?

Practice Test

<u>Multiple Choice Items</u>: *Please write the letter corresponding to your answer in the space to the left of each item.*

_____ 1. Sara and Frank are competing for the same new job. They both very much want the job and believe that it would substantially help their careers. Frank isn't sure that he has the job or interview skills needed to get the job and as a result, he puts a little less effort into his resume and job interview. Sara on the other hand believes that she has good interview skills and thinks that she has the talent to get the job. As a result, she prepares at bit harder for this position. The expectancy x value theory of motivation would **most likely** explain this difference in motivation as being due to ____.

    a. their different expectations regarding their goal-related behaviors
    b. their different growth needs
    c. the different values they placed on the job
    d. their different internal drives

_____ 2. Tim is just learning to play the piano and somewhat surprisingly, he already enjoys playing it even though he isn't very good. Tim's parents would like to see him develop his skills so they decide to pay Tim $10.00 at the end of each week if he has satisfactorily practiced all his lessons. Motivation theorists familiar with the overjustification hypothesis would argue that the rewards being offered by Tim's parents may ____ Tim's interest in piano by ____ motivation.

    a. increase; enhancing his extrinsic
    b. decrease; undermining his extrinsic
    c. increase; enhancing his intrinsic
    d. decrease; undermining his intrinsic

_____ 3. Initial research suggested that the _____ was a "hunger on" center in the brain but more recent research has revealed that neurons in the ____ play an important role in triggering and reducing hunger.

    a. ventromedial hypothalamus (VMH); lateral hypothalamus (LH)
    b. ventromedial hypothalamus (VMH); paraventricular nucleus (PVN)
    c. lateral hypothalamus (LH); paraventricular nucleus (PVN)
    d. lateral hypothalamus (LH); ventromedial hypothalamus (VMH)

_____ 4. For people who are overweight, their bodies tend to respond to the food deprivation often involved in dieting by ____ the rate of basal metabolism. As fat mass decreases, leptin levels _____, which stimulates appetite and makes it harder to keep dieting.

    a. decreasing; decrease
    b. decreasing; increase
    c. increasing; decrease
    d. increasing; increase

_____ 5. Research on the prevalence of anorexia and bulimia has determined that these disorders are
_____.

    a. most common in industrialized cultures where beauty is equated with thinness
    b. equally common in almost all cultures of the world
    c. most common in cultures that have to deal with food scarcity and famine
    d. most common in cultures where people lack personal control and freedom

_____ 6. During the _____ phase of the sexual response cycle, physiological arousal builds
rapidly and blood flow increases to the organs in and around the genitals in a process called
vasocongestion.

    a. plateau
    b. excitement
    c. arousal
    d. resolution

_____ 7. According to Masters and Johnson, in proper order, the four stages of the human sexual
response cycle are _____, _____, _____, and _____.

    a. plateau; excitement; orgasm; resolution
    b. plateau; excitement; resolution; orgasm
    c. excitement; orgasm; resolution; plateau
    d. excitement; plateau; orgasm; resolution

_____ 8. The fact that children in the Marquesas Islands of French Polynesia have ample opportunity to
observe sexual behavior and boys in this society are sometimes masturbated by their parents
when the boys are distressed **best demonstrates** how _____ factors can impact sexual behavior.

    a. genetic
    b. personal psychological
    c. cultural
    d. biological

_____ 9. Real world correlational evidence gathered on the effect of pornography on behavior _____.

    a. provides clear support for the social learning theory position
    b. provides clear support for the psychoanalytic position
    c. does not clearly support either the social learning theory or psychoanalytic position
    d. provides clear support for both the social learning theory and psychoanalytic positions

_____ 10. All of the following findings have been observed in research on sexual orientation **except**
the finding that homosexual _____.

    a. children seem to know early in life that they are somehow different from their same-sex
       peers.
    b. children are more likely to engage in gender nonconforming behaviors.
    c. and heterosexual males have different adult levels of sex hormones.
    d. women are more likely to be considered "tomboys" and to be interested in boy's toys.

_____ 11. Two common perspectives on attraction are that "birds of a feather flock together" and "opposites attract." Scientific research on attraction has revealed that _____.

a. both of these statements are equally supported.
b. neither or these statements is supported.
c. the evidence is overwhelmingly consistent with "opposites attract."
d. the evidence is overwhelmingly consistent with "birds of a feather flock together."

_____ 12. Jeff and Mary have been dating for several weeks and are both considering making their relationship exclusive and not seeing other people. According to social penetration theory, their relationship will tend to grow closer and deeper if _____.

a. there is sexual intimacy but no self-disclosure
b. the relationship exceeds their respective comparison levels
c. there are no other reasonable alternative relationships for both of them
d. there is enough self-disclosure

_____ 13. Jean is happy in a romantic relationship but feels that there is likely another relationship that would make her even more content. Applying the concepts of social exchange theory, if we **only** examine the comparison level of Jean's current relationship, we would predict that she would _____ the relationship. If we look **solely** at her comparison level for alternatives, we would likely guess that she would _____ the relationship.

a. stay in; stay in
b. stay in; leave
c. leave; stay in
d. leave; leave

_____ 14. Fran really would like to do well in this course. She isn't so much motivated by wanting to get better grades and test scores than her classmates nor is she afraid of doing poorly but she is very much interested in learning and gaining some expertise for the material, even though some of the content is quite challenging for her. Fran appears to have a _____ and her particular way of manifesting this suggests that she is motivated by _____ goals.

a. strong fear of failure; mastery
b. high need for achievement; competitive
c. strong motive for success; competitive
d. high need for achievement; mastery

_____ 15. In cultures that encourage _____, such as China and Japan, measures of achievement motivation more strongly represent the desire to fit into the family and social group and to meet the expectations and work goals of these groups.

a. intrinsic motivation
b. mastery goals
c. collectivism
d. individualism

_____ 16. Hez I. Tent is having a hard time telling his girlfriend, Gofour Itt, that he loves her and wants to commit to her. From the perspective of exchange theory, this is likely because Hez is _____.

a. looking at his comparison level for alternatives
b. suffering from the "four horsemen of the apocalypse"
c. securely attached
d. not passionately in love

_____ 17. Although their marriage at one time consisted of all three components of Sternberg's (1988) love triangle, Jane and George Jetson feel that all of the passion has gone out of their relationship since George's unfortunate accident with that exploding space sprocket. Visiting space-age psychotherapist Dr. Ploo Toe, they would discover that they still would have _____ love in their relationship if the other two components of Sternberg's love triangle remain.

a. companionate
b. consummate
c. erotic
d. romantic

_____ 18. Having divorced formerly faithful wife Wilma because of her fling with pool shark Joe Rockhead, Fred Flintstone goes back into the dating pool. According to the evolutionary theory of mate selection, Fred would be most attracted to _____.

a. lifelong buddy and bosom pal Barney Rubble
b. the rich 65-year-old wife of boss Mr. Slate, Sandstone Slate
c. the 61-year-old but gorgeous Ms. Granite Pebbles
d. 23-year-old Miss Bedrock, Shale Limestone

_____ 19. According to the proximity effect, Snow White should be most attracted to _____.

a. Cinderella's husband, the man formerly known as "The Prince"
b. that evil, vain, mirror-loving queen
c. Johnny Appleseed
d. the Seven Dwarfs, with whom she lives

_____ 20. Tilly Seaker likes to bungee jump off of skyscrapers in the nude every few days. Tilly's behavior is probably best explained by _____.

a. drive theory
b. sensation-seeking theory
c. the desire to maintain homeostasis
d. avoidance-avoidance conflicts

_____ 21. _____ represent environmental stimuli that "pull" an organism toward a goal.

    a. Drives
    b. Incentives
    c. Homeostatic states
    d. Intrinsic motivators

_____ 22. At the top of Maslow's pyramid, the need to fulfill our potential is called _____.

    a. self-actualization
    b. a cognitive need
    c. an aesthetic need
    d. an esteem need

_____ 23. When _____ levels decline, hunger is likely to be felt when _____ levels increase, eating diminishes.

    a. CCK; blood glucose
    b. leptin; blood glucose
    c. blood glucose; CCK
    d. blood glucose; LH

_____ 24. Of the following, the one which is not a <u>psychological</u> factor that regulates food intake is _____.

    a. CCK
    b. attitudes
    c. habits
    d. psychological needs

_____ 25. A disorder in which a person has an intense fear of being fat and thus severely restricts their food intake to the point of self-starvation is called _____.

    a. bulimia nervosa
    b. CCK
    c. leptin
    d. anorexia nervosa

_____ 26. The hormones that appear to have the primary influence on sexual desire are the _____.

    a. estrogens
    b. leptins
    c. androgens
    d. initiators

_____ 27. Repeated exposure to a stimulus typically increases our liking for it, according to studies of _____.

    a. the mere exposure effect
    b. the similarity effect
    c. parental investment theory
    d. social penetration theory

_____ 28. _____ love involves emotion, arousal, and yearning for the partner without a sense of intimacy or commitment.

   a. Companionate
   b. Passionate
   c. Consummate
   d. Fatuous

_____ 29. A goal setting technique used by managers that involves combining goal setting with employee participation and feedback is called _____.

   a. task significance
   b. job feedback
   c. task identity
   d. management by objectives

_____ 30. At this point in your review of this chapter, you have to decide to answer the rest of the practice test questions (a very undesirable alternative) or study for your biology test (another undesirable alternative) You are experiencing a(n) _____ conflict.

   a. approach-approach
   b. approach-avoidance
   c. avoidance-avoidance
   d. hopeless

True/False Items: *Write T or F in the space provided to the left of each item.*

_____ 1. According to Hull's drive theory, drives are produced by physiological disruptions to homeostasis.

_____ 2. Performing an activity to obtain an external reward or to avoid punishment is called intrinsic motivation.

_____ 3. Studies of the lateral hypothalamus and the ventromedial hypothalamus have definitively shown that they are "hunger-on" and "hunger-off" centers respectively.

_____ 4. According to Fredrickson and Roberts' (1997) objectification theory, American culture teaches women to view their bodies as objects.

_____ 5. Sensation-seeking refers to the motivation to seek out stimulation and novelty.

_____ 6. The four stage pattern of sexual response described by Masters and Johnson (1966) includes excitement, plateau, orgasm, and resolution.

_____ 7. Repeated exposure to a stimulus typically increases our liking of it.

_____ 8. According to social penetration theory, as relationships progress they become narrower and shallower.

_____ 9. Affection, deep caring about a partner's well-being, and a commitment to "being there" for the other is called passionate love.

_____ 10. An approach-approach conflict involves making a choice between two attractive alternatives.

Short Answer Questions

1. What role may homeostasis play in motivation?

2. What are the psychological aspects of hunger?

3. How are hormones involved in sexual motivation?

4. How does social exchange theory explain behavior in relationships?

5. Distinguish between the three different types of motivational conflict.

Essay Questions

1. Describe the physiological processes involved in hunger.

2. How are both genetics and environmental factors involved in obesity?

3. Describe three psychological processes involved in initial attraction.

4. Describe the triangular theory of love.

5. How can employers enhance work motivation?

Answer Keys

Answer Key for Key Terms

Perspectives on Motivation
Hunger and Weight Regulation
Sensation-Seeking

1. o
2. p
3. l
4. d
5. e
6. f
7. k
8. c
9. r

10. b
11. g
12. m
13. j
14. a
15. h
16. n
17. i
18. q

Sexual Motivation
The Desire for Affiliation and Intimacy
Achievement Motivation
Motivation in the Workplace
Motivational Conflict

1. a
2. s
3. u
4. t
5. n
6. m
7. b
8. q
9. r
10. g
11. f

12. p
13. h
14. l
15. c
16. d
17. e
18. k
19. j
20. i
21. o
22. v

Answer Key for Review at a Glance

1. Motivation
2. instinct
3. drive
4. homeostasis
5. Extrinsic
6. intrinsic
7. need hierarchy
8. self actualization
9. metabolism
10. glucose
11. CCK (cholecystokinin)
12. leptin

21. estrogens
22. Sexual orientation
23. matching
24. mere exposure
25. parental investment
26. social structure
27. social penetration
28. social exchange
29. Passionate
30. companionate
31. triangular
32. Need for achievement

13. lateral hypothalamus
14. ventromedial
15. paraventricular
16. anorexia nervosa
17. bulimia nervosa
18. sensation seeking
19. sexual response cycle
20. androgens

33. fear
34. job enrichment
35. intrinsic
36. management by objectives
37. approach-approach
38. avoidance-avoidance
39. approach-avoidance

Answer Key for Practice Test Multiple Choice Questions

1. a
2. d
3. c
4. b
5. a
6. b
7. d
8. c
9. c
10. c
11. d
12. d
13. b
14. d
15. c

16. a
17. a
18. d
19. d
20. b
21. b
22. a
23. c
24. a
25. d
26. c
27. a
28. b
29. d
30. c

Answer Key for Practice Test True/False Questions

1. T
2. F
3. F
4. T
5. T

6. T
7. T
8. F
9. F
10. T

Answer Key for Practice Test Short Answer Questions

1. Homeostasis is a state of internal physiological equilibrium that the body strives to maintain. Homeostatic regulation involves both unlearned and learned behaviors. According to drive theory, physiological disruptions to homeostasis produce drives, which motivate organisms to behave in ways that reduce drive.

2. From a behavioral perspective, eating is positively reinforced by good taste and negatively reinforced by hunger reduction. We have expectations that eating will be pleasurable, so cognitions about eating are important in motivation. Our beliefs, attitudes, and cultural standards about caloric intake as well as body image are important factors affecting eating.

3. The pituitary gland secretes hormones called gonadotropins into the bloodstream. These hormones affect the rate at which the gonads (testes in the male and ovaries in the female) secrete androgens and estrogens. These sex hormones have both organizational effects on the body by directing the development of the sex organs and activational effects by stimulating sexual desire and behavior.

4. According to Thibaut and Kelley's (1967) social exchange theory, relationships are governed by rewards and costs. Outcomes are evaluated against one's comparison level, which is the outcome that a person has come to expect from the relationship as well as against one's comparison level for alternatives, which focuses on potential alternatives to the relationship. For example, if one's rewards are less than one would expect, and the comparison level for alternatives suggests more rewards elsewhere, one will not be very commited to a relationship.

5. Approach-approach conflicts involve having to choose between two attractive alternatives. Avoidance-avoidance conflicts involve choosing between two undesirable alternatives. Approach-avoidance conflicts involve being attracted to and repelled by the same goal.

Answer Key for Practice Test Essay Questions

1. One key ingredient affecting hunger is glucose. Studies have determined that a temporary drop-rise pattern in blood glucose levels occurs prior to experiencing hunger and may be a signal to the brain that helps initiate feeding. As we eat, stomach and intestinal distention provide satiety signals to the brain, suggesting that we are getting full. The intestines respond to food by releasing peptides that help terminate a meal. For example, CCK (cholecystokinin) is released into the bloodstream, travels to the brain, and stimulates receptors in several brain regions, resulting in the cessation of eating. Leptin signals influence neural pathways to decrease appetite and increase energy expenditure. Many pathways involving the paraventricular nucleus (PVN) may also regulate food intake.

2. Over 200 genes have been identified as possible contributors to human obesity. The combined effects of some of those genes rather than a single gene itself may produce an increased risk of obesity. Societal and cultural factors such as an abundance of inexpensive, tasty, high-fat foods; a cultural emphasis on things like "supersizing," and technological advances that decrease the need for daily physical activity interact with genetic propensities to influence the development of obesity.

3. Proximity is the best predictor of who we will cross paths with and ultimately be attracted to. Proximity increases the chances of frequent encounters, and the mere exposure effect suggests that repeated exposures to a stimulus increase our liking for it. A second factor deals with similarity. Despite the popular notion that "opposites attract," there is far more evidence that suggests that people who are similarly physically attractive and/or are similar on other qualities such as attitudes, are attracted to each other. We are also more attracted to physically attractive people.

4. Robert Sternberg's triangular theory of love suggests that three components: intimacy, passion, and commitment are the most important aspects of love relationships. If we just have intimacy, we like a person. If we just have passion, we experience infatuation. If we just have commitment, we have an empty love. Other types of love are combinations of these components. Romantic love springs from a combination of intimacy and passion. Companionate love springs from intimacy and commitment. Fatuous love is a combination of passion and commitment. Finally, consummate love occurs if all three components are present in a relationship. Sternberg argues that consummate love is the ultimate form of love.

5. There are a number of ways that employers can enhance job motivation. Job enrichment programs attempt to increase intrinsic motivation by making jobs more fulfilling and providing workers with

opportunities for personal growth. Increasing skill variety such that a worker can use many talents and skills seems to be a successful way of increasing job motivation. Similarly, increasing a worker's sense of task identity, his or her sense of completing a job from start to finish, can help. Other ways of increasing motivation involve increasing a worker's sense of task significance, increasing worker autonomy, and providing clear feedback about job performance. Management by objectives programs attempt to increase motivation by combining goal setting with employee participation and feedback. Finally, improving external incentives such as pay and bonuses can increase motivation.

Chapter 10
EMOTION, STRESS, AND HEALTH

Learning Objectives: *These questions, with a few additions, are taken from the directed questions found in the margins of the chapter. After reading the chapter, you should be able to answer these questions.*

1. What is an emotion?

2. How are emotions related to motivation?

3. What are the adaptive functions of positive and negative emotions?

4. In what ways are emotions modes of communication?

5. Name the four major components of emotions, including the two classes of behavioral responses.

6. In what sense can eliciting stimuli be external or internal? What is the role of biological and learning factors?

7. How do cognitive appraisals enter into emotion? Do they need to involve conscious thought?

8. What evidence exists for (a) universal and (b) culturally determined appraisals? Provide examples of each.

9. How strongly are wealth, health, relationships, intelligence, and religiosity related to happiness?

10. Describe the role of comparison processes in happiness.

11. What evidence is there that genetics and culture can influence happiness?

12. Which subcortical and cortical structures are involved in emotion? How does LeDoux's theory explain unconscious emotional phenomena?

13. What experimental and clinical evidence supports the role of the amygdala in emotional learning?

14. Which neurotransmitters are involved in specific emotional responses?

15. What clinical and research evidence is there to support an "L+, R-" theory of hemispheric activation differences for positive and negative emotions?

16. How are the sympathetic and endocrine systems involved in emotion? Do different emotions have different patterns of autonomic arousal?

17. What considerations and research evidence challenges the validity of the "lie detector?" What kinds of errors are most likely?

17.1* What is empathy?

18. What evidence exists for fundamental emotional patterns of expression? How do they fit into an emotional hierarchy?

19. What important research results concerning emotional perception, sex differences, and universal expressions of emotion have occurred using the FACS?

20. What are cultural display rules? How do they affect emotional behavior?

20.1* What are instrumental behaviors?

21. What two general principles capture relations between emotional arousal, task complexity, and task performance?

22. Compare the James-Lange (somatic) and Cannon-Bard explanations for emotional perception and labeling.

23. How does research on animals and people deprived of sensory feedback bear on the validity of the James-Lange and Cannon-Bard theories?

24. What is the facial feedback hypothesis? What research evidence supports it? What might be the role of vascular feedback?

25. According to Schachter, what influences perceptions of emotional intensity? What tells us which emotion we are experiencing?

26. How did Lazarus et al. show that appraisals influence level of arousal? How did Schachter & Wheeler show that arousal level can affect appraisals?

27. Describe three ways that theorists have defined the term _stress_?

27.1* What are some different types of stressors? How do researchers measure stressful life events?

28. What four types of appraisal occur in response to a potential stressor? How do these correspond to primary and secondary appraisal?

29. Describe the three stages of Selye's GAS.

29.1* How do some evolutionary theorists explain the current detrimental effects of stress?

30. What are the characteristics of the rape trauma syndrome?

31. Describe three possible causal paths between self-reported stress and distress.

32. By what physiological and behavioral mechanisms can stress contribute to illness?

33. Differentiate between vulnerability and protective factors, and give examples of each.

34. What evidence exists that social support is a protective factor? In what ways can it protect against stressful events?

35. Can disclosing upsetting experiences to others enhance well-being? Cite relevant data.

36. What three beliefs underlie the protective factor called hardiness?

37. What four types of information increase coping self-efficacy?

38. What evidence is there that optimism-pessimism affect response to stress?

39. In what ways do spiritual and religious beliefs affect response to stressful events?

40. Define and give an example of the three major classes of coping strategies.

41. How does controllability influence the effectiveness of coping strategies?

42. How do gender and cultural factors affect the tendency to use particular coping strategies?

43. What coping skills can be used to control (a) cognitive appraisal and (b) physiological arousal components of the stress response? Describe the integrated coping response.

Chapter Overview

The Nature and Functions of Emotions

Emotions are positive or negative affect states consisting of a pattern of cognitive, physiological, and behavioral reactions to events that have relevance to important goals or motives. Emotions have important adaptive functions. Negative emotions may help us to narrow attention and actions to deal with a threatening situation. Positive emotions may help us to broaden our thinking and behavior so that we explore, consider new ideas, try out new ways to achieve goals, play, and savor what we have. The emotions we have share four common features: they are responses to stimuli, they involve cognitive appraisal, they involve physiological responses, and they include behavioral tendencies. Innate biological factors and learning may both influence which eliciting stimuli elicit which emotions. Appraisal processes relate to what we think is desirable and undesirable. Culture can also affect appraisal.

Biological factors also play an important role in emotions. Subcortical structures such as the hypothalamus, amygdala, and other limbic system structures are particularly involved. The ability to regulate emotion depends heavily on the prefrontal cortex. Joseph LeDoux has discovered that the thalamus sends messages along two independent neural pathways: to the cortex and to the amygdala. This dual system means that emotional responses can occur both through cortex interpretation and through a more primitive system through the amygdala, which is likely important for survival. Left-hemisphere activation may underlie certain positive emotions, and right-hemisphere activation might influence negative ones. Such activation may also underlie subjective well-being.

Autonomic and hormonal processes may also influence emotions. Some basic emotions, such as anger and fear, show distinctive autonomic processes. The behavioral component of emotions involves expressive behaviors, or emotional displays. Modern evolutionary theorists stress the adaptive value of such displays and suggest that some fundamental emotional patterns may be innate. Paul Ekman's studies of emotional expressions have shown a wide degree of cross-cultural agreement in evaluations of expressions. The studies also show that different parts of the face provide the best clues for certain emotions and that women are generally more accurate judges of emotional expression. Different cultures have different display rules for emotions.

Interactions Among the Components of Emotion

According to the James-Lange theory of emotion, which today lives on as the somatic theory of emotion, bodily reactions produce perceptions of emotional states. An offshoot, the facial-feedback hypothesis, suggests that feedback to the brain from facial muscles produces emotions. The Cannon-Bard theory stresses the simultaneous messages sent by the thalamus to the cortex and the body's internal organs. Schachter's two-factor theory stresses cognitive appraisal of physiological arousal and situational cues leading to perception of an emotion.

Stress, Coping, and Health

Stimuli that place strong demands on us are called stressors. Stress involves a pattern of cognitive appraisals, physiological responses, and behavioral tendencies that occurs in response to a perceived imbalance between situational demands and the resources needed to cope with them. Four aspects of the appraisal process are of particular significance: appraisal of demands of a situation (primary appraisal), appraisal of coping resources (secondary appraisal), judgment of the consequences of the situation for us, and appraisal of the personal meaning of the situation for us. Stress has important effects on health. For example, traumatic events such as rape or war experiences can have long-lasting health implications. Stress can combine with other physical and psychological factors to influence a large number of physical illnesses. Vulnerability factors increase people's susceptibility to stressful events while protective factors help people cope more effectively. Social support is a particularly strong protective factor, as are hardiness, coping self-efficacy, optimism, and finding meaning in stressful life events. People cope with stress through dealing with the problem directly (problem-focused coping), dealing with emotions (emotion-focused coping), and through seeking social support. A sense of controllability and coping efficacy seem to be particularly important in helping people to cope with stressful events. Men are more likely to rely on problem-focused coping, while women are more likely to use emotion-focused coping and to seek social support. Cultural differences in coping styles have also been found.

Chapter Outline

The Nature and Functions of Emotions
    The Adaptive Value of Emotions
    The Nature of Emotions
        Eliciting Stimuli
        The Cognitive Component
            Appraisal Processes
            Culture and Appraisal
    Psychological Frontiers: What Makes People Happy?
        The Physiological Component
            Brain Structures and Neurotransmitters
            Hemispheric Activation and Emotion
            Autonomic and Hormonal Processes
            "I cannot tell a lie": the Lie Detector Controversy
        The Behavioral Component
            Expressive Behaviors
            Evolution and Emotional Expression

Key Terms: *Write the letter of the definition next to the term in the space provided.*

1. ____ cognitive appraisal
2. ____ coping self-efficacy
3. ____ display rules
4. ____ downward comparison
5. ____ emotion
6. ____ emotion-focused coping
7. ____ empathy
8. ____ expressive behaviors
9. ____ facial feedback hypothesis
10. ____ fundamental emotional patterns

a. positive or negative affective states
b. interpretation of eliciting stimuli
c. people's emotional responses and their degree of satisfaction with various aspects of their lives
d. an instrument that measures physiological responses
e. emotional displays
f. occur when others' emotional displays can evoke similar emotional reactions in us
g. innate patterns of emotions
h. norms for emotional expression within a given culture
i. behaviors directed at achieving a goal
j. theory that bodily reactions cause our emotions

11. ___ general adaptation syndrome

12. ___ hardiness

13. ___ instrumental behaviors

14. ___ life event scales
15. ___ neuroticism

16. ___ polygraph

17. ___ primary appraisal

18. ___ problem-focused coping

19. ___ protective factors
20. ___ rape trauma syndrome

21. ___ secondary appraisal
22. ___ seeking social support

23. ___ self-instructional training

24. ___ somatic theory of emotions

25. ___ stress

26. ___ stressors

27. ___ subjective well-being

28. ___ two-factor theory of emotion

29. ___ upward comparison

30. ___ vascular theory of emotional feedback

31. ___ vulnerability factors

k. idea that facial muscular feedback to the brain plays a key role in the nature and intensity of emotion

l. theory that tensing facial muscles alters the temperature of blood entering the brain, thus influencing emotion

m. theory that emotions are caused by arousal and cognitive labeling

n. events that place strong demands on us

o. a pattern of appraisals, physiological responses, and behaviors that occurs in response to a perceived imbalance between situational demands and coping resources

p. ask people to indicate whether an event occurred, their appraisal of it, and whether it was a major event

q. initial view of a situation as benign, neutral, or threatening

r. examining perceived ability to cope with a situation

s. consists of alarm, resistance, and exhaustion

t. a reaction in which victims feel nervous and fear another attack

u. increase people's susceptibility to stressful events

v. environmental or personal resources that help people cope more effectively

w. a stress-protective factor consisting of commitment, control, and challenge

x. the conviction that we can perform the behaviors necessary to cope successfully

y. strategies that attempt to directly deal with the demands of the situation

z. strategies that attempt to manage the emotional consequences of a stressful situation

aa. turning to others for assistance and emotional support in times of stress

bb. a strategy in which people talk to themselves and guide their behavior in ways that make them cope more effectively

cc. seeing ourselves as better off than the standard for comparison

dd. a heightened tendency to experience negative emotion and to get oneself into stressful situations through maladaptive behaviors

ee. view ourselves as worse off than our standard of comparison

Review at a Glance: *Write the term that best fits the blank to review what you learned in this chapter.*

The Nature and Functions of Emotions

(1) _____ are positive or negative affect states consisting of a pattern of cognitive, physiological, and behavioral reactions to events that have relevance to important goals or motives. Emotional responses result from our interpretation or (2) _____ _____ of stimuli. We often infer an internal state in another person by examining his or her emotional displays, or (3) _____ behaviors. Others' emotional displays can evoke similar emotional responses in us, a process known as (4) _____. Modern evolutionary theorists stress the adaptive value of emotional expression. Humans have innate emotional patterns, which are also known as (5) _____ _____ patterns. Culture also affects emotional displays. The norms for emotional expression within a given culture are called (6) _____ _____. Emotional reactions may give rise to (7) _____ behaviors, which are directed at achieving a goal.

Interactions Among the Components of Emotion

According to the (8) _____ or (9) _____ theory of emotion, bodily reactions determine emotions, rather than the other way around. According to the (10) _____ hypothesis, facial muscles involved in emotional expression send messages to the brain, which then interprets the pattern as an emotion. The (11) _____ theory of emotional feedback suggests that this occurs because tensing facial muscles alters the temperature of blood entering the brain. The (12) _____ theory of emotion proposed that when we encounter an emotion-arousing situation, the thalamus simultaneously sends sensory messages to the cerebral cortex and to the body's internal organs. Schachter's (13) _____ theory of emotion states that physiological arousal and cognitive labeling of the arousal produces an emotion.

Stress, Coping, and Health

Eliciting stimuli that place strong demands on us are called (14) _____. (15) _____ is a pattern of cognitive appraisals, physiological responses, and behavioral tendencies that occurs in response to a perceived imbalance between situational demands and the resources needed to cope with them. Lazarus suggests that when we first encounter a situation, we engage in (16) _____ appraisal, by which we perceive the situation as either benign, neutral, or threatening. Our perception of our ability to cope with a situation is called (17) _____ appraisal. Hans Selye was a pioneer in examining the body's response to stress. His work found three phases: alarm, resistance, and exhaustion in a system he called the (18) _____ _____ syndrome. Some individuals cope better with stress than do others. (19) _____ factors increase people's susceptibility to stress, while (20) _____ factors are environmental or personal resources that help people cope more effectively. A stress-protective factor termed (21) _____ by Kobasa consists of commitment, control, and challenge. The conviction that we can perform behaviors necessary to cope, called (22) _____ _____ and optimism can also influence coping. (23) _____ - _____ coping strategies attempt to directly deal with the problem, while (24) _____ - _____ strategies attempt to manage the emotional aspects of the

problem. A third class of coping strategies involves (25) _____ _____ _____,
turning to others for assistance and emotional support in times of stress.

Apply What You Know

1. Using Study Sheet 10.1, keep a journal of your emotions throughout one day. Describe what behaviors and thoughts you are engaged in as you are experiencing your emotions at that particular time. What patterns of behaviors and thoughts seem to emerge for both positive and negative emotions as you examine your own data? Does your data support any of the theories of emotions described in your textbook? If so, which ones, and why?

2. Describe a stressful situation that you recently encountered. Using Lazarus' model, describe how the processes of primary appraisal and secondary appraisal were involved in your experience. Describe how you used methods of coping described in the textbook to deal with the stressful situation.

Stretching Your Geographies

1. Interview people of different backgrounds from your own to determine how display rules for emotions are different in their culture than they are in your own. Describe your findings.

Practice Test

<u>Multiple Choice Items</u>: *Please write the letter corresponding to your answer in the space to the left of each item.*

_____ 1. According to many evolutionary psychologists, such as Barbara Fredrickson (1998), ____.

    a. positive and negative emotions have no adaptive significance
    b. positive and negative emotions have very similar adaptive functions
    c. only negative emotions have adaptive significance
    d. positive and negative emotions have different and distinct adaptive functions

_____ 2. Of the following statements regarding the correlates of happiness, the one which is **most accurate** is that health ____.

    a. is strongly associated with happiness but wealth and intelligence are not
    b. ,wealth, and intelligence are only weakly related to happiness
    c. and wealth are strongly associated with happiness but intelligence is not
    d. ,wealth, and intelligence are all highly associated with happiness

_____ 3. Jan gets a good score of 85% on her test, but when talking to her friends, she learns that two people in her class of 45 students did better than her. If she were to focus on the fact that two people scored better than her, Jan would be engaging in what is technically called a _____ comparison process and we would expect her to feel dissatisfied.

    a. competitive
    b. primary
    c. downward
    d. upward

_____ 4. All of the following brain structures were mentioned as playing important roles in the regulation and production of emotion **except** the ____.

    a. hypothalamus
    b. cerebellum
    c. hippocampus
    d. amygdala

_____ 5. LeDoux's research on the brain mechanisms involved in emotion determined that sensory input from the thalamus is routed independently to both the cortex and the amygdala. This specific neural wiring could account for the fact that ____.

    a. cognitive appraisals for various emotions tend to be very similar across different cultures
    b. different people can respond with different emotions to the same stimulus
    c. physiological arousal can produce both instrumental and expressive behavioral responses
    d. we can have separate conscious and unconscious emotional reactions to the same stimuli

_____ 6. The fact that children who are blind from birth express the basic emotions in roughly the same way as sighted children was presented to demonstrate that _____.

    a. even the emotions of children are based largely on cognitive appraisals
    b. basic human emotions are determined by sensory information sent directly to the amygdala
    c. the emotional responses of children appear to largely be learned
    d. humans may have innate fundamental emotion patterns

_____ 7. In the United States, someone who sticks her thumb up is likely trying to hitchhike or is telling someone that everything is OK. However, in Greece, this same gesture is considered obscene. This difference **best demonstrates** how culturally based norms called _____ can influence emotional expressions.

    a. eliciting stimuli
    b. display rules
    c. primary appraisals
    d. instrumental behaviors

_____ 8. The _____ theory of emotion asserts that the thalamus sends messages directly to the cortex and these messages determine the experience of emotion. The physiological arousal that accompanies the emotion is determined by separate messages sent from the thalamus to the body's internal organs.

    a. James-Lange
    b. Cannon-Bard
    c. facial feedback
    d. somatic

_____ 9. Lazarus' theory of emotion and Schachter's two-factor theory of emotion are similar in that they both _____.

    a. minimize the importance of cognitive appraisals
    b. view emotion as primarily a physiological process
    c. contradict the Cannon-Bard theory of emotion
    d. acknowledge the importance of situational cues in determining emotions

_____ 10. Research has shown that excessive levels of stress can have detrimental effects on both psychological and physical health. Evolutionary theorists speculate that this may be because the physical mobilization system that was shaped by evolution to help people cope with life-threatening _____ stressors may not be adaptive for coping with the _____ stressors that characterize the modern world.

    a. emotional; physical
    b. physical; psychological
    c. psychological; emotional
    d. emotional; physical

_____ 11. People who are high in the personality trait of _____ have a heightened tendency to experience negative emotions and to get themselves into stressful situations. This variable may explain in part why there is a positive correlation between negative life events and distress.

a. depression
b. neuroticism
c. anxiety
d. pessimism

_____ 12. A major study by House et al. (1988) of almost 37,000 people in the United States, Finland, and Sweden found that people with low levels of _____ were twice as likely to die during the 12 year period of the study and that the relationship between this variable and health was _____ for men than for women.

a. personal coping skills; stronger
b. pessimism; weaker
c. social support; stronger
d. optimism; weaker

_____ 13. Jan is about to compete in a triathlon. Though such a competition would likely inspire fear and nervousness in most people, Jan is feeling good about the race because she believes she has the skills to successfully complete it. Psychologist Albert Bandura would **most likely** say that Jan has high _____.

a. self-efficacy
b. self-esteem
c. self-confidence
d. self-control

_____ 14. Research on the impact of religious beliefs have suggested that they have the most positive effects in helping people to deal with _____ but can function to increase the stress of people dealing with ___.

a. illnesses; losses
b. losses; marital problems
c. marital problems; personal setbacks
d. marital problems; illnesses

_____ 15. Norm and Cliff have both recently been through relationship break ups. Norm decides to go to his favorite bar and talk with his friends about what's been happening. Cliff on the other hand, decides to go home and meditate in order to deal with his negative feelings. Based on the information provided, we would say that Norm is involved in ___ while Cliff is involved in ___.

a. seeking social support; emotion-focused coping
b. seeking social support; problem-focused coping
c. emotion-focused coping; seeking social support
d. emotion-focused coping; problem-focused coping

_____ 16. After being fed curds and whey by Little Miss Muffett, Little Jack Horner's heart starts to race, he sweats, and his pupils get really big. Attributing these reactions to Muffett, Jack believes that he is deeply in love with Muffett, a development that would support the _____ theory of emotion.

  a. instinct
  b. two-factor
  c. James-Lange
  d. Cannon-Bard

_____ 17. Selye, in his general adaptation syndrome theory, argued that animals will go through all of the following stages except _____ in dealing with an environmental stressor.

  a. empathy
  b. resistance
  c. exhaustion
  d. alarm

_____ 18. Due to a few excessive keg parties this year on Old McDonald's farm, the cows have gotten a little skittish about jumping over the moon during the Barnyard Games. They therefore go to animal psychotherapist Dr. Dish N. Spoon, who discovers that they are worried about their ability to deal with the stress caused by this event in the Games (because of their general drunkenness). According to work by Lazarus, the cows are using _____ to determine that they may not have what it takes this year for the big jump.

  a. primary appraisal
  b. emotion-focused coping
  c. secondary appraisal
  d. problem-focused coping

_____ 19. All but the _____ is/are thought to play a role in the psychophysiology of emotion.

  a. empathy
  b. sensory nerves
  c. adrenal glands
  d. heart

_____ 20. People's degree of satisfaction with various aspects of their lives is called _____.

  a. self-esteem
  b. self-efficacy
  c. subjective well-being
  d. downward comparison

_____ 21. Polygraphs measure all of the following except _____.

  a. respiration
  b. heart rate
  c. skin conductance
  d. brain waves

_____ 22. Others' emotional displays can evoke similar emotional responses in us, a process known as
_____.

    a. emotional intelligence
    b. a fundamental emotional pattern
    c. an instinct
    d. empathy

_____ 23. Behaviors directed at achieving some goal are called _____ behaviors.

    a. emotional
    b. instrumental
    c. empathic
    d. instinctual

_____ 24. Results of studies examining the facial feedback hypothesis are best explained by _____.

    a. the two-factor theory
    b. cognitive-affective theories
    c. the vascular theory of emotional feedback
    d. Lazarus' theory of coping

_____ 25. Factors that increase people's susceptibility to stressful events are known as _____ factors.

    a. protective
    b. stress
    c. vulnerability
    d. stressor

_____ 26. The conviction that we can perform the behaviors necessary to cope successfully is known as
_____.

    a. hardiness
    b. optimism
    c. coping self-efficacy
    d. primary appraisal

_____ 27. All of the following except _____ seem to be involved in a person's hardiness.

    a. commitment
    b. self-esteem
    c. control
    d. challenge

_____ 28. Studies of stressors suggest that _____.

    a. everyone experiences stress in the same way
    b. there is little evidence that stressors have long-term effects
    c. stressors can have long-term and strong psychological impact
    d. there is little evidence that environmental factors produce stress

_____ 29. The discovery that many victims of rape experience the rape trauma syndrome provides evidence that _____.

    a. everyone experiences stress in the same way
    b. there is little evidence that stressors have long-term effects
    c. stressors can have long-term and strong psychological impact
    d. there is little evidence that environmental factors produce stress

_____ 30. Studies of social support suggest that all of the following except _____ influence the relationship between receiving social support and coping with stress.

    a. improved immune system functioning
    b. experiencing a greater sense of meaning and identity in one's life
    c. having someone to talk to about upsetting experiences
    d. an increase in vulnerability factors

True/False Items: *Write T or F in the space provided to the left of each item.*

_____ 1. Psychophysiological findings suggest that left hemisphere activation might underlie certain positive emotions.

_____ 2. Polygraphs are extremely accurate in measuring lying.

_____ 3. The fact that expressions of certain emotions are similar across a variety of cultures supports theories of the biological bases of emotions.

_____ 4. According to the James-Lange theory, subcortical activity in the thalamus leads to autonomic arousal and emotion.

_____ 5. Results of studies examining the facial feedback hypothesis support the James-Lange theory.

_____ 6. Stressors are specific kinds of eliciting stimuli that place demands on us and endanger our well-being.

_____ 7. Appraising our ability to cope with the demands of a situation is called primary appraisal.

_____ 8. Social support is an example of a vulnerability factor.

_____ 9. Commitment, control, and challenge make up the factor called hardiness.

_____ 10. Studies of coping have shown that both problem-focused coping and seeking social support are associated with favorable adjustment to stressors.

Short Answer Questions

1. What is the adaptive value of emotions?

2. What are cultural display rules?

3. What does the two-factor theory of emotions say?

4. How does the text define stress?

5. Distinguish between primary and secondary appraisal.

Essay Questions

1. How are appraisal processes involved in emotion?

2. How does physiology affect the experience of emotions?

3. How does stress affect health?

4. What protective factors help people cope with stress?

5. How do gender and culture affect coping strategies?

Study Sheet 10.1   Emotions Throughout The Day

Time	Emotions Experiencing	Thoughts	Behaviors
8:00 a.m.			
10:00 a.m.			
12:00 noon			
2:00 p.m.			
4:00 p.m.			
6:00 p.m.			
8:00 p.m.			
10:00 p.m.			

Answer Keys

Answer Key for Key Terms

1. b
2. x
3. h
4. cc
5. a
6. z
7. f
8. e
9. k
10. g
11. s
12. w
13. i
14. p
15. dd
16. d
17. q
18. y
19. v
20. t
21. r
22. aa
23. bb
24. j
25. o
26. n
27. c
28. m
29. ee
30. l
31. u

Answer Key for Review at a Glance

1. Emotions
2. cognitive appraisal
3. expressive
4. empathy
5. fundamental emotional
6. display rules
7. instrumental
8. James-Lange
9. somatic
10. facial feedback
11. vascular
12. Cannon-Bard
13. two-factor
14. stressors
15. Stress
16. primary
17. secondary
18. general adaptation
19. Vulnerability
20. protective
21. hardiness
22. coping self-efficacy
23. Problem-focused
24. emotion-focused
25. seeking social support

Answer Key for Practice Test Multiple Choice Questions

1. d
2. b
3. d
4. b
5. d
6. d
7. b
8. b
9. d
10. b
11. b
12. c
13. a
14. b
15. a
16. b
17. a
18. c
19. a
20. c
21. d
22. d
23. b
24. c
25. c
26. c
27. b
28. c
29. c
30. d

Answer Key for Practice Test True/False Questions

1. T
2. F
3. T
4. F
5. T

6. T
7. F
8. F
9. T
10. T

Answer Key for Practice Test Short Answer Questions

1. Emotions signal that something important is happening, and they direct our attention to that event. Because of that, we are more likely to engage in behaviors to help us cope with the situation, increasing the chances of our survival. Fredrickson argues that negative emotions narrow our attention so that we can respond to it with particular responses. Positive emotions, on the other hand, may broaden our thinking and behavior so that we can explore new things.

2. Cultural display rules are the norms for emotional expression within a given culture. Display rules dictate when and how particular emotions are to be expressed.

3. The two-factor theory of emotion states that both physiological arousal and cognitive labeling create an emotional experience. Situational cues provide us with the necessary information we need to understand and label the nature of the physiological response that we are feeling.

4. Stress is defined as a pattern of cognitive appraisals, physiological responses, and behavioral tendencies that occur in response to a perceived imbalance between situational demands and the resources needed to cope with them. Thus, primary and secondary appraisal processes, coping behaviors, and physiological factors such as increased heart rate, increased breathing rate etc. interact to influence our perceptions of stress.

5. Primary appraisal involves determining the extent to which a situation is benign, neutral, irrelevant, or threatening. Secondary appraisal involves determining one's ability to cope with the situation by examining one's coping resources.

Answer Key for Practice Test Essay Questions

1. Appraisals relate to what we think is desirable or undesirable for us or for the people we care about. Some appraisals are more automatic, particularly for emotions such as fear. This may be because of the instinctual nature of some emotions. Other appraisals are more cognitively based and include evaluative and personal dimensions. This is why different people may have entirely different emotional reactions to the same stimuli.

2. Subcortical structures such as the hypothalamus, amygdala, hippocampus, and other structures in the limbic system play major roles in emotions. The prefrontal cortex likely plays an important role in our ability to regulate emotion. The thalamus sends messages via two independent neural pathways, one to the cortex and one to the amygdala. This dual system for processing means that some emotions likely do not involve conscious thought while others do. Other theorists argue that neurotransmitters such as dopamine, serotonin, norepinephrine, and endorphins play major roles in the experience of emotion. Some research findings suggest that left hemisphere activation might underlie certain

positive emotions while right hemisphere activation might underlie some negative ones. Finally, the release of hormones into the bloodstream likely also influence emotions by triggering physiological responses.

3. Stress can affect health in a number of ways. First of all stress affects psychological well-being. People who have experienced traumatic life events are more likely to develop disorders such as anxiety and depression. People high in the personality trait of neuroticism have a heightened tendency to experience anxiety and to get themselves into stressful situations, increasing the chances of developing health problems. Stress can also combine with other psychological factors as well as physical factors to influence a wide variety of physical illnesses, from common colds to cancer. One of the reasons for this is that stressors can result in physiological responses that directly harm various body systems.

4. Protective factors are environmental or personal resources that help people to cope more effectively with stressful events. These include social support, coping skills, and optimism. People who have social support may experience a greater sense of identity and meaning in their lives, which results in greater psychological well-being. Having social networks also reduce exposure to other risk factors like loneliness. Friends can also bring social pressure to bear so that people don't engage in maladaptive behaviors. Social support can also give us someone to talk to about upsetting experiences. Coping skills such as hardiness and coping self-efficacy are important resources. Having a sense of control, part of hardiness, seems to be particularly important in helping us to cope with stressful circumstances. Having a sense of coping self-efficacy, the conviction that we can perform the behaviors necessary to cope, is an important protective factor. Optimistic people are at lower risk for anxiety and depression when they encounter stress in their lives.

5. Although men and women both used problem-focused and emotion-focused coping, men are more likely to rely on problem-focused coping to deal with stress, while women are more likely to use emotion-focused coping and seeking social support to deal with stress. North Americans and Europeans are more likely to use problem-focused coping than are Asian and Hispanic peoples, who rely more on emotion-focused coping and social support. Asians also seem to be more likely to use avoidance of stress as a coping mechanism.

Chapter 11
DEVELOPMENT OVER THE LIFE SPAN

Learning Objectives: *These questions, with a few additions, are taken from the directed questions found in the margins of the chapter. After reading the chapter, you should be able to answer these questions.*

1.   Describe four broad issues that guide developmental research.

2.   Explain how cross-sectional, longitudinal, and sequential designs differ.

2.1*   What are the three stages of prenatal development?

3.   What determines the sex of a child?

4.   How do STDs, alcohol, and other drugs affect prenatal development? Identify other broad classes of teratogens.

5.   How can scientists measure newborns' sensory capabilities and perceptual preferences? What are some of those preferences?

6.   Can newborns learn through classical conditioning, operant conditioning, and modeling?

7.   Explain how nature and nurture jointly influence physical growth and motor development during infancy.

8.   Describe assimilation and accommodation. How are they related to cognitive development?

9.   How do infants develop cognitively during the sensorimotor stage?

10.   Identify some achievements and limitations of the preoperational stage.

11.   How does thinking change during the concrete and formal operational stages?

12.   In what major ways does research support and contradict Piaget's basic ideas?

13.   What is the "zone of proximal development" and why is it important?

14.   Describe how information-processing capabilities improve during childhood. How is this relevant to the continuity-discontinuity debate?

15.   At what age do children begin to understand other people's thinking? How have researchers established this?

16.   How do preconventional, conventional, and postconventional moral reasoning differ?

17.   What aspects of Kohlberg's model have been supported? What are its limitations?

18.   What does Erickson's model imply regarding the stability of personality?

19.   Does infants' temperament predict their childhood behavior? Does children's temperament predict their adult functioning?

20.   How does imprinting illustrate the concept of critical periods?

21.   How did Harlow demonstrate the importance of contact comfort?

22.   According to Bowlby, what are the phases of attachment in infancy?

22.1*   Distinguish between stranger and separation anxiety. Which one occurs first?

23.   Does separation anxiety follow a similar pattern across cultures? What is the adaptive value of separation anxiety?

24.   What is the "strange situation?" Describe the styles of attachment identified by this procedure.

25.   How do studies of monkey and child isolates, and of children in orphanages, help us resolve whether attachment involves critical or sensitive periods?

26.   Why might Victor's recovery have been so limited, as compared to that of the Czech twins?

27.   Does daycare impair infants' attachment? Does it seem to have any long-term effects on children?

28.   In the short- and long-term, how do children generally respond to parental divorce? What factors enhance their adjustment to divorce and remarriage?

29.   What parenting styles are associated with the most and least positive child outcomes?

30.   How does socialization shape children's beliefs about gender?

31.   Describe some factors that influence adolescents' psychological reaction to experiencing puberty.

32.   Discuss how adolescents' reasoning abilities change, and the ways in which their thinking is egocentric.

33.   Identify some of the different ways that adolescents approach the challenge of establishing an identity.

34.   To what extent are parent-teen relationships characterized by "storm and stress?"

35.   How do peer relationships change during adolescence?

36.   What are some of the major bodily changes that occur from early through late adulthood?

36.1*   Discuss some of the controversy surrounding the possible "fifth stage" of development that some cognitive theorists believe occurs in adulthood.

37.   Discuss how information processing abilities and memory change throughout adulthood.

38.   How do intellectual abilities change with age? To what extent does the answer depend on the research design used?

39.   Identify some factors associated with greater retention of cognitive abilities during late adulthood.

40.   Does theory of mind research support the notion that elderly adults are "older but wiser?"

41.   According to Erickson, what are the three major developmental challenges of adulthood?

42.   How does marital satisfaction typically change over time? What major events are associated with these changes?

43.   Describe some major differences between women and men's typical career paths.

44.   Is midlife crisis a myth? Discuss the evidence.

45.   Does retirement cause psychological problems for most retirees? Under what situations are such problems most likely?

45.1*   What are Kubler-Ross's five stages of coping with impending death?

46.   Why is it incorrect to say that there is a "normal" or "proper" way to confront death?

Chapter Overview

Major Issues and Methods

Developmental psychology examines biological, physical, social, and behavioral changes that occur with age. Four broad issues: nature and nurture, critical and sensitive periods, continuity versus discontinuity, and stability versus change guide developmental research. Developmental psychologists employ both cross-sectional research to study cohorts at the same point in time and longitudinal research to study the same cohort at different points in time.

Prenatal Development

Prenatal development consists of three stages: zygote, embryo, and fetus. The 23rd pair of chromosomes in the zygote determines the child's sex. The pairing of two X chromosomes creates a female, and the pairing of X and Y chromosomes creates a male. Teratogens like nicotine, alcohol, other drugs, mercury, lead, and radiation can cause abnormal prenatal development.

Infancy and Childhood

The visual systems of neonates are poor but develop quickly. They are equipped with many reflexes to respond to specific stimuli. Physical and motor development of newborns follow both the cephalocaudal and proximodistal principles. Environmental and cultural influences affect physical and motor development as well and interact with biological factors. Swiss psychologist

Jean Piaget suggested that children learn about the world through their schemas. Assimilation is the process by which new experiences are incorporated into existing schemas, while accomodation is the process by which schemas are changed by new experiences. Piaget's stage model of cognitive development proposes that infants in the sensorimotor stage learn about the world through their sensory processes and movements. During this stage, children also attain a sense of object permanence. Symbolic thought develops in the preoperational stage, while during the concrete operational stage children begin to be able to perform basic mental operations, such as reversibility and serial ordering. Abstract reasoning and the systematic use of hypotheses first occur during the formal operational stage. Research on Piaget's theory has found that the general cognitive abilities he suggested occur in the same order across cultures, but children acquire many cognitive skills much earlier than he suggested. Furthermore, children may perform skills that indicate they may be at one stage in some ways and in another in other ways.Lev Vygotsky proposed a zone of proximal development in which children, with assistance, may do more than they might be capable of independently. Information processing approaches to cognitive development stress developmental changes in information-search strategies, information-processing speed, memory capabilities, and metacognition. Kohlberg's stage model of moral development suggests that children develop morally from reasoning based on anticipated rewards and punishments to reasoning based on social expectations and laws to the highest level of moral reasoning based on general principles. Kohlberg's critics claim that the theory is culturally and gender biased. Erikson argued that social development occurs throughout the lifespan in eight major psychosocial stages, each of which involves a particular "crisis" in how we relate to others. Much recent research in developmental psychology has focused on attachment, the strong emotional bond between children and their caregivers. British theorist John Bowlby hypothesized that attachment develops through indiscriminate attachment to discriminate attachment behavior to specific attachment to specific caregivers. Mary Ainsworth's research using the strange situation to measure attachment and anxiety has revealed different patterns of attachment, including securely attached, insecurely attached, anxious-resistant, and anxious-avoidant infants. There is much research showing the effects of early attachment styles on later behaviors. Studies of isolates and children raised in orphanages suggest that infancy is a sensitive, but not critical, period during which attachment forms most easily and can facilitate subsequent development. Studies have found that day-care children do not show less attachment to their parents than children raised exclusively in the home. High-quality day-care can also aid children from disadvantaged backgrounds, but the quality of family experiences is often more important in predicting social adjustment and academic performance. Styles of parenting including authoritative, authoritarian, indulgent, and neglectful can also influence children's development. Through cognitive maturation and socialization, children develop gender identity and gender constancy, which influence their sense of what it means to be a girl or a boy.

Adolescence

Adolescence begins at puberty, at which time hormonal secretions stimulate the development of both primary and secondary sex characteristics. Such physical changes have important psychological ramifications for adolescents. Adolescent thinking can become highly self-focused, resulting in adolescent egocentrism. The search for one's identity can be a major goal of adolescence. During this time, relationships with parents and peers can change.

Adulthood

Physical status typically peaks during one's twenties and then declines at midlife. Perceptual speed, memory for new factual information, and recall often decline as one ages. Fluid intelligence seems to decline steadily beginning in young adulthood, while crystallized intelligence declines later. Regular exercise and perceptual-motor activities help people to retain cognitive functioning at later ages. Social clocks influence whether we are satisfied with our lives by setting expectations for when we should marry and have children, amongst other life goals. Research on the "mid-life crisis" suggest that it is largely a myth. People at all ages experience conflict, disappointments, and frustrations. Retirement can be a "golden" time for those who desire it. Eventually, everyone will die. Elisabeth Kübler-Ross' pioneering work emphasized several distinct stages people work through as they approach death, although the sequence and the existence of all stages for all people is questionable. Nevertheless, death has many psychological ramifications for people.

Chapter Outline

Major Issues and Methods

Prenatal Development
      Genetics and Sex Determination
      Environmental Influences

Infancy and Childhood
      The Amazing Newborn
            Sensory Capabilities and Perceptual Preferences
            Reflexes and Learning
      Physical, Motor, and Brain Development
            Environmental and Cultural Influences
      Cognitive Development
            Piaget's Stage Model
                  Sensorimotor Stage
                  Preoperational Stage
                  Concrete Operational Stage
                  Formal Operational Stage
            Stages, Ages, and Culture
            Vygotsky: The Social Context of Cognitive Development
            Information-Processing Approaches
            Theory of Mind: Children's Understanding of Mental States
      Moral Development
            Kohlberg's Stage Model
            Culture, Gender, and Moral Reasoning
      Personality and Social Development
            Erikson's Psychosocial Theory
            Psychological Frontiers: You Were Such a Fussy Baby: Does Early Temperament Predict Adult Functioning?
            Attachment
                  The Attachment Process
                  Variations in Attachment
                  Attachment and Later Behavior
            Attachment Deprivation
                  Isolate Monkeys and Children
                  Children Raised in Orphanages
            The Day-Care Controversy
            Applications of Psychological Science: Understanding How Divorce and Remarriage Affect Children

Styles of Parenting
Gender Identity and Socialization

Adolescence
Physical Development and Its Psychological Consequences
Cognitive Development
Abstract Reasoning Abilities
Social Thinking
Social and Personality Development
The Search for Identity
Relationships With Parents
Peer and Friendship Relationships

Adulthood

Physical Development
Cognitive Development
Information Processing and Memory
Intellectual Changes
Use it or Lose it? Maintaining Cognitive Functioning
Research Close-Up: Older But Wiser? Mind-Reading in Elderly and Young Adults
Social and Personality Development
Stages and Critical Events
Marriage and Family
Cohabitation
What's Love Got to Do With it? Culture and Marriage
Marital Satisfaction, Parenthood, and the Empty Nest
Establishing a Career
Midlife Crisis: Fact or Fiction?
Retirement and the Golden Years
Death and Dying

Key Terms: *Write the letter of the definition next to the term in the space provided.*

Major Issues and Methods
Prenatal Development

1.	___ critical period	a.	an age range during which certain experiences must occur for development to proceed normally
2.	___ cross-sectional design	b.	an optimal age range for certain experiences
3.	___ embryo	c.	used to compare people of different ages at the same point in time
4.	___ fetal alcohol syndrome	d.	used to repeatedly assess the same cohort as it grows older
5.	___ fetus	e.	a fertilized egg
6.	___ longitudinal design	f.	name for the cell mass from the second through the eighth week after conception
7.	___ sensitive period	g.	name for the developing organism from the ninth week after conception until birth

8. ___ teratogen

    h. environmental agents that can cause abnormal prenatal development

9. ___ zygote

    i. a severe group of abnormalities that result from prenatal exposure to alcohol

Infancy and Childhood

1. ___ accommodation

    a. automatic, inborn behaviors that occur in response to specific stimuli

2. ___ assimilation

    b. the genetically programmed biological process that governs our growth

3. ___ attachment

    c. reflects the tendency for development to proceed in a head-to-foot direction

4. ___ authoritarian parenting

    d. states that development begins along the innermost parts of the body and continues outward

5. ___ authoritative parenting

    e. organized patterns of thought and action

6. ___ cephalocaudal principle

    f. the process by which new experiences are incorporated into existing schemas

7. ___ concrete operational stage

    g. the process by which new experiences cause existing schemas to change

8. ___ conservation

    h. stage in which infants understand their world through sensory experiences and physical interactions with objects

9. ___ conventional moral reasoning

    i. an infant's understanding that an object continues to exist even when it can't be seen

10. ___ egocentrism

    j. stage in which children begin to symbolically represent the world through words and mental images

11. ___ formal operational stage

    k. the principle that basic properties of objects stay the same even thought their outward appearance may change

12. ___ gender constancy

    l. difficulty in viewing the world from someone else's perspective

13. ___ gender identity

    m. stage at which children can perform basic mental operations involving tangible objects and situations

14. ___ imprinting

    n. stage at which individuals can think both concretely and abstractly and can form and test hypotheses

15. ___ indulgent parenting

    o. the difference between what a child can do independently and with assistance

16. ___ maturation

    p. a person's beliefs about the mind and ability to understand others' mental states

17. ___ neglectful parenting

    q. moral reasoning based on anticipated punishment or rewards

18. ___ object permanence

    r. moral reasoning based on conformity to social expectations, laws, and duties

19. ___ postconventional moral reasoning

    s. moral reasoning based on general moral principles

20. ___ preconventional moral reasoning

    t. a series of stages that involve "crises" of how we view ourselves in relation to others

21. ___ preoperational stage

    u. a biologically based general style of reacting emotionally and behaviorally to the environment

22. ___ proximodistal principle

    v. a biologically primed form of attachment

23. ___ psychosocial stages

w. the strong emotional bond between children and their primary caregivers

24. ___ reflexes

x. when approached by an unfamiliar person, becoming afraid, crying, and reaching for the caregiver; occurs from 6-7 months to about 1 _ years old

25. ___ schemas

y. becoming anxious and crying when separated from a primary caregiver

26. ___ sensorimotor stage

z. a standard procedure for examining infant attachment

27. ___ separation anxiety

aa. parenting that is controlling but warm

28. ___ sex-role stereotypes

bb. parenting that is controlling and cold

29. ___ socialization

cc. parenting that is warm, caring, and permissive

30. ___ strange situation

dd. parenting that is rejecting and permissive

31. ___ stranger anxiety

ee. a sense of "maleness" and "femaleness"

32. ___ temperament

ff. the understanding that being male or female is a permanent part of a person

33. ___ theory of mind

gg. beliefs about characteristics and behaviors that are sex appropriate

34. ___ zone of proximal development

hh. the process by which we acquire the beliefs, values, and behaviors of a group

Adolescence
Adulthood

1. ___ adolescent egocentrism

a. an overestimation of the uniqueness of feelings and experiences and a feeling of being "on stage"

2. ___ postformal thought

b. a period of rapid maturation in which a person becomes capable of sexual reproduction

3. ___ puberty

c. a set of cultural norms concerning the optimal age range for work, marriage, parenthood, and other major life experiences

4. ___ social clock

d. a fifth stage of cognitive development in which people can reason logically about opposing points of view and accept contradictions and irreconcilable differences

Review at a Glance: *Write the term that best fits the blank to review what you learned in this chapter.*

Major Issues and Methods

Developmental psychologists examine changes that occur as we age. A (1) _____ _____ is an age range during which certain experiences must occur for development to proceed normally. A (2) _____ period is an optimal age range for certain experiences. Developmental psychologists use both (3) _____ - _____ designs, which compare people of different cohorts at the same time and (4) _____ designs, which repeatedly test the same people as they grow older.

Prenatal Development

A fertilized egg is known as a (5) _____. From the second through the eighth week after conception, the cell mass is called an (6) _____, and after that the developing organism is called a (7) _____. Environmental influences can affect prenatal development. (8) _____ are environmental agents that can cause abnormal development, such as (9) _____ _____ _____, which results from prenatal exposure to alcohol.

Infancy and Childhood

Newborn children, or neonates, are equipped with automatic, inborn behaviors, or (10) _____ that help them to respond to specific stimuli. The genetically programmed biological process that governs our growth is called (11) _____. Physical and motor development follow both the (12) _____ principle, which reflects the tendency for development to proceed in a head-to-foot direction and the (13) _____ principle, which states that development begins on the innermost parts of the body and proceeds toward the outermost parts. Cognitive development was studied most famously by (14) _____. He argued that children organize the world in terms of (15) _____. (16) _____ is the process by which new information causes existing schemas to change, while (17) _____ is the process by which new experiences are incorporated into existing schemas. Piaget suggested that children go through four distinct cognitive stages. In the (18) _____ stage, infants understand their world through their sensory experiences and movements. During this stage, an infant comes to understand that an object continues to exist even when it cannot be directly experienced, a concept Piaget called (19) _____ _____. Children enter the (20) _____ stage around the age of two and begin to represent the world symbolically through words and mental images. Preoperational children also show (21) _____, which reflects their difficulty in viewing the world from any perspective other than their own. In the (22) _____ _____ stage, children can now perform basic mental functions involving tangible objects and situations. Finally, in the (23) _____ operational stage, individuals can think abstractly and can use the hypothetico-deductive process to solve problems. Another theorist, (24) _____, argued that there is a zone of (25) _____ _____, the difference between what a children can do independently and what they can do with assistance. Kohlberg's theory of moral development suggests that children proceed from a stage of morality based on anticipated punishments or rewards, called (26) _____ moral reasoning, to conformity based on social expectations, laws, and duties, called (27) _____ moral reasoning, to the highest level of moral reasoning, (28) _____ moral reasoning, which is based on general moral principles. Theorist Erik Erikson proposed that people develop through eight major (29) _____ stages. (30) _____ refers to the strong emotional bond that develops between children and their primary caregivers. As an infant's attachment develops, two types of anxiety occur. (31) _____ anxiety occurs first, followed by (32) _____ anxiety. A standard procedure used to measure attachment developed by Mary Ainsworth and colleagues is called the (33) _____ _____. Four parenting styles have been associated with different patterns of child-rearing. Controlling but warm parents are called (34) _____, while controlling but cold parents are called (35) _____. Parents who have warm, caring relationships with their children but who provide little or no rules or guidance are called (36) _____ parents, and parents who are cold toward their children and who provide little or no rules of guidance are called (37) _____ parents. Parents also help their children develop a sense of "femaleness" or "maleness" called (38) _____ _____. As gender identity develops, children acquire beliefs about characteristics and behaviors that are appropriate for girls and for boys. These beliefs are known as (39) _____ _____.

Adolescence

Adolescents tend to think that their experiences and feelings are unique, which is known as the (40) _____ _____. They also tend to believe that everyone else is watching what they are doing. The two phenomena together are what Elkind calls (41) _____ _____.

Adulthood

Several theorists have proposed a fifth stage of cognitive development called (42) _____ thought, in which people can reason logically about opposing points of view. Neugarten has suggested that people match what is going on in their lives with a (43) _____ _____, which is a set of cultural norms conerning the optimal age for marriage, parenthood, and other life goals.

Apply What You Know

1. Find four children who should be in different Piagetian cognitive stages. Observe their behavior and interview them to determine what behaviors and thoughts correspond to those suggested by Piaget as appropriate for that particular stage. Determine some behaviors and thoughts that don't correspond to what Piaget believed. Use Study Sheet 11.1.

2. Study Sheet 11.2 provides Neugarten's findings about social clocks in the 1970's. Devise a survey for measuring student's social clocks for the same events today, and compare and contrast your findings to what Neugarten observed.

Stretching Your Geographies

1. Kohlberg's moral development theory has been criticized on the basis that it reflects a male-oriented pattern of moral development and on the basis that it is culturally biased toward more of a Western sense of moral development. Interview both males and females and people of different cultural backgrounds to determine whether these are fair criticisms of Kohlberg's theory. What do you find?

2. Using Study Sheet 11.2, give the survey you developed for "Apply What You Know" question #2 above and survey people of different cultural backgrounds. What differences do you see?

Practice Test

Multiple Choice Items: *Please write the letter corresponding to your answer in the space to the left of each item.*

_____ 1. In developmental research, a _____ period is an age range during which specific experiences must take place if normal development is to occur. This is in contrast to a ____ period, where it is optimal although not necessarily essential for these experiences to occur.

    a. sensitive; critical
    b. critical; receptive
    c. critical; sensitive
    d. explicit; sensitive

_____ 2. A self-esteem researcher is interested in how self-esteem varies across the life span and decides to conduct a survey comparing people of different ages to address this issue. He recruits participants to be in one of four different age groups (20-29, 30-39, 40-49, 50-59), has them complete a self-esteem survey, and then analyses the data to see if any patterns emerge. This study would be considered an example of a ____ design.

    a. longitudinal
    b. double-blind
    c. cross-sectional
    d. sequential

_____ 3. If a zygote receives a Y chromosome from its father, this means that the egg ____.

    a. will be a female
    b. will be a male
    c. could be either a male or a female, depending on the contribution of the mother
    d. will have the characteristics of both a male and a female

_____ 4. Consistent with the concept of _____ , a study found that children over age three who grew up with older brothers or sisters performed _____ on a cognitive task than children with no siblings or younger siblings.

    a. a zone of proximal development; better
    b. egocentrism; worse
    c. animism; better
    d. irreversibility; worse

_____ 5. Results from studies examining the information-processing abilities of young children are often used to argue that cognitive development is _____, but there are some theorists who assert that children still learn new ways of processing information as they age.

    a. determined by sensitive periods
    b. schema-driven
    c. discontinuous
    d. continuous

_____ 6. In response to the moral dilemma where a man must decide if he should steal a medication to save his dying wife, a child says that he shouldn't steal the medication because if he does, he'll be punished. This child would be classified as being in Kohlberg's _____ level of moral reasoning.

a. preconventional
b. preoperational
c. conventional
d. concrete operational

_____ 7. _____ refers to the strong emotional bond that develops between human children and their primary caregivers and its creation appears to be governed by a ____ period since it is most easily established during the first 1- to 2-years of a child's life.

a. Attachment; sensitive
b. Attachment; critical
c. Imprinting; sensitive
d. Imprinting; critical

_____ 8. _____ anxiety refers to how young toddlers become upset when they are apart from their primary caregivers and it appears to follow ____ patterns in different cultures.

a. Stranger; similar
b. Separation; similar
c. Stranger; different
d. Separation; different

_____ 9. Nguyen is participating in an attachment experiment involving the strange situation. When his mother is present with the stranger, Nguyen explores the room and is friendly with the stranger. However, when the mother leaves, he becomes upset and starts to cry. When she returns, Nguyen happily greets her and then returns to his previous explorations. Nguyen would most likely be classified as a(n) ____ child.

a. resistant-avoidant
b. anxious-resistant
c. anxious-avoidant
d. securely attached

_____ 10. A couple with three kids is considering divorce but is wondering if they should remain together for the sake of their children. Research suggests that the **most important** factor that they should take into consideration is ____.

a. how old the children are.
b. how long they have been married.
c. the amount of conflict in the relationship.
d. whether or not adultery is involved.

_____ 11. Ned is growing up in a family where his parents provide him with a great deal of warmth and he feels that he has very close relationships with both of his parents. In terms of discipline, his parents are relatively lax and allow him to do as he pleases. As result, Ned is somewhat immature and self-centered. Diana Baumrind would **most likely** classify Ned's parent's as using a(n) _____ parenting style.

    a. tolerant
    b. indulgent
    c. lenient
    d. liberal

_____ 12. A father believes that there are certain behaviors that are more appropriate for boys than for girls. His wife has heard him share these beliefs and she wonders if they are partly responsible for the fact that he actually relates differently to his son, with whom he tends to use more verbal and physical prohibition, than he does with his daughter. In this example the father's beliefs would be examples of _____ while the fact that he treats his children differently depending on their gender demonstrates the concept of _____.

    a. gender identities; gender constancies
    b. sex-role stereotypes; gender preferences
    c. sex-role stereotypes; sex typing
    d. gender identities; sex typing

_____ 13. _____ who reach puberty ___ their peers tend to be more popular and have more positive body images.

    a. Boys; earlier than
    b. Boys; at the same time as
    c. Boys; later than
    d. Girls; earlier than

_____ 14. Your Grandmother is just about to have her 77th birthday. According to results from studies examining information processing changes that occur with age, of the following areas the one which you would expect to be **least impaired** by the process of aging would be ____.

    a. memory for new information
    b. recall memory
    c. memory for familiar information
    d. speed of processing

_____ 15. Studies indicate that most people who retire ____ more likely to become anxious, depressed, or lonely. The risks that are associated with retirement become more likely when the retirement is ____.

    a. are not; forced
    b. are not; voluntary
    c. are; forced
    d. are; voluntary

_____ 16. Piaget was one of the first to suggest that children actively interpret information about their environments. They likely do this through the processes of _____ and _____.

a. accommodation; assimilation
b. moral development; accommodation
c. object permanence; assimilation
d. developing an anxious style of attachment; developing a zone of proximal development

_____ 17. Running out of chickens to grace the menus at his many worldwide establishments, a desperate Private Sanders (young son of legendary Colonel Sanders) tries to determine what will make chickens cross the road. Hypothesizing that chickens, like people, are attracted by sexy images, he believe that chickens wearing skimpy, sexy bikini underwear will entice other chickens to cross the road and constructs a study to see if this is actually the case. According to Piaget's theory, Private has reached the _____ stage of development.

a. sensorimotor
b. preoperational
c. concrete operational
d. formal operational

_____ 18. People who develop a secure attachment style when they are infants tend to have better adult romantic relationships (e.g. Hazan & Shaver, 1987; Collins & Read, 1990). This is most likely because of a positive resolution of the _____ developmental conflict.

a. trust vs. mistrust
b. generativity vs. stagnation
c. identity vs. role confusion
d. integrity vs. despair

_____ 19. Vygotsky believed that _____.

a. development occurs in discrete stages for everyone
b. cognitive development depends on the people in a child's world and the tools that the culture provides to support thinking
c. the learning of language does not influence cognitive development
d. children should learn on their own and should not be assisted

_____ 20. The developmental period that begins at approximately 35-45 years of age and extends into the sixties is known as _____ and is the time of the _____ psychosocial conflict, according to Erikson's theory.

a. early adulthood; intimacy vs. isolation
b. middle adulthood; generativity vs. stagnation
c. middle adulthood; intimacy vs. isolation
d. early adulthood; generativity vs. stagnation

_____ 21. The prenatal period that begins approximately 2 months after conception and continues until birth is known as the _____.

a. zygote stage
b. embryonic period
c. fetal period
d. germinal phase

_____ 22. Of the following, the one which is <u>not</u> an important way in which the information processing of children increases as they grow older is in _____.

a. speed
b. capacity
c. automaticity
d. schematic simplicity

_____ 23. Apparently having a few too many rocks in their heads, Fred and Wilma Flintstone let daughter Pebbles hang out to all hours with boyfriend Bamm-Bamm. They allow her to let her bedroom become a filthy, rotting mess of empty pizza boxes, and, when she comes home after winning the title of Miss Bedrock, ignore her pleas for praise in order to concentrate on planning their latest trip to Rock Vegas. Fred and Wilma's parenting style would best be described as

_____.

a. authoritarian
b. authoritative
c. indulgent
d. neglectful

_____ 24. Having eaten only a small amount of porridge, young Baby Bear is distracted for a moment by the morning antics of the Teletubbies and moves into the Bear living room to watch TV. During this time, devious parents Papa and Mama Bear remove Baby Bear's porridge and put it in the freezer. Returning to the table after boring soap operas come on, Baby Bear sees that his porridge is no longer there and believes that it has vanished forever. Baby Bear has not yet developed _____, which develops during the _____ period.

a. object permanence; sensorimotor
b. centration; preoperational
c. object permanence; preoperational
d. centration; sensorimotor

_____ 25. Looking back over a long life of violence before he says his final "Hasta la vista, baby," an old, wrinkled, stooped-over Terminator wonders if his life would have been better if he had been a florist. Term is experiencing Erikson's _____.

a. generativity vs. stagnation
b. integrity vs. despair
c. identity vs. role confusion
d. industry vs. inferiority

_____ 26. Males are <u>least</u> likely to be better than females at _____.

a. solving Rubik's Cube, a three dimensional cubic puzzle, in which the solver must determine how to make all squares on each side of the cube the same color
b. Scrabble, a game which requires a good vocabulary size and spelling ability
c. visualizing how furniture might look in a room before it is actually placed there
d. spatial geometry

_____ 27. I recently observed a 4-year-old girl at the local fast food establishment "Taco Bell." At the conclusion of their meal, she asked her mother if they should "leave money on the table." Her mother responded that they didn't do that at this place even though they did do so at other restaurants. The girl nodded her head. In this case, Piaget would argue that the little girl was using _____ in her development of knowledge of what to do at "restaurants."

a. accomodation
b. object permanence
c. sensorimotor thought
d. gender identity

_____ 28. By definition, adolescence begins at ____.

a. the time a child gets his or her first job
b. hormonal sensitization of brain structures
c. the initial development of primary sex characteristics
d. puberty

_____ 29. Adolescents' overestimation of their uniqueness and their feeling of being "on stage" are part of Elkind's (1978) notion of ____.

a. puberty
b. intimacy vs. isolation
c. adolescent egocentrism
d. identity diffusion

_____ 30. Studies of men's and women's careers show that ____.

a. women are more likely to have "career gaps" due to pregnancy and taking care of elderly relatives
b. men are more likely to have "career gaps"
c. the first stage of most careers is a "maintenance" stage
d. men experience more "interrole conflict" than women do

True/False Items: *Write T or F in the space provided to the left of each item.*

_____ 1. A critical period is an age range during which certain experiences must occur for development to proceed normally.

_____ 2. A longitudinal design is used to compare people of different ages at the same point in time.

_____ 3. Smoking during pregnancy is an example of a teratogen.

_____ 4. The proximodistal principle stresses that development proceeds in a head-to-foot direction.

_____ 5. According to Piaget, assimilation is the process by which new experiences cause existing schemas to change.

_____ 6. In the preoperational stage, children learn how to use abstract reasoning.

_____ 7. Studies of children's information processing show that metacognition declines with age.

_____ 8. Studies of Kohlberg's model of moral development find that the stages he proposed are equally common in all cultures, supporting a biological basis for moral development.

_____ 9. Cross-cultural studies support the hypothesis that most infants are insecurely attached.

_____ 10. Research into the relationships between adolescents and their parents has found that "storm and stress" is the rule rather than the exception.

Short Answer Questions

1. What is object permanence?

2. What is the zone of proximal development?

3. What is attachment?

4. What changes in cognitive development are hypothesized to take place in adolescence?

5. What intellectual changes occur in adulthood?

Essay Questions

1. How do both genetics and environmental influences affect prenatal development?

2. What major changes take place in each of Piaget's stages of cognitive development?

3. Describe Kohlberg's stage model of moral development.

4. Describe Erikson's stages of psychosocial development.

5. What does the research on the developmental effects of day-care indicate?

Study Sheet 11.1   Using Piaget's Theory

<u>Supporting</u>   <u>Not Supporting</u>

Sensorimotor

Preoperational

Concrete Operational

Formal Operational

Study Sheet 11.2   **Social Clocks**

	Late 70's*		Today	
	Men	**Women**	**Men**	**Women**
Best Age for a Man to Marry (20-25)	42%	42%		
Best Age for a Woman to Marry (19-24)	44%	36%		
When Should Most People Become Grandparents (45-50)	64%	57%		
Best Age for Most People to Finish School and Go To Work (20-22)	36%	38%		
When Most Men Should Be Settled On a Career (24-26)	24%	36%		
When Most Men Hold Their Top Jobs (45-50)	38%	31%		
When Most People Should Be Ready To Retire (60-65)	66%	41%		
When a Man Has the Most Responsibilities (35-50)	49%	50%		
When a Man Accomplishes the Most (40-50)	46%	41%		
The Prime of Life for a Man (35-50)	59%	66%		
When a Woman Has the Most Rcsonsibilities (25-40)	59%	53%		
When a Woman Accomplishes the Most (30-45)	57%	48%		

*Data are taken from a study by Passuth, Mines, & Neugarten, 1984). Percentages refer to the percentages of the sample who agreed with the statement that the age range in parentheses is the appropriate age range for the event.

Answer Keys

Answer Key for Key Terms

Major Issues and Methods
Prenatal Development

1. a
2. c
3. f
4. i
5. g

6. d
7. b
8. h
9. e

Infancy and Childhood

1. g
2. f
3. w
4. bb
5. aa
6. c
7. m
8. k
9. r
10. l
11. n
12. ff

13. ee
14. v
15. cc
16. b
17. dd
18. i
19. s
20. q
21. j
22. d
23. t
24. a

25. e
26. h
27. y
28. gg
29. hh
30. z
31. x
32. u
33. p
34. o

Adolescence
Adulthood

1. a
2. d

3. b
4. c

Answer Key for Review at a Glance

1. critical period
2. sensitive
3. cross-sectional
4. longitudinal
5. zygote
6. embryo
7. fetus
8. Teratogens
9. fetal alcohol syndrome
10. reflexes
11. maturation
12. cephalocaudal
13. proximodistal
14. Piaget

23. formal
24. Vygotsky
25. proximal development
26. preconventional
27. conventional
28. postconventional
29. psychosocial
30. Attachment
31. Stranger
32. separation
33. strange situation
34. authoritative
35. authoritarian
36. indulgent

15. schemas
16. Accommodation
17. assimilation
18. sensorimotor
19. object permanence
20. preoperational
21. egoentrism
22. concrete operational

37. neglectful
38. gender identity
39. sex-role stereotypes
40. personal fable
41. adolescent egocentrism
42. postformal
43. social clock

Answer Key for Practice Test Multiple Choice Questions

1. c
2. c
3. b
4. a
5. d
6. a
7. a
8. b
9. d
10. c
11. b
12. c
13. a
14. c
15. a

16. a
17. d
18. a
19. b
20. b
21. a
22. d
23. d
24. a
25. b
26. b
27. a
28. d
29. c
30. a

Answer Key for Practice Test True/False Questions

1. T
2. F
3. T
4. F
5. F

6. F
7. F
8. F
9. F
10. F

Answer Key for Practice Test Short Answer Questions

1. Object permanence is the belief that children develop during the sensorimotor stage of cognitive development that an object continues to exist even when it no longer can be seen.

2. Zygotsky's idea of the zone of proximal development is the difference between what a child can do independently and what he or she can do with some assistance. Thus, a child may be able to do more than someone thinks he or she can, if some help is given.

3. Attachment refers to the strong emotional bond that develops between children and their primary caregivers.

4. There are several cognitive changes that occur in adolescence. Piaget proposed that adolescents acquire formal operational thinking, which is characterized by more abstract and hypothetical

thought. Elkind (1978) proposed that adolescents engage in adolescent egocentrism, which involves an overestimation of the uniqueness of one's feelings and experiences and a feeling of being "on stage."

5. Fluid intelligence begins to decline steadily in young adulthood, whereas crystallized intelligence peaks during middle adulthood and declines after that. Poorer perceptual speed, memory, vision, and hearing may contribute to these intellectual declines. People who have above-average education, cognitively stimulating jobs, are involved in cognitively-stimulating activities on a regular basis, marry spouses with greater intellectual abilities than their own, and maintain a higher level of perceptual processing speed tend to have less steep declines in cognitive functioning. Regular physical exercise and perceptual-motor activities also help to preserve cognitive abilities.

Answer Key for Practice Test Essay Questions

1. At conception an egg and sperm unite to form the zygote. The 23rd pair of chromosomes determine the baby's sex. If the union produces an XY combination in the 23rd pair, the resulting child will be a boy. If the combination is XX, the resulting child will be a girl. The TDF gene on the Y chromosome initiates the development of testes in the male at 6-8 weeks after conception. If there is no Y chromosome (and thus no TDF gene), testes do not form, and if there is an absence of sufficient androgen activity in this critical period, a female pattern of organ development occurs. Environmental agents called teratogens can cause abnormal prenatal development. Teratogens include things like nicotine, alcohol consumption, mercury, lead, and radiation.

2. During the sensorimotor period, children come to understand their world through their sensory processes and through motor behavior (movements like crawling, walking, touching things etc.). During this stage they develop object permanence and start to develop the basic skills of language. During the preoperational stage beginning about the age of 2, children start to be able to represent the world through symbols such as words and numbers. During this stage children can also start to think about past and future events and engage in pretend play. They have difficulty understanding the principle of conservation. Children's thinking at this time also reflects their egocentrism. Children in the concrete operational stage understand the concept of reversibility, the serial ordering of objects (e.g. smallest to largest) and can form mental representations of a series of steps needed to accomplish a goal, an important step in problem-solving. Finally, children in the formal operational stage can use abstract and hypothetico-deductive thought.

3. Kohlberg believed that people pass through three main levels of moral development. The first stage is called preconventional moral reasoning and is based on anticipated punishments and rewards. Individuals in this stage are simply interested in getting rewards and avoiding punishments and see morality in those terms. The second level is called conventional moral reasoning and is the stage that Kohlberg felt most people reach as adults. Conventional moral reasoning is based on conformity to social expectations. Thus, a person in this level behaves morally because he or she seeks to gain approval from others and feels that it is one's duty to show respect for authority and to maintain order. The third level is called postconventional moral reasoning. This level is based on well-thought-out moral principles. These are principles that can be above laws and rules and are often based on principles of justice and equality.

4. Erikson argued for eight psychosocial stages of development. The first is called trust vs. mistrust and is characterized by the development of a sense of trust toward others based on experiences in the first year of life. Autonomy versus shame and doubt follows as children start to exercise their individuality. Parents who don't allow that may have children who develop shame and doubt. From ages three to six, children's curiosity about the world shows up in initiative versus guilt. Given

freedom to explore, children will develop a sense of initiative. From six to puberty, a child who experiences pride will develop "industry," a striving to achieve. Without this, a child will develop a sense of inferiority. In adolescence, the major issue is "identity versus role confusion" as adolescents try to develop a sense of identity, "who they are." In young adulthood (20-40), the major issue is "intimacy versus isolation" and involves making connections with others, particularly in terms of finding a life partner and developing a family. In middle adulthood (40-65), the major issue is "generativity versus stagnation" as people feel they are moving forward with family and career or are not. Finally, the last stage is called "integrity versus despair," as people look back over their lives and experience a sense of satisfaction or regret.

5. Research into the day-care controversy has revealed some interesting results. Day care does not seem to disrupt infants' attachments to their parents unless the day care is poor, the child spends many hours there, parents are not sensitive to their child at home, and the child has multiple day-care arrangements. Infants and toddlers are slightly less engaged with their mothers and less sociable toward them if they attend day-care. Infants and pre-schoolers from low income families seem to benefit socially and cognitively from high-quality day-care. For infants from middle- and upper-income homes, day-care, regardless of quality, seems to have little subsequent effect (positively or negatively) on children once they enter elementary school. The quality of home and family experiences seem to be more important predictors of development for these children.

Chapter 12
BEHAVIOR IN A SOCIAL CONTEXT

Learning Objectives: *These questions, with a few additions (indicated with an asterisk), are taken from the directed questions found in the margins of the chapter. After reading the chapter, you should be able to answer these questions.*

1. When does the mere presence of others people enhance or impair performance? Why?

2. How do norms and roles guide our behavior?

3. Explain the difference between informational and normative social influence.

4. Identify some situational factors that influence people's degree of conformity.

5. When is the minority most likely to influence the majority?

6. Describe Milgram's obedience experiment. Do you believe the results would be similar today? Why or why not?

7. What situational factors increase obedience?

8. Describe deindividuation and how conditions in the Stanford Prison Study may have fostered it.

9. What is social loafing and when is it most likely to occur?

10. Identify two causes of group polarization.

11. What are some causes, symptoms, and consequences of groupthink?

12. Why did LePiere's study raise doubts about attitude-behavior consistency?

13. Discuss the three broad conditions under which attitudes best predict behavior.

14. What causes cognitive dissonance, and how can it produce attitude change?

15. According to self-perception theory, why does counterattitudinal behavior produce attitude change?

16. What evidence supports dissonance theory? What evidence favors self-perception theory?

17. Identify communicator and message characteristics that increase persuasiveness.

18. Describe the central and peripheral routes to persuasion. For whom is the central route most likely to be effective?

19. How are the norm of reciprocity, door-in-the-face, and foot-in-the-door techniques, and lowballing used to manipulate behavior?

20. What types of information lead us to form a situational, rather than personal attribution?

21. Describe the fundamental attribution error and the self-serving bias. How do cultural norms affect these attributional tendencies?

22. Why do primacy effects occur in impression formation? How can they be reduced?

23. How do mental sets shape the way we perceive people? How do stereotypes create mental sets?

24. Explain how our incorrect expectations can become self-fulfilling.

25. How do psychologists use reaction time tasks to detect people's covert prejudices?

26. Identify cognitive processes that foster prejudice.

27. How can people maintain their stereotypes in the face of contradictory information?

28. According to realistic conflict theory and social identity theory, what are the motivational roots of prejudice?

29. Discuss how self-fulfilling prophecies and stereotypes threaten to perpetuate prejudice.

30. According to sociobiologists, what is the evolutionary basis for helping behavior?

31. How do social norms, self-reinforcers, and empathy influence helping behavior?

32. Identify two key ways (2 stages of intervention) in which the "bystander effect" often inhibits people from responding to emergency.

32.1* What additional factors help to explain why bystanders may be helpful?

33. Who are we most likely to help? How might the belief in a just world inhibit us from helping?

33.1* What factors serve to increase prosocial behavior?

34. What evidence supports a genetic role in aggression?

35. Discuss some brain regions and body chemicals that play a role in aggression.

36. Identify some major types of environmental stimuli that increase the risk of aggression.

37. Discuss how reinforcement and modeling contribute to aggression.

38. How do cognitive factors determine whether we respond to a stimulus aggressively?

38.1 Define the term catharsis and how it is related to Megargee's concept of overcontrolled hostility?

39. According to the catharsis and social learning viewpoints, what role does media violence play in regulating human aggression?

40. Based on research, how does media violence affect people's behavior and attitudes?

41. According to learning principles, how might violent video games teach people to behave aggressively? Does evidence support this view?

Chapter Overview

Social Influence

One major topic of social psychology is the study of how other people influence our behavior, which is called social influence. Studies of social facilitation suggest that both animals and humans have an increased tendency to perform their dominant response in the presence of others. When performing easy tasks or complex tasks that we have mastered, our dominant response usually is correct, so the presence of others enhances performance. At unlearned complex tasks, our dominant response usually is to make errors, so the presence of others impairs performance. We are also affected by both social norms and social roles, both of which prescribe how we *should* behave. Two major topics in the area of social influence are conformity and obedience. We conform because of both informational social influence (i.e. conforming because we believe others are right) and because of normative social influence (i.e. conforming because we want others to accept us). Group size affects conformity to a certain point, and the presence of a dissenter can reduce conformity. Milgram's classic studies on obedience point to a number of situational factors that influence obedience, including remoteness of victims, closeness and legitimacy of an authority figure, and being a "cog in a wheel." Personal characteristics do not seem to explain obedience as well as such situational factors. Deindividuation, resulting from the increased anonymity that sometimes accompanies being in a crowd, can also fuel destructive behavior. Finally, both social loafing, which is the tendency to expend less effort when working in a group than when working alone, and groupthink, which is the tendency for group members to suspend critical thinking to create a sense of group unanimity are social psychological phenomena that affect people in groups.

Social Thinking and Perception

Attitudes are positive or negative evaluative reactions toward stimuli. Attitudes are most predictive of behavior when situational factors are weak, when subjective norms support our attitudes, and when we believe behaviors are under our control, according to the Theory of Planned Behavior. Additionally attitudes best predict behavior when we are aware of them and general attitudes best predict general classes of behavior, and specific attitudes best predict specific behaviors. Other theories such as cognitive dissonance theory and self-perception theory focus on how our behavior influences our attitudes. Specifically, they predict that we mold our attitudes to be consistent with how we have already behaved. Studies of persuasion suggest three major components in the persuasive process: the communicator, the message, and the audience. Communicator credibility, largely determined by perceived expertise and trustworthiness, is a key to persuasion. Two-sided communications, which present both sides of an issue, have been found to be more persuasive than one-sided messages in many situations. Audience factors play a role in whether the central or the peripheral route to persuasion is a better technique for persuasion. When people are motivated to critically examine arguments, the central route is the better technique. Marketers use several persuasion techniques, including the norm of reciprocity, the door-in-the-face technique, the foot-in-the-door technique, and lowballing. Attributions are judgements about the causes of behavior. One distinction we make is between personal and situational attributions. When we make a personal attribution, we believe the cause of someone's behavior is a personal characteristic of theirs. Situational attributions are made to environmental causes. A number of biases, including the fundamental attribution error (the tendency to overestimate personal causes of behavior) affect our judgements. Forming and maintaining impressions is another aspect of social thinking and perception. The initial information we learn about a person greatly influences our perceptions of them (primacy effect). Stereotypes and self-fulfilling prophecies can bias the way that we perceive individuals.

Social Relations

Prejudice and discrimination remain major problems in American society. Categorization into ingroups and outgroups and the use of the outgroup homogeneity bias (the belief that the members of our outgroups are all very similar to one another) are major cognitive sources of prejudice and discrimination. Realistic conflict theory explains the motivational source of prejudice and discrimination as due to competition between groups for limited resources, while social identity theory explains prejudice and discrimination as due to a need to enhance our self-esteem (by making sure that our ingroup does well and that our outgroup does poorly). Prosocial behavior is affected by biological predispositions, learning, and by personality characteristics such as empathy. Other factors that influence helping include simply noticing a problem, social comparison, feeling a sense of responsibility to help, and a sense of self-efficacy in dealing with the situation. Biological, environmental, and psychological factors all affect aggressive behavior. The hypothalamus, amygdala, and other subcortical structures seem to affect the likelihood of engaging in aggression. Recent studies have also implicated the role of the frontal lobes (site of reasoning, forethought, and impulse control) in aggressive behavior. Serotonin and testosterone have also been found to be related to aggression, although the effects are often weak in humans. Environmental stimuli that cause frustration or pain can increase aggression, as can other environmental factors such as provocation and exposure to aggressive models. Attributions of intentionality for someone's negative behavior toward us, a lack of empathy, and the ability to regulate emotions are important psychological factors in affecting aggressive behavior. Studies of media violence are controversial, but several assertions regarding the link between media and violence have been made: viewers learn new aggressive behaviors through modeling, viewers believe that aggression is rewarded, viewers become desensitized to violence and suffering, and viewers' fears of becoming targets of crime and violence increase.

Chapter Outline

Social Influence
    The Mere Presence of Others
    Social Norms: The Rules of the Game
        Culture and Norm Formation
    Conformity and Obedience
        Why Do People Conform?
        Factors That Affect Conformity
        Minority Influence
        Obedience to Authority
        Research Close-Up: The Dilemma of Obedience: When Conscience Confronts
        Malevolent Authority

Key Terms: *Write the letter of the definition next to the term in the space provided.*

1. ___ attitude

2. ___ attributions

3. ___ bystander effect

4. ___ catharsis

5. ___ central route to persuasion

6. ___ deindividuation

7. ___ door-in-the-face technique

8. ___ empathy altruism hypothesis

9. ___ foot-in-the-door technique

10. ___ frustration-aggression hypothesis

11. ___ fundamental attribution error

12. ___ group polarization

13. ___ groupthink

14. ___ informational social influence

15. ___ just world hypothesis

16. ___ kin selection

17. ___ lowballing

18. ___ negative state relief model

19. ___ normative social influence

20. ___ peripheral route to persuasion

a. an increased tendency to perform one's dominant response in the presence of others

b. shared expectancies of how people should think, feel, and behave

c. set of norms that characterizes how people ought to behave

d. conforming because we believe others are right

e. conforming because we want to be accepted by others

f. an increase in anonymity that leads to disinhibited behavior in a group or crowd

g. the tendency to expend less effort when working in a group than when working alone

h. the tendency for the average opinion of group members to become more extreme after group discussion

i. the tendency of group members to suspend critical thinking because they are striving for agreement

j. a positive or negative evaluative reaction toward a stimulus

k. theory that our intention to engage in a behavior is strongest when we have a positive attitude, when subjective norms support our attitudes, and when we believe that we control the behavior

l. theory that people strive for consistency in their cognitions

m. theory that we determine our attitudes by observing our behavior

n. occurs when people think carefully about a message and are influenced because they find the arguments compelling

o. occurs when people do not scrutinize persuasive arguments

p. making a large request that is sure to be rejected followed by a smaller request

q. compliance with a small request is followed by a larger request

r. ask for commitment to an action and then raise the cost of the behavior before the behavior is performed

s. judgements about the causes of our own and others' behaviors

t. underestimating the impact of the situation and overestimating the role of personal factors in explaining behavior

21. ___ prejudice

22. ___ primacy effect

23. ___ realistic conflict theory

24. ___ self-fulfilling prophecy

25. ___ self-perception theory

26. ___ self-serving bias

27. ___ social facilitation

28. ___ social identity theory

29. ___ social loafing

30. ___ social norms

31. ___ social role

32. ___ stereotype

33. ___ stereotype threat

34. ___ theory of cognitive dissonance

35. ___ theory of planned behavior

u. making relatively more personal attributions for our successes and situational attributions for our failures

v. our tendency to attach more importance to the intitial information we learn about a person when forming impressions

w. a generalized belief about a group or category of people

x. occurs when people's erroneous beliefs lead them to act toward others in a way that brings about the expected behaviors

y. a negative attitude toward people based on their membership in a group

z. theory that competition for limited resources fosters prejudice

aa. theory that prejudice stems from a need to enhance our self-esteem

bb. idea that stereotypes create a fear and self-consciousness among stereotyped group members that they will live up to stereotypes

cc. principle that organisms are most likely to help others with whom they share the most genes

dd. hypothesis that altruism is produced by empathy

ee. theory that helping others allows us to reduce our own personal distress caused through empathy

ff. the finding that the presence of bystanders inhibits a person's tendency to help

gg. hypothesis that people perceive that others get what they deserve and deserve what they get

hh. hypothesis that frustration leads to aggression

ii. principle that performing an act of aggression discharges aggressive energy and temporarily reduces aggressive impulses

Review at a Glance: *Write the term that best fits the blank to review what you learned in this chapter.*

Social Influence

One major aspect of social psychology is the exploration of how other people influence our behavior, a phenomenon called (1) _____ _____. Researchers such as Zajonc have found that the mere presence of others can affect the behavior of both animals and humans. When humans and animals perform simple tasks or complex learned tasks better in the presence of others but difficult or unlearned tasks worse in the presence of others, the phenomenon called (2) _____ _____ has occurred. All societies have rules for proper behavior. (3) _____ _____ are shared expectations about how people should think, feel, and behave. (4) _____ _____ are sets of norms that characterize how people in a given social position "ought" to behave. People will generally conform to social norms and expectations because of both (5) _____ _____ _____, by which people conform because they think others are right, and (6) _____ _____

_____, by which people conform because they want to be accepted by others. People's behavior can also be affected by the greater sense of anonymity they feel in crowds, leading to disinhibition. This phenomenon is called (7) _____. Yet another phenomenon of social influence by which people work less hard in groups than they do when working alone is called (8) _____ _____. Good decision-making is sometimes impaired by group dynamics. When a group of like-minded people discusses an issue, the initial tendency of the group tends to become more extreme, a process called (9) _____ _____. Social psychologist Irving Janis described a process by which groups suspend good critical thinking in the name of group unanimity, a process he calls (10) _____.

Social Thinking and Perception

A second major topic of social psychology is how people come to perceive their world. An (11) _____ is a positive or negative evaluative reaction toward a stimulus. Much research has been done to examine the relationship between attitudes and behaviors. According to the theory of (12) _____ _____, our intentions to engage in a behavior are strongest when subjective norms support our attitudes, when we have a positive attitude toward the behavior, and when we believe the behavior is under our control. We tend to believe that our attitudes cause our behaviors, but there is some evidence that behavior influences what we believe our attitudes to be. According to the theory of (13) _____ _____, people strive for consistency in their cognitions, such that, for example, when people's cognitions about their attitudes and behaviors are not consistent with one another, people are motivated to change either attitudes or behaviors to bring them into line with one another. Similarly, Daryl Bem argued in his (14) _____ _____ theory, that we make inferences about our own attitudes by examining our own behavior. Much research in social psychology has examined the process of persuasion. The three components that have been studied the most are the communicator, the message, and the audience. Studies of communicator credibility have indicated that communicators are most credible if we believe that they are (15) _____ and (16) _____. In general, studies of messages indicate that (17) _____ - _____ messages are the most effective kinds. Petty and Cacioppo have argued that there are two routes that audiences use when examining messages. The (18) _____ route occurs when people think carefully about the message, while the (19) _____ route occurs when people do not scrutinize the message but are persuaded by other factors, such as the speaker's attractiveness or the emotional content of the message. Social psychologists have also studies several persuasive tactics used by salespersons. People often feel that if someone has done something nice for them, they should do the same for that person, a phenomenon known as the (20) _____ _____ _____. When someone firsts asks you for a large request, which you typically refuse, and then asks you to comply with a smaller request (the real target behavior), that individual is using the (21) _____ _____ _____ _____ technique. The opposite technique, which requires compliance first with a small request before a larger request is made, is called the (22) _____ _____ _____ _____ technique. When a persuader gets us to commit to an action and then increases the cost of the behavior before we actually have performed the behavior, (23) _____ has occurred. Social psychologists also study the process of (24) _____, by which we make judgements about the causes of our own and other's behaviors. One major distinction made by social psychologist Fritz Heider was between attributions to personal charactistics, called (25) _____ attributions, and attributions to environmental causes of behavior, called (26) _____ attributions. We can be quite biased in the way that we explain behavior. A bias by which we tend to underestimate situational factors of behavior when judging the causes of other people's behavior is called the (27) _____ _____ _____. When it comes to explaining our own behavior, we tend to protect our self-esteem by using the (28) _____ _____ _____, making more personal attributions for success and more situational ones for failure. As social beings, we constantly form impressions of others. The tendency to attach more importance to the initial information we learn about a person is called the (29) _____ effect. Generalized beliefs about a group or category of people are called (30) _____. When people's erroneous expectations about a person or group of people leads them to act toward others in a way that brings about the expected behavior, a (31) _____ _____ _____ has occurred.

Social Relations

(32) _____ refers to a negative attitude toward people based on their membership in a certain group. Social categorization of individuals leads to a differentiation between groups to which we believe we belong, or (33) _____ - _____, and groups to which we believe we do not belong, or (34) _____ _____. A tendency to view the members of groups to which we believe we do not belong as being more similar to one another than members of groups to which we believe we do belong is called the (35) _____ _____ bias. Two major theories of why prejudice occurs have been identified. According to (36) _____ _____ theory, competition for limited resources fosters prejudice. According to (37) _____ _____ theory, prejudice occurs because of our basic need to maintain and enhance our self-esteem, which is done by making sure our in-group succeeds (often at the expense of our out-group). Social psychologists have also studied why and when people help each other. According to the principle of (38) _____ _____, people (and animals) are most likely to help others with whom they share the most genes. According to the (39) _____ _____ hypothesis, helping is influenced by our ability to understand things from another's perspective. Studies of helping in crowds suggest a (40) _____ _____, by which the presence of many people decreases the likelihood of any individual helping, largely because of a lack of individual felt responsibility to help. Often people won't help others because they feel that others get what they deserve, a phenomenon best explained by the (41) _____ _____ hypothesis. Studies of aggression have suggested both biological and psychological causes. According to the original (42) _____ - _____ hypothesis, frustration inevitably leads to aggression, and all aggresion is the result of frustration (both assertions were eventually found to be false). Other psychological factors in aggression include (43) _____ _____, by which aggressors blame the victim for some problem, thus convincing themselves that the victims deserved the aggression, and (44) _____ _____ _____, by which aggressors believe that they have been deliberately provoked by others.

Apply What You Know

1. Choose three television commercials. Describe each commercial and how communicator, message, and audience factors play roles in the persuasive process of the ad. Use Study Sheet 12.1 to record your answers.

2. Describe how you would design a study to examine whether the primacy or recency effect was more important in the forming of impressions.

3. Using Study Sheet 12.2, watch three children's cartoons and record the number of aggressive acts that you see in each program. Make sure that you operationally define each category. What aggressive acts occur most often? Did the results surprise you? Why or why not?

Stretching Your Geographies

1. Research an African or Asian country of your choice and describe how the social norms of that country are different from those of the United States.

2. Conflicts in the Balkans and in the Middle East have been sources of international concern for some time. Choosing one conflict in either place, describe the prejudices and discrimination that occur on both sides of the conflict.

Practice Test

<u>**Multiple Choice Items:**</u> *Please write the letter corresponding to your answer in the space to the left of each item.*

_____ 1. The fact that Japanese individuals typically sit farther apart when conversing than Americans do and that Greeks are more likely to touch during a social interaction than Europeans are **best considered** as examples of _____.

    a. groupthink
    b. stereotype threat
    c. social norms
    d. informational social influence

_____ 2. Suppose you were designing an obedience study and wanted to reduce or lower the obedience rates found by Milgram. Of the following, the one which would **most likely** decrease participants' obedience would be to _____.

    a. have an authority figure that is perceived to be legitimate
    b. have the participants feel fully responsible for the victim's welfare
    c. place the victims in a separate room where the participant can't see them
    d. have your participants all be women

_____ 3. The fact that guards in the Stanford Prison study did not use their actual names, did not know that they were being observed, and wore reflective sunglasses that prevented direct eye contact all suggest that _____ may have played a key role in producing the results obtained in this experiment.

    a. the self-fulfilling prophecy
    b. social facilitation
    c. perceived legitimacy of the authority figures
    d. deindividuation

_____ 4. The belief that one's individual performance within a group is **not** being monitored and having a task goal that is not very meaningful or valuable to a person are two factors that are **most likely** to increase the chance of _____.

    a. groupthink
    b. social loafing
    c. minority influence
    d. group polarization

_____ 5. A group of public officials is meeting to decide what to do about a budget shortage. The principle of group polarization would predict that this group of people would be **most likely** to reach a highly conservative decision if _____.

a. the group has a relatively small number of people in it (4-5)
b. the group members believe that their individual performance with in the group is being monitored
c. the group members are generally conservative to begin with
d. the group has an authority figure who is perceived to be legitimate

_____ 6. In the case of the Space Shuttle Challenger disaster, the NASA official who gave the final go-ahead for the mission was never informed about the many engineers who initially opposed the launch. The fact that this information never reached the official **best illustrates** the groupthink process of _____.

a. direct pressure
b. the illusion of unanimity
c. self-censorship
d. mind guarding

_____ 7. Don went to three different dances this past week. Prior to this, he had a slightly negative attitude towards dancing but after observing his behavior, he starts to conclude that he must in fact enjoy it otherwise he wouldn't have attended so many. This change in Don's attitude is **most consistent** with the predictions of _____.

a. social identity theory
b. cognitive dissonance theory
c. the theory of planned behavior
d. self-perception theory

_____ 8. Alison is at a workshop where a presenter is attempting to persuade people to make a rather risky but potentially profitable financial investment. After carefully considering the presenter's arguments, Alison finds this person's idea sound and compelling and decides to invest. This example **best demonstrates** the _____.

a. peripheral route to persuasion
b. norm of reciprocity
c. central route to persuasion
d. door-in-the-face technique

_____ 9. A phone solicitor calls and asks if you would be interested in volunteering to work on a local political campaign. The job involves working 20 hours per week, you must work on the both Saturday and Sunday for the next 6 months, and you receive no financial compensation. After politely refusing this request, the solicitor asks if you would be willing to work one evening a month on the campaign. This example **best demonstrates** the persuasion strategy known as _____.

a. the foot-in-the-door
b. the door-in-the-face
c. the norm of reciprocity
d. lowballing

_____ 10. A person on campus walks up to you and asks if you would be willing to wear a ribbon to show support for her cause. Though the ribbon is a bit unattractive, it is small so you agree to wear it. After agreeing to this request, the solicitor then asks you if you would be willing to make a donation of $15. This example best demonstrates the persuasion technique called _____.

    a. the foot-in-the-door
    b. the door-in-the-face
    c. the norm of reciprocity
    d. lowballing

_____ 11. Juan is in the process of forming an opinion about someone when a friend who is taking a psychology class tells him to avoid making snap judgements and to carefully consider the evidence. The net result of this advice is that Juan feels more accountable for his opinions. The advice of Juan's friend should **most likely** decrease the _____.

    a. recency effect
    b. primacy effect
    c. fundamental attribution error
    d. self-serving bias

_____ 12. A person with covert prejudicial feelings towards gays and lesbians would most likely have the **slowest** reaction times to which of the _____ word pairs presented using the implicit association test.

    a. gay-wrong
    b. straight-right
    c. lesbian-bad
    d. gay-good

_____ 13. A mother risks her own life by rushing into a burning building to save her son. According to the _____, she is **most likely** performing this altruistic behavior because _____.

    a. norm of social responsibility; she feels she should help when others treat her kindly
    b. concept of reciprocal altruism; she feels she should contribute to the welfare of society
    c. norm of reciprocity; it increases the likelihood of receiving help in return
    d. principle of kin selection; she shares genes with her child

_____ 14. In his study of murderers, Adrian Raine (1998) found that impulsive murderers had _____ than murders who had committed their crimes as a planned predatory act.

    a. lower frontal lobe activity
    b. greater frontal lobe activity
    c. less subcortical activity
    d. more subcortical activity

_____ 15. Realistic conflict theory argues that _____.

a. we use the outgroup homogeneity bias to classify outgroups
b. prejudice is due to illusory correlations
c. prejudice and discrimination exist because groups of people are competing for the same things
d. prejudice and discrimination are due to repressed frustrations that people have

_____ 16. Through the use of _____, a persuader gets us to commit to some action and then, before we actually perform the behavior, he or she increases the "cost" of the same behavior.

a. cognitive dissonance theory
b. the door-in-the-face strategy
c. lowballing
d. the foot-in-the-door strategy

_____ 17. The inventor of "Preparation K," a new potion for dealing with that nagging   hemorrhoid problem suffered by many Klingons, is looking for a new spokesperson. Turning to the world of Earth TV for help in pitching his product to the Klingon population, the inventor would be most advised to choose _____, according to studies of the three components in persuasion.

a. out-of-control former starship Enterprise captain James T. Kirk, who hates Klingons because they killed his son David
b. human cartoon characters George Jetson, his boy Elroy, daughter Judy, and Jane, his wife, who have never suffered from hemorrhoids in their entire lives
c. Lieutenant Worf, a Klingon officer, and show him casually discussing his hemorrhoid problems with Dr. Beverly Crusher
d. 10-year-old child actress, Cher Lee Temple

_____ 18. Really wanting her dwarfs to buy her a new Porsche, the formerly pure Snow White first asks them to buy an inexpensive bicycle. The dwarafs realize that Snow is using the foot-in-the-door technique and come to believe that Snow is acting as she does because she is a manipulative person. The dwarfs have just made a _____.

a. recency effect
b. self-serving bias
c. personal attribution
d. situational attribution

_____ 19. Shared expectations about how people should think, feel, and behave are called _____.

a. social norms
b. informational social influences
c. normative social influences
d. self-perceptions

_____ 20. Going along with a group's opinion because we believe the group is "right" is called _____.

    a. a social norm
    b. informational social influence
    c. normative social influence
    d. a self-perception

_____ 21. Studies of the effect of group size on conformity have suggested that _____.

    a. group size has no effect on conformity
    b. a group of ten produces more conformity that a group of five
    c. the larger the group the less likely there is to be a dissenter
    d. group size increases conformity up to about five people in a group, but after that increasing group size does not increase conformity

_____ 22. Studies of personal characteristics in obedience have found that _____.

    a. more intelligent people are less likely to be obedient
    b. more religious people are more likely to be obedient
    c. more outgoing people are less likely to be obedient
    d. gender is not related to obedience rates

_____ 23. A generalized belief about a group of category of people is called a(n) _____.

    a. stereotype
    b. self-perception
    c. self-schema
    d. self-fulfilling prophecy

_____ 24. According to the outgroup homogenity bias, _____.

    a. people's erroneous expectations lead them to act toward other in such a way that brings about the expected behaviors, thereby confirming the original impression
    b. people form a negative attitude toward someone because of their membership in a group
    c. people view members of groups to which they do not belong as more similar to one another than are members of groups to which they feel they do belong
    d. people underestimate the role of the situation and overestimate the role of personal factors in explaining others' behavior

_____ 25. According to _____ theory, prejudice stems from a need to enhance our self-esteem.

    a. social facilitation
    b. social identity
    c. norm of reciprocity
    d. attribution

_____ 26. On an icy day, a crash occurs at an intersection. A person who did not see or hear the crash is asked why she thought it occurred. She says that it was probably because the person was drunk. This woman is subject to the _____.

a. fundamental attribution error
b. self-serving bias
c. primacy effect
d. recency effect

_____ 27. People are most likely to help those who share their genes, a principle called _____.

a. the norm of reciprocity effect
b. kin selection
c. social loafing
d. the empathy-altruism hypothesis

_____ 28. The idea that we help others because it helps us to reduce our own personal distress is called _____.

a. the norm of reciprocity effect
b. kin selection
c. the negative state relief model
d. the empathy-altruism hypothesis

_____ 29. The belief that people get what they deserve and deserve what they get is called the _____.

a. bystander effect
b. just-world hypothesis
c. catharsis hypothesis
d. negative-state relief model

_____ 30. Studies of media effects on violence have found that _____.

a. viewers learn new aggressive behaviors through modeling
b. the fear of becoming a target of violent crime decreases with more TV watching
c. viewers learn that aggression is rarely rewarded
d. fears that viewers will become desensitized to violence are unfounded

True/False Items: *Write T or F in the space provided to the left of each item.*

_____ 1. The mere presence of others does not affect human behavior.

_____ 2. Normative social influence occurs when people conform because they want to be accepted by others.

_____ 3. The presence of a dissenter tends to increase conformity.

_____ 4. Personal characteristics have been found to be more important than situational characteristics in obedient behavior.

_____ 5. Social loafing is more likely to occur when people believe that individual performance is not being monitored.

_____ 6. Groupthink is more likely to occur when groups are under high stress to reach a decision.

_____ 7. Cognitive dissonance produces motivation to reduce inconsistency between attitudes and behaviors.

_____ 8. The peripheral route to persuasion occurs when people carefully scrutinize the content of a message.

_____ 9. Stereotypes are not types of schemas.

_____ 10. We are more likely to help people who are similar to us.

Short Answer Questions

1. What is the difference between social facilitation and social loafing?

2. Why do influence processes produce conformity?

3. What does cognitive dissonance theory argue?

4. What are the cognitive roots of prejudice?

5. What is kin selection?

Essay Questions

1. What group dynamics affect group decision-making?

2. How do our attitudes influence our behavior?

3. What processes are involved in forming and maintaining impressions?

4. When do people help?

5. What psychological factors are involved in aggression?

Study Sheet 12.1
Commercials

Commercial	Communicator	Message	Audience

Study Sheet 12.2

Cartoon	Physical Aggression (Definition:)	Verbal Aggression (Definition:)

Answer Keys

Answer Key for Key Terms

1. j
2. s
3. ff
4. ii
5. n
6. f
7. p
8. dd
9. q
10. hh
11. t
12. h
13. i
14. d
15. gg
16. cc
17. r
18. ee
19. e
20. o
21. y
22. v
23. z
24. x
25. m
26. u
27. a
28. aa
29. g
30. b
31. c
32. w
33. bb
34. l
35. k

Answer Key for Review at a Glance

1. social influence
2. social facilitation
3. Social norms
4. Social roles
5. informational social influence
6. normative social influence
7. deindividuation
8. social loafing
9. group polarization
10. groupthink
11. attitude
12. planned behavior
13. cognitive dissonance
14. self-perception
15. trustworthy
16. expert
17. two-sided
18. central
19. peripheral
20. norm of reciprocity
21. door-in-the-face
22. foot-in-the-door
23. lowballing
24. attribution
25. personal
26. situational
27. fundamental attribution error
28. self-serving bias
29. primacy
30. stereotypes
31. self-fulfilling prophecy
32. Prejudice
33. in-groups
34. out-groups
35. outgroup homogencity
36. realistic conflict
37. social identity
38. kin selection
39. empathy-altruism
40. bystander effect
41. just world
42. frustration-aggression
43. self-justification
44. attribution of intentionality

Answer Key for Practice Test Multiple Choice Questions

1.	c	16.	c
2.	b	17.	c
3.	d	18.	c
4.	b	19.	a
5.	c	20.	b
6.	d	21.	d
7.	d	22.	d
8.	c	23.	a
9.	b	24.	c
10.	a	25.	b
11.	b	26.	a
12.	d	27.	b
13.	d	28.	c
14.	a	29.	b
15.	c	30.	a

Answer Key for Practice Test True/False Questions

1.	F	6.	T
2.	T	7.	T
3.	F	8.	F
4.	F	9.	F
5.	T	10.	T

Answer Key for Practice Test Short Answer Questions

1. Social facilitation is an increased tendency to perform one's dominant response in the mere presence of others. Social loafing is the tendency for people to expend less effort when working in groups than when working alone.

2. People conform because of both informational and normative social influence. When people conform because they believe others are right, informational social influence has occurred. When people conform because they want to be accepted by others, normative social influence has occurred.

3. Cognitive dissonance theory argues that people strive for consistency in their cognitions. When two or more cognitions contradict one another, people are motivated to change them so that they are consistent. Thus, cognitive dissonance motivates attitude and behavior change.

4. People tend to categorize the world into "in-groups," groups to which we feel we belong, and "out-groups," groups to which we don't feel that we belong. We tend to believe that the members of a given outgroup are quite similar to one another, which is called the outgroup homogeneity bias. Stereotypes are formed through this process. Exceptions to the stereotypes tend to be placed in a special subcategory so that we may maintain the stereotype.

5. Kin selection refers to the preference for helping others who share our genes.

Answer Key for Practice Test Essay Questions

1. Group polarization effects occur when the group's initial position becomes more extreme with discussion. Both normative and informational social influence play a role in the process. Groupthink occurs when groups suspend critical thinking when they are striving to seek agreement. Janis has proposed that groupthink occurs when a group is under high stress to make a decision, is insulated from outside input, has a directive leader who promotes his or her personal agenda, and has high cohesion.

2. Attitudes have been found to influence behaviors more strongly when counteracting situational factors are weak, when we are aware of them and when they are strongly held, and when general attitudes are used to predict general classes of behavior and specific attitudes are used to predict specific behaviors. According to the theory of planned behavior, behavioral intentions are predicted by subjective norms, attitudes toward the behavior, and perceptions of personal control.

3. The primacy effect refers to our tendency to attach more importance to the initial information that we learn about a person. Mental sets and schemas can bias what we perceive about another person. Self-fulfilling prophecies occur when our expectations about others lead us to act toward others in such a way that brings about the expected behaviors, thus confirming the original impression.

4. People are more likely to help when there is a close genetic connection with others. According to Darley and Latane's bystander intervention model, helping occurs when people notice a problem, decide it is an emergency, asssume responsibility to intervene, feel self-efficacy in dealing with the situation, and believe that the perceived costs of the situation should not prevent help. We are more likely to help people who are similar to us and when we believe that people's troubles are beyond their control. Women are more likely to receive help if the bystander is male.

5. People often use self-justification in their aggressive behavior by blaming victims for imagined wrongs. If we perceive that others have intentionally wronged us, we are more likely to aggress against them, as will a lack of empathy toward them. Finally, our ability to regulate our emotions influences our aggressive tendencies.

Chapter 13
PERSONALITY

Learning Objectives: *These questions, with a few additions (indicated with an asterisk), are taken from the directed questions found in the margins of the chapter. After reading the chapter, you should be able to answer these questions.*

1.   What two common observations give rise to our definition of personality?

1.1*   Define personality. What three characteristics do the behaviors associated with personality typically have?

2.   What three standards are used to evaluate the usefulness of a personality theory?

3.   Which clinical phenomena convinced Freud of the power of the unconscious mind?

3.1*   What methods did Freud use to uncover unconscious material?

4.   How did hydraulic systems of his time contribute to Freud's psychodynamic concepts?

4.1*   Differentiate between conscious, preconscious, and unconscious mental events. Be able to give an example of each.

5.   Discuss the roles of the pleasure principle, the reality principle, and identification in relation to Freud's three personality structures.

6.   Why is the ego sometimes referred to as the "executive of the personality?"

7.   How and why do defense mechanisms develop? What specific forms do they take?

8.   How does each of Freud's psychosexual stages contribute to adult personality?

8.1*   What is a major shortcoming of Freud's psychoanalytic theory?

9.   Describe how Shevrin et al. tried to establish the existence of unconscious psychodynamics. What were their findings?

10.   What are the major difficulties in testing psychoanalytic theory? What are the current status of unconscious processes and psychosexual development?

11.   Explain how the neoanalytic theorists Adler and Jung departed from Freudian theory. What is the focus of the object relations approach?

12.   What is meant by self-actualization? How does this concept conflict with Freud's conception of human nature?

13.   Describe the roles of self-consistency and congruence in Rogers's self theory. How do these concepts relate to adjustment?

14. How do conditions of worth develop and how can they hinder adjustment?

15. How do differences in self-esteem affect behavior? What conditions affect self-esteem development?

16. Define self-verification and self-enhancement. What research evidence is there to support these processes? Under what conditions are they pitted against one another?

17. What cultural and gender differences have been found in self-concept research?

17.1* What criticisms does the book present regarding humanistic theories of personalities?

17.2* What did Rogers' studies of the difference between the ideal self and the perceived self of psychotherapy clients reveal?

18 How is factor analysis based on correlation, and how is it used to identify personality traits?

19. What does *OCEAN* stand for in the five factor model?

20. What are the predictive advantages of (a) broad general traits and (b) narrow, specific ones? What's the research evidence?

21. In Eysenck's theory, what are the biological bases for individual differences in extraversion and stability.

22. What do twin studies suggest about the respective roles of (a) genetic factors, (b) family environment, and (c) individual environment in personality traits?

23. According to evolutionary theorists, what is the origin of the Big Five factors?

24. How does research evidence bear on the assumption of stability across time and across situations?

25. What three factors influence behavioral stability predicted from personality traits?

25.1* What challenges confront the trait approach to personality?

26. Describe Type A, Type B, and Type C personalities, as well as the risk factors inherent in the Type A and Type C patterns.

27. How do differences in optimism-pessimism and conscientiousness relate to health and longevity?

27.1* What is the social cognitive approach to personality? Name some prominent social cognitive theorists.

28. How does reciprocal determinism apply to Julia's personality pattern? Specify the two-way causal links.

29. Define expectancy and reinforcement value and explain how they influence behavior in Rotter's theory.

30. Describe Rotter's concept of locus of control and how it affects behavior.

31.   Define self-efficacy. What four sources of information influence efficacy beliefs?

32.   Summarize 6 principles of effective goal setting.

33.   Describe the 5 person variables that constitute the CAPS?

34.   What are behavioral signatures? How do they explain situational consistency and inconsistency in behavior?

34.1*   What are some strengths of the social cognitive approach to personality?

35.   How do the personality perspectives differ in terms of (a) the structure of personality, (b) major personality processes; (c) personality development, and (d) roots of maladjustment.

36.   Cite 6 methods that can be used to measure personality variables.

37.   What is a structured interview? What are its advantages over informal approaches?

38.   How are behavioral assessments designed, and what 3 questions are they designed to answer?

39.   Describe remote behavioral sampling procedures and the types of reports that can be collected.

40.   Contrast the rational and empirical approaches to personality test development. Give an example of a test developed by each approach.

41.   What is the assumption underlying projective tests? Describe two widely used projective tests.

42.   What kinds of personality measures are favored within the various perspectives?

Chapter Overview

What is Personality?

Personality refers to the relatively enduring and distinctive ways of thinking, feeling, and acting that characterize a person's responses to life situations.

The Psychodynamic Perspective

Freud believed strongly in the ideas of unconscious processes and psychic energy as motivators of behavior. Freud's structural theory of personality suggests that three interacting structures (id, ego, and superego) form the core of personality. The id operates according to the pleasure principle, seeking immediate gratification for its sexual and aggressive impulses. The ego, operating primarily at a conscious level, operates according to the reality principle, finding ways that the id can safely discharge its impulses. The superego is the moral arm of personality and strives to check the desires of the id. Freud believed that the interaction between all three structures of personality, along with the release of psychic energy not only motivated behavior but also could result in anxiety if the three structures of personality don't work together in harmony. Defense mechanisms such as repression are used by the ego to deal with anxiety. Freud also proposed a series of psychosexual stages through which children develop. Sexual pleasure is focused on different parts of the body during these stages (oral, anal, phallic, latency, and genital). Needless to say, Freud's theory has been controversial in the field of psychology. Much research does not support the basic suppositions of the theory, but some research does support the importance of the unconscious in motivating behavior. Former Freudian disciples who grew disenchanted with Freudian theory developed their own theories, and, as a group, they became known as the neoanalysts. These theorists suggested that social and cultural factors play a far more important role in the development of personality than Freud had believed and argued that Freud had placed too much importance on childhood events in his theory. Important neoanalysts include Jung and the object relations theorists, including Melanie Klein.

The Humanistic Perspective

Humanistic psychologists stress people's striving for self-actualization, the realization of one's potential. One of the most important theorists, Carl Rogers, believed that we have needs for self-consistency (in self-perceptions) and congruence (between self-perceptions and experience). Inconsistency creates threat and anxiety. Rogers believed that we are born with a need for positive regard from others and that conditional positive regard, which means that others give us approval only if we behave or think in ways that they approve of, can hurt us in a number of ways. Research on the self has pointed to the importance of self-esteem for healthy functioning. People try to self-verify their perceptions and engage in self-enhancement behaviors to develop their self-esteem.

Trait and Biological Perspectives

Two of the more prominent theories of traits are Cattell's sixteen personality factors theory and the five factor model, which, not surprisingly, argue that there are sixteen different personality factors and five different personality factors, respectively. Biological explanations for traits focus on three different causes: activity of the nervous system, genes, and evolution. Studies of brain activity have indicated some differences between introverts and extraverts. Twin studies have indicated that monozygotic twins are far more alike in personality than are dizygotic twins, suggesting a genetic basis of personality traits. Evolutionary personality theory suggests that traits developed throughout human history because they helped us to physically survive and because they aid in reproduction.

Social Cognitive Theories

Social cognitive theories, as the name would indicate, combine behavioral and cognitive theories in an attempt to understand behavior. According to Bandura's principle of reciprocal determinism, person factors (including personality and cognitive processes), the environment, and behavior all affect each other. Julian Rotter argued that the likelihood that we will engage in a certain behavior is governed by expectancy and how much we desire or dread the expected outcome of our behavior. Locus of control is a term that Rotter devised to refer to the degree to which we believe that internal or external factors control our behavior. Bandura has suggested that self-efficacy strongly affects how people regulate their lives. Performance experiences, observational learning, emotional arousal, and verbal persuasion all affect one's sense of self-efficacy. Mischel and Shoda have described a five person variable cognitive-affective personality system (CAPS). The interactions of these five factors result in distinctive behavioral signatures, which are consistent ways of responding to situations. These five factors are encoding strategies, expectancies and beliefs, goals and values, affects (emotions), and self-regulatory processes and competencies.

Personality Assessment

Personality assessment is accomplished through a number of means, including interviews, behavioral assessment, personality scales, and projective tests. In behavioral assessment, elaborate coding systems are used by psychologists in observing behaviors of interest. Objective personality scales, such as the Minnesota Multiphasic Personality Inventory follow the empirical approach to the study of personality. Projective tests, such as the Rorschach inkblot test and the Thematic Apperception Test are tests of interpretations of ambiguous stimuli. People's responses to the stimuli are thought by some psychologists to be "projections" of inner needs, feelings, and ways of viewing the world.

Chapter Outline

What is Personality?

The Psychodynamic Perspective
    Freud's Psychoanalytic Theory
        Psychic Energy and Mental Events
        The Structure of Personality
        Conflict, Anxiety, and Defense
        Psychosexual Development
        Research on Psychoanalytic Theory
        Research Close-Up: Using Neuropsychology to Study Unconscious Psychodynamics
        Evaluating Psychoanalytic Theory
        Freud's Legacy: Neoanalytic and Object Relations Approaches

The Humanistic Perspective
    Carl Rogers's Self Theory
        The Self
        The Need for Positive Regard
        Fully Functioning Persons
    Evaluating Humanistic Theories

Trait and Biological Perspectives
    Cattell's Sixteen Personality Factors
    The Five Factor Model
    Eysenck's Extraversion-Stability Model
    Traits and Behavior Prediction
    Biological Foundations of Personality Traits
        Personality and the Nervous System
        Behavior Genetics and Personality
        Evolutionary Approaches
    The Stability of Personality Traits
    Evaluating the Trait Approach
    Psychological Frontiers: Personality and Health

Social Cognitive Theories
     Julian Rotter: Expectancy, Reinforcement Value, and Locus of Control
         Locus of Control
     Albert Bandura: Social Learning and Self-Efficacy
         Self-Efficacy
     Applications of Psychological Science: Increasing Self-Efficacy Through Systematic Goal-Setting
     Walter Mischel and Yuichi Shoda: The Cognitive-Affective Personality System
         Encoding Strategies
         Expectancies and Beliefs
         Goals and Values
         Affects (Emotions)
         Self-Regulatory Processes and Competencies

Personality Assessment
     Interviews
     Behavioral Assessment
     Remote Behavior Sampling
     Personality Scales
     Projective Tests
         Rorschach Inkblots
         Thematic Apperception Test
     Personality Theory and Personality Assessment

Key Terms: *Write the letter of the definition next to the term in the space provided.*

What is Personality?
The Psychodynamic Perspective

1. ___ analytic psychology

    a. the distinctive and relatively enduring ways of thinking, feeling, and acting that characterize a person's responses to life situations

2. ___ archetypes

    b. powers the mind and constantly presses for direct or indirect release

3. ___ defense mechanisms

    c. the innermost core of the personality that is the source of all psychic energy

4. ___ ego

    d. the seeking of immediate gratification or release, regardless of reality

5. ___ Electra complex

    e. the part of personality that tests reality to decide how best to allow the id to satisfy its desires

6. ___ id

    f. the realization that id impulses should only be satisfied in societally appropriate ways

7. ___ object relations theories

    g. the moral part of the personality

8. ___ Oedipal complex

    h. strategies used by the ego to deny or to distort reality

9. ___ personality

    i. a defense mechanism by which the ego uses some of its energy to prevent anxiety-arousing memories, feelings, and impulses from entering consciousness

10. ___ pleasure principle

    j. a defense mechanism by which a repressed impulse is released in the form of a socially acceptable behavior

11. ___ psychic energy

12. ___ psychosexual stages

13. ___ reality principle

14. ___ repression
15. ___ sublimation
16. ___ superego

k. stages during which psychic energy is focused on particular erogenous zones of the body

l. consists of a boy's erotic feelings toward his mother, guilt, and castration anxiety

m. consists of a girl's erotic feelings toward her father, guilt, and anxiety

n. Jung's theory of personality

o. inherited tendencies to interpret experiences in certain ways

p. theories that focus on the images or mental representations that people form of themselves and other people as a result of early experience with caregivers

The Humanistic Perspective

1. ___ conditions of worth
2. ___ congruence

3. ___ fully functioning person
4. ___ gender schema
5. ___ need for positive regard

6. ___ need for positive self-regard
7. ___ self

8. ___ self-actualization
9. ___ self-consistency
10. ___ self-enhancement

11. ___ self-esteem
12. ___ self-verification

13. ___ threat
14. ___ unconditional positive regard

a. the total realization of one's human potential
b. an organized, consistent set of perceptions and beliefs about oneself

c. an absence of conflict among self-perceptions
d. consistency between self-perception and experience
e. evoked by any experience that is inconsistent with our self-concept

f. need for acceptance, sympathy, and love from others

g. communicates that love is independent of how the child behaves

h. wanting to feel good about ourselves
i. dictate when we approve or disapprove of ourselves
j. people who do not hide behind masks or adopt artificial roles

k. how positively or negatively we feel about ourselves
l. need to preserve self-concept by maintaining self-consistency and congruence

m. a tendency to gain and preserve a positive self-image
n. organized mental structures that contain our understanding of the attributes and behaviors that are appropriate and expected for males and females

Traits and Biological Perspectives
Social Cognitive Theories
Personality Assessment

1. ___ behavioral assessment

2. ___ behavioral signatures

3. ___ cognitive-affective personality system

a. a statistical tool that identifies clusters of correlated behaviors

b. theory that traits exist because of their historical aid in physical survival and reproduction

c. paying attention to situational cues and adapting behavior appropriately

4. ___ empirical approach

    d. a personality type of people who live under great pressure and are very demanding of themselves

5. ___ evolutionary personality theory

    e. a personality type that may be a risk factor for cancer

6. ___ factor analysis

    f. theory that stresses the interaction of thought and environmental influences

7. ___ internal-external locus of control

    g. principle that the person's behavior and the environment influence each other

8. ___ Minnesota Multiphasic Personality Inventory

    h. an expectancy concerning the degree of personal control we have in our lives

9. ___ rational approach

    i. beliefs concerning ability to perform behaviors needed to achieve desired outcomes

10. ___ reciprocal determinism

    j. an organization of five person factors that account for how a person might respond to a given situation

11. ___ remote behavioral sampling

    k. consistent ways of responding to particular classes of situations

12. ___ self-efficacy

    l. internal, self-administered rewards and punishments

13. ___ self-monitoring

    m. an observation of behaviors

14. ___ self-reinforcement processes

    n. self-reports of behavior from respondents' natural environments using "beeper" or computer prompts

15. ___ social cognitive theory

    o. creating items for a personality test based on a theorist's conception of a personality trait

16. ___ Type A personality

    p. choosing test items that are answered differently by groups that differ on the personality variable of interest

17. ___ Type C personality

    q. the most widely used personality inventory; based on the empirical approach

Review at a Glance: *Write the term that best fits the blank to review what you learned in this chapter.*

The Psychodynamic Perspective

According to Freud, instinctual drives generate (1) _____ _____, which powers the mind and presses for release. Freud divided the personality into three separate but interacting structures. The (2) _____ exists totally within the unconscious mind and operates according to the (3) _____ principle. The (4) _____ operates primarily at a conscious level, testing reality and trying to satisfy the id's desires in appropriate ways, according to the (5) _____ _____. The moral arm of personality is called the (6) _____. As the personality involves a dynamic interaction between all three personality structures, anxiety may occur if they do not work in harmony. The ego may resort to (7) _____ _____, which may distort reality when a person feels anxiety. For example, in (8) _____, the ego uses some of its energy to prevent anxiety-provoking memories, feelings, and impulses from entering consciousness. Another technique the ego uses is

(9) _____, by which the sinister underlying impulses are completely masked. Freud believed that much of adult personality structure is set during childhood. He proposed that children pass through five (10) _____ stages of development: oral, anal, phallic, latency, and genital. During the phallic stage, boys sexually desire their mothers but fear castration by their father, resulting in the (11) _____ _____, while girls similarly sexually desire their fathers but fear their mother's response, resulting in the (12) _____ _____. Successful resolution of these complexes leads to identification with the same-sex parent, according to Freud. Neo-Freudians, who broke away from Freudian theory, developed their own ideas about personality. Carl Jung developed his theory of (13) _____ psychology. Jung believed that all humans have a collective unconscious that consists of memories accumulated throughout the entire history of the human race. These memories are represented as (14) _____, inherited tendencies to interpret experiences in certain ways. (15) _____ _____ theorists believe that early experiences with caregivers influence the images that people form of themselves and of others.

The Humanistic Perspective

Humanistic psychologists believe that humans are motivated to realize their full potential, a process called (16) _____ _____. They believe that we have a tendency to maintain our self-concept after it is established and thus have a need for an absence of conflict among self-perceptions, or (17) _____ _____, and a need for consistency between self-perceptions and experience, or (18) _____. A prominent humanistic theorist, Carl Rogers, believed that we are born with an innate need for (19) _____ _____, that is, for acceptance, sympathy, and love from others. (20) _____ _____ _____ from parents communicates to the child that he or she is inherently worthy of love. However, when other people withhold approval unless an individual thinks or acts in a certain way, they have placed (21) _____ _____ _____ on that individual. People who had achieved self-actualization were called (22) _____ - _____ persons by Rogers. Research on the self has shown that how positively or negatively we feel about ourselves, or our sense of (23) _____ - _____ has important implications for our lives. The proposition that people are motivated to preserve their self-concept and maintain their self-consistency and congruence is called (24) _____ - _____. Processes used to gain and maintain a positive self-image are called (25) _____ - _____ activities.

Trait and Biological Perspectives

A statistical approach often used by trait theorists that identifies clusters of specific behaviors that are associated with one another so that they are seen as reflecting a basic trait on which people can vary is called (26) _____ _____. One of the most popular trait theories is called Big Five theory, which suggests that there are five major personality traits. The acronym (27) _____ can be used to remember the traits: Openness, Conscientiousness, Extraversion, Agreeableness, and Neuroticism. Eysenck believed that the factors of introversion-extraversion and stability-instability (neuroticism) underlie normal personality. Biological approaches have suggested that activity of the nervous system, genetics, and evolution all play a role in the development of personality traits. According to (28) _____ _____ theory, human personality traits have come to exist because of the role they play in both survival and reproduction.

Social Cognitive Theories

According to Bandura's principle of (29), _____ _____, the person, the person's behavior, and the environment all influence one another in a pattern of two-way causal links. Julian Rotter believed that a sense of personal control plays an important influence on our behaviors. People with an (30) _____ locus of control believe that they control their own behavior, while people with an (31) _____ locus of control believe that external factors control their behavior. Bandura also believed that people who believe that they have abilities to perform the behaviors needed to achieve desired outcomes have a good sense of (32) _____ - _____. Mischel and Shoda have developed a social cognitive model of personality called the (33) _____ - _____ _____ _____, or CAPS for short. The CAPS model suggests that encoding strategies, expectancies and beliefs, goals and values, affects, and personal competencies and self-regulatory processes affect behavior. As a result of interactions between the personality system and situations, people exhibit distinctive (34) _____ _____, which are outward manifestations of a person's identity.

Personality Assessment

There are many techniques used to assess personality. (35) _____ are particularly valuable for the direct personal contact established between researcher and respondent. In (36) _____ _____, psychologists use an explicit coding system to code the behaviors of interest. Through (37) _____ _____ _____, researchers and clinicians collect samples of behavior from respondents as they live their daily lives. Personality scales, such as the most widely used personality inventory, the (38) _____, are developed in two major ways. In the (39) _____ approach, items are based on the theorist's conception of the personality trait to be measured, while in the (40) _____ approach, items are chosen because previous research has shown that the items were answered differently by groups of people known to differ in the personality characteristic of interest. Tests that assume that when a person is presented with an ambiguous stimulus, his or her interpretation of it will indicate inner feelings, anxieties, or desires are called (41) _____ tests.

Apply What You Know

1. Using Study Sheet 13.1, rate both your actual and ideal characteristics. Using the principles of humanistic psychology, describe how you could move your "actual self" toward your "ideal self."

2. Describe how Rotter's principles of expectancy, reinforcement value, and locus of control can be used to change an undesirable behavior that you have.

3. Describe how you might use the Cognitive-Affective Personality System proposed by Mischel and Shoda to do the same thing.

Stretching Your Geographies

1. Why might traits predict behavior better in some cultures than in others?

Practice Test

Multiple Choice Items: *Please write the letter corresponding to your answer in the space to the left of each item.*

_____ 1. When confronted by potentially overwhelming urges, the ego may resort to what are called _____ in order to reject or distort reality and thus effectively reduce the anxiety that accompanies these urges.

    a. free associations
    b. subliminal psychodynamic activations
    c. archetypes
    d. defense mechanisms

_____ 2. During a conversation with a friend, Al starts to get angry but this is an emotion that he considers inappropriate and childish. As a result, instead of noticing his own anger, he unknowingly starts to believe that his friend is becoming angry and excited, even though she is doing no such thing. This example **best demonstrates** the defense mechanism of _____.

    a. reaction formation
    b. projection
    c. sublimation
    d. displacement

_____ 3. Freud speculated that someone who receives very lax toilet training during the anal stage of development will tend to be _____.

    a. a messy, pessimistic, and controlling adult
    b. an obsessive and orderly adult
    c. a talkative, orally-focused adult
    d. a well-adjusted, healthy adult

_____ 4. Neoanalytic theorists such as Alfred Adler and Carl Jung departed from traditional psychoanalytic theory in that they _____.

    a. were less optimistic than Freud regarding human nature
    b. assumed that personality is almost entirely shaped during childhood
    c. believed childhood sexuality needed to emphasized even more
    d. believed that Freud did **not** place enough emphasis on social and cultural factors

_____ 5. Bob thinks that he is a good tennis player and his results support this belief. His is better than almost all of the people in his tennis club and he wins most of his tennis matches. This agreement between Bob's beliefs and his actual experience would **best be considered** as an example of Carl Roger's concept of _____.

    a. self-actualization
    b. congruence
    c. self-consistency
    d. a condition of worth

_____ 6. Sarah has the belief that she is good in math, but she has just received her first D grade in her freshman calculus class. This inconsistency between Sarah's self-belief and her actual experience will most likely generate what Carl Rogers termed _____.

   a. self-actualization
   b. a condition of worth
   c. threat
   d. a need for unconditional self-regard

_____ 7. A person who is intellectural, imaginative, and has a broad range of interests would **mostly likely** score highly on a measure of _____.

   a. Openness
   b. Agreeableness
   c. Extraversion
   d. Conscientiousness

_____ 8. Research conducted with twins indicates that genetic factors appear to account for approximately _____ of the variation in traits while unique or individual environments account for about _____.

   a. 80-90%; 10-20%
   b. 20-30%; 20-30%
   c. 30-40%; 50-60%
   d. 40-50%; 40-50%

_____ 9. Greg doesn't think he has much of a chance of getting into his top choice for medical school. However, he still very much likes this school and desires very much to go there. Based on Rotter's concept of _____, we would expect Greg **not** to apply to this school while Rotter's concept of _____ suggests that Greg would apply to this school.

   a. internal locus of control; external locus of control
   b. expectancy; reinforcement value
   c. self-consistency; self-efficacy
   d. reinforcement value; self-efficacy

_____ 10. Ralph tends to be a rather passive person. Though he is happy and content with himself, he doesn't really believe that his actions make much of a difference in the word. For instance, he doesn't vote because he assumes that most governments are run by a few powerful people and there is very little he can do to change things. Ralph would **most accurately** be classified as having _____.

   a. low self-esteem
   b. high self-monitoring skills
   c. an external locus of control
   d. an internal locus of control

_____ 11. Steve is an athlete who always seems to perform well under pressure. When the heat is on, he knows that he has the skills needed to succeed and tends to experience an energized excitement that allows him to play his best. According to the CAPS model of personality, Steve's belief about his skills would be classified a(n)_____ while his energized excitement would be seen as a(n) _____.

    a. personal competency; affect
    b. expectation; value
    c. goals; value
    d. affect; encoding

_____ 12. When using _____ to assess personality and/or behaviors, researchers will create explicit coding systems that contain the particular behavioral categories in which they are interested.

    a. the interview method
    b. psychological tests
    c. the behavioral assessment method
    d. projective tests

_____ 13. The basic assumption underlying projective tests is that if you present someone with a(n) _____ stimulus, the interpretation for this stimulus will come from within and thus presumably represent or reflect their inner needs and feelings.

    a. sexual
    b. ambiguous
    c. psychodynamically meaningful
    d. provocative

_____ 14. According to Freud, the ego _____.

    a. is responsible for creating instincts
    b. operates according to the pleasure principle
    c. is created after the resolution of the Oedipal or Electra complexes
    d. operates according to the reality principle

_____ 15. The psychoanalytic term for unconscious methods by which the ego distorts reality, thereby protecting a person from anxiety is a(n) _____.

    a. catharsis
    b. defense mechanism
    c. extrinsic motivation
    d. competence motivation

_____ 16. Having had it drummed into her for years that sex is bad, bad, bad, Frig Id has a very uncomfortable and unhappy wedding night. Freud would probably suggest that the major reason for Frig's problems is that she has a _____.

a. very strong libido
b. very strong superego
c. lot of neurotic anxiety
d. strong defense mechanism

_____ 17. The idea that human beings, across cultures, may <u>unconsciously</u> share certain ideas such as the concept of "evil" is part of _____.

a. Jung's analytic psychology
b. Rogers's self theory
c. Rotter's social cognitive theory
d. Freud's structural model

_____ 18. <u>Eysenck's</u> trait theory includes all of the following dimensions of personality <u>except</u> _____.

a. introversion
b. neuroticism
c. agreeableness
d. psychoticism

_____ 19. In their Big 5 theory, Costa and McCrae (1988) have argued that there are five major personality factors. Of the following, the one which is <u>not</u> one of the Big 5 factors is _____.

a. neuroticism
b. extraversion
c. openness
d. dominance

_____ 20. Of the following, the person who is probably most <u>fully functioning</u> is a person who _____.

a. is worried about his performance
b. feels that she is free to realize her potential
c. dislikes trying new things
d. hates everyone

_____ 21. Of the following, the one which is an example of <u>conditional</u> positive regard is _____.

a. helping another person with a problem
b. trying to understand another person
c. a parent giving approval to a child only if the child brings home straight "A's"
d. a parent giving approval to a child regardless of what the child does

_____ 22. The personality dimension shared by both Eysenck's theory and Big 5 theory is _____.

a. introversion-extraversion
b. openness
c. dominance
d. psychoticism

_____ 23. How positively or negatively we feel about ourselves is called _____.

a. self-esteem
b. self-verification
c. self-enhancement
d. self-actualization

_____ 24. Personality traits exist in human beings today because they have historically aided in both survival and reproduction, according to _____ theory.

a. humanistic personality
b. Big 5
c. evolutionary personality
d. Cattell's sixteen personality factor

_____ 25. The personality trait that affects whether or not people tailor their behavior to what is called for by the situation is called _____.

a. self-verification
b. self-enhancement
c. self-actualization
d. self-monitoring

_____ 26. A personality type that may be related to the propensity to develop cancer is called _____.

a. Type A
b. Type B
c. Type C
d. Type D

_____ 27. According to Bandura's principle of reciprocal determinism, _____.

a. behavior determines personality but not vice-versa
b. personality determines behavior but not vice-versa
c. the environment does not affect behavior
d. the environment, person factors, and behavior all affect each other

_____ 28. Bandura has suggested that performance experiences, observational learning, emotional arousal, and verbal persuasion all affect _____.

a. locus of control
b. self-efficacy beliefs
c. the cognitive-affective personality system
d. self-actualization

_____ 29. Consistent ways of responding to particular classes of situations are called _____.

   a. CAPS
   b. loci of control
   c. behavioral signatures
   d. personalities

_____ 30. Ambiguous stimuli are used as part of _____.

   a. projective tests
   b. CAPS
   c. MMPI-2
   d. objective tests of personality

True/False Items: *Write T or F in the space provided to the left of each item.*

_____ 1. Personality is defined as the relatively enduring ways of thinking, feeling, and acting that characterize a person's response to life situations.

_____ 2. Freud believed that instincts generate psychic energy.

_____ 3. Freud believed that children are sexual beings.

_____ 4. Rogers believed that people are motivated for self-consistency but not for congruence.

_____ 5. Conditional positive regard communicates that a person is inherently worthy of love regardless of what he or she does.

_____ 6. Biological factors do not affect the development of personality traits.

_____ 7. The degree of behavioral consistency across situations is affected by how important a given trait is to a person.

_____ 8. Coronary heart disease has been associated with Type A personality.

_____ 9. Rotter argued that both expectancy and reinforcement value affect the likelihood that we will engage in a behavior.

_____ 10. Through remote behavior sampling, researchers and clinicians can collect samples of behavior from respondents as they live their daily lives.

Short Answer Questions

1. What were Freud's ideas about psychic energy and mental events?

2. What did Rogers argue about positive regard?

3. What are the Big Five factors in the five-factor model of personality?

4. What is locus of control?

5. What are projective tests used for?

Essay Questions

1. What were Freud's ideas on the structure of personality?

2. How do the neoanalytic and object relations theories differ from Freudian theory?

3. What are the biological foundations of personality traits?

4. What is the cognitive-affective personality system?

5. How are personality scales constructed?

Study Sheet 13.1
Real and Ideal Selves

Please rate both your actual self (your perception of yourself right now) and your ideal self (how you would like to be) by using the following scale:

1	2	3	4	5	6	7
poor						excellent

Actual _____ Ideal

_____ 1. Sensitivity

_____ 2. Body

_____ 3. Sense of humor

_____ 4. Weight

_____ 5. Friendliness

_____ 6. Face

_____ 7. Honesty

_____ 8. Smile

_____ 9. Being understanding

_____ 10. Chest

_____ 11. Patience

_____ 12. Legs

_____ 13. Being Outgoing

_____ 14. Eyes

_____ 15. Being caring

Answer Keys

Answer Key for Key Terms

What is Personality?
The Psychodynamic Perspective

1. n
2. o
3. h
4. e
5. m
6. c
7. p
8. l

9. a
10. d
11. b
12. k
13. f
14. i
15. j
16. g

The Humanistic Perspective

1. i
2. d
3. j
4. n
5. f
6. h
7. b

8. a
9. c
10. m
11. k
12. l
13. e
14. g

Trait and Biological Perspectives

1. m
2. k
3. j
4. p
5. b
6. a
7. h
8. q
9. o

10. g
11. n
12. i
13. c
14. l
15. f
16. d
17. e

Answer Key for Review at a Glance

1. psychic energy
2. id
3. pleasure
4. ego
5. reality principle
6. superego
7. defense mechanisms
8. repression
9. sublimation
10. psychosexual
11. Oedipus complex

22. fully-functioning
23. self-esteem
24. self-verification
25. self-enhancing
26. factor analysis
27. OCEAN
28. evolutionary personality
29. reciprocal determinism
30. internal
31. external
32. self-efficacy

12. Electra complex
13. analytic
14. archetypes
15. Object relations
16. self-actualization
17. self-consistency
18. congruence
19. positive regard
20. Unconditional positive regard
21. conditions of worth

33. cognitive-affective personality system
34. behavioral signatures
35. Interviews
36. behavioral assessment
37. remote behavior sampling
38. MMPI
39. rational
40. empirical
41. Projective

Answer Key for Practice Test Multiple Choice Questions

1. d
2. b
3. a
4. d
5. b
6. c
7. a
8. d
9. b
10. c
11. a
12. c
13. b
14. d
15. b

16. b
17. a
18. c
19. d
20. b
21. c
22. a
23. a
24. c
25. d
26. c
27. d
28. b
29. c
30. a

Answer Key for Practice Test True/False Questions

1. T
2. T
3. T
4. F
5. F

6. F
7. T
8. T
9. T
10. T

Answer Key for Practice Test Short Answer Questions

1. Freud believed that instincts created psychic energy, which powers the mind and presses for direct or indirect release.

2. Rogers believed that all of us are born with a need for positive regard, a need for acceptance, sympathy and love from others. A need for positive self-regard also develops, whereby we want to feel good about ourselves. Unconditional positive regard promotes our sense of well-being, while conditions of worth impede our development.

3. The five factors can be remembered through use of the acronym OCEAN: Openness, Conscientiousness, Extraversion, Agreeableness, and Neuroticism.

4. Locus of control refers to our expectancies of the degree of personal control we believe we believe we have over our behavior. People with an external locus of control believe that environmental circumstances control their behavior, while people with an internal locus of control believe that they have internal control over their own behavior.

5. Projective tests use ambiguous stimuli to help therapists and clients uncover unconscious aspects of their personalities.

Answer Key for Practice Test Essay Questions

1. Freud divided the personality into three separate but interacting structures: the id, the ego, and the superego. The id operates according to the pleasure principle, seeking immediate gratification, and is the source of all psychic energy. The ego has both unconscious and conscious aspects and seeks to satisfy the id's desires while dealing with environmental realities. Thus, the ego operates according to the reality principle. The superego is the moral arm of the personality and consists of values and ideals of society.

2. The neoanalysts, including Jung, Adler, Horney, Erikson, and Jung argued that Freud did not give social and cultural factors enough emphasis in his theories and that he stressed infantile sexuality and the events of childhood too much as explanations of adult personality. Object relationships theorists, in particular, focus on the images or mental representations that people form of themselves through interactions with caregivers. These images form "mental models" that influence their behavior.

3. Eysenck believed that differences in biological arousal within the brain underscores personality trait differences. Twin and adoption studies have conclusively shown that genetics play an important role in the development of traits. Evolutionary personality theory suggests that the traits we see in humans today exist because they have been historically useful in both survival and reproduction.

4. Mischel and Yoda have developed a model of personality called the cognitive-affective personality system (CAPS). They argue that five factors: encoding strategies, expectancies and beliefs, goals and values, affects, and personal competencies and self-regulatory processes interact with situational factors to produce distinctive behavioral signatures for each person. These behavioral signatures are consistent ways of responding to particular classes of situations.

5. Personality scales are constructed through two main approaches. In the rational approach, items are chosen for the test because of the way the theorist conceptualizes the trait. In the empirical approach, the items are chosen because they have previously been determined to distinguish those who have the trait from those who do not.

Chapter 14
PSYCHOLOGICAL DISORDERS

Learning Objectives: *These questions, with a few additions (indicated with an asterisk), are taken from the directed questions found in the margins of the chapter. After reading the chapter, you should be able to answer these questions.*

1.   Describe the demonological perspective on abnormal behavior and its implications for dealing with deviant behavior?

2.   What was the historical importance of discovering the cause of general paresis?

3.   What concepts are used by the psychodynamic, behavioral, cognitive, humanistic, and sociocultural perspectives to explain abnormal behavior?

4.   How does the vulnerability-stress model illustrate person-situation interactions?

5.   Cite the "three Ds" that typically underlie judgements that behavior is abnormal.

6.   What is meant by reliability and validity of diagnostic classification systems?

7.   How do the five axes of DSM-IV describe an individual's abnormal behavior and factors that may contribute to it or predict its future course?

8.   What effects do psychiatric labeling have on social- and self-perceptions?

9.   Differentiate between the legal concepts of competency and insanity. What is the current burden of proof in insanity hearings?

10.   Describe the three components of anxiety.

11.   What is a phobia, and what are the three major types of phobias?

12.   How does a generalized anxiety disorder differ from a phobic disorder?

13.   What occurs in a panic disorder, and how do these experiences frequently result in development of agoraphobia?

14.   Differentiate between obsessions and compulsions. How are they typically related to one another?

15.   Describe the four common features of PTSD.

16.   What evidence is there for a genetic predisposition to anxiety disorders. What form might the vulnerability factor take?

17. How might GABA be related to anxiety disorders? How might the biochemical factor in panic disorder be different?

18. What factors might produce the sex difference seen in the prevalence of the anxiety disorders?

19. How does psychoanalytic theory explain the development of anxiety disorders? What research support exists for these ideas?

20. How do cognitive factors enter into the anxiety disorders, particularly panic disorder? What research supports these explanations?

21. Explain anxiety disorders in terms of classical conditioning, negative reinforcement, and modeling influences.

22. Describe four culture-bound disorders that involve anxiety.

23. Differentiate between major depression and dysthymia.

24. Describe the four classes of symptoms that characterize (a) depression, and (b) mania.

25. How prevalent is depression in men and women? Why the difference? What is its course if left untreated, and it's likelihood of recurrence?

26. What evidence exists for a genetic factor in depression?

27. What biochemical processes might underlie depression? Mania?

28. What evidence is there to support the notion that early losses create a risk factor for later depression?

29. What might help explain the dramatic increase in depression among people born after 1960?

30. Describe (a) the cognitive triad and (b) the depressive attributional pattern described by Beck.

31. According to learned helplessness theory, what kinds of attributions trigger depression?

32. How does Lewinsohn's learning theory explain the spiraling course downward that occurs in depression?

33. How are cultural factors related to prevalence, manifestations, and sex differences in depression?

34. What is the relation between depression and suicide? What are the major motives and risk factors for suicide? Describe four practical guidelines for helping a suicidal person.

35. Describe three varieties of somatoform disorders. What causal factors might be involved in somatoform disorders?

36. What is the central feature of dissociative disorders? Describe the three major types of dissociative disorders.

37.   How does the trauma-dissociation theory account for the development of DID?

38.   On what grounds have critics questioned the validity of DID, and what explanations do they offer instead?

39.   What is meant by the term schizophrenia? What are the major cognitive, behavioral, emotional, and perceptual features of these disorders?

40.   Describe the four major types of schizophrenic disorders.

41.   Distinguish between Type I and Type II schizophrenia. How are positive and negative symptoms related to past history and future prognosis?

42.   Describe the evidence for genetic and neurological factors in schizophrenia?

43.   What is the dopamine hypothesis, and what evidence supports it?

44.   What concepts do (a) psychoanalytic and (b) cognitive theorists use to explain the symptoms of schizophrenia?

45.   How successful have researchers been in identifying family factors that cause schizophrenia? What role does expressed emotion play as a family variable?

46.   Contrast the social causation and social drift hypotheses concerning social class and prevalence of schizophrenia.

47.   Describe three important characteristics of the antisocial personality disorder.

48.   How are biological factors implicated in the antisocial personality disorder?

49.   How are classical conditioning and modeling concepts used to account for the development of antisocial personality disorder?

50.   Describe the psychological and physiological characteristics of the two types of battering men discovered by Jacobson and Gottman.

Chapter Overview

Historical Perspectives on Psychological Disorders

Ancient humans believed that abnormal behavior is caused by supernatural forces. Up until fairly recent history, people with psychological disorders were branded as witches and hunted down and often killed. Early biological views, such as those of the Greek physician Hippocrates, suggested that psychological disorders are diseases just like physical disorders. Early psychological theories focused on the use of psychoanalytic, behavioral, cognitive, and humanistic theories to explain abnormality. Today most clinical psychologists and counselors believe in the vulnerability/stress model, which suggests that biological, psychological, and environmental and sociocultural factors all play a role in the development of psychological disorders.

Defining and Classifying Psychological Disorders

Judgements about what an "abnormal" behavior is are often difficult to make and can vary from culture to culture and can change as societies develop. A current working definition for abnormal behavior is "behavior that is personally distressful, personally dysfunctional, and/or so culturally deviant that other people judge it to be inappropriate or maladaptive." The most widely used diagnostic system for classifying mental disorders in the United States is called the Diagnostic and Statistical Manual of Mental Disorders (DSM-IV). DSM-IV uses five axes (primary diagnosis, personality/developmental disorders, relevant physical disorders, severity of psychosocial stressors, and global assessment of functioning) to help clinicians understand disorders.

Anxiety Disorders

In anxiety disorders, the frequency and intensity of anxiety responses are out of proportion to the situations that trigger them, and the anxiety interferes with daily life. Anxiety disorders have cognitive, physiological, and behavioral components. Phobias are strong and irrational fears of certain objects or situations. Generalized anxiety disorder is a chronic state of anxiety (called 'free-floating') that is not attached to specific situations or objects. Panic disorders involve sudden and unpredictable anxiety that is extremely intense. Obsessive-compulsive disorder involves repetitive and unwelcome thoughts, images, and impulses and repetitive behavioral responses. People who have been exposed to traumatic live events may develop posttraumatic stress disorder. Biological factors including genetics, neurotransmitters, and evolutionary factors have all been implicated in the development of anxiety disorders. Psychological factors such as cognitive processes and learning also play important roles in the development of anxiety disorders, while sociocultural factors can also play a role.

Mood (Affective Disorders)

Depression involves emotional, cognitive, motivational, and somatic (body) symptoms. Major depression may lead people to be unable to function, while a less intense form of depression called dysthymia has less dramatic effects on personal functioning. Bipolar disorder involves both depression and periods of mania, which is a state of excited mood and behavior. Biological factors, including genetics and neurotransmitters play an important role in the development of mood disorders. Low levels of neurotransmitters such as serotonin, dopamine, and norepinephrine may be particularly likely to influence the development of mood disorders. Psychological factors including personality, cognitive processes, and learning also play roles. Sociocultural factors can affect the prevalence of depressive disorders and the ways in which depression is manifested.

Somatoform Disorders

Somatoform disorders involve physical complaints or disabilities that suggest a medical problem, but which have no known biological cause.

Dissociative Disorders

Dissociative disorders involve a breakdown of the normal integration of personality. These disorders include psychogenic amnesia, psychogenic fugue, and dissociative identity disorder, which used to be called multiple personality disorder. According to trauma-dissociation theory, dissociative disorders develop due to response to severe stress in a person's life.

Schizophrenia

Schizophrenia is a psychotic disorder that involves severe disturbances in thinking, speech, perception, emotion, and behavior. DSM-IV differentiates between four major types of schizophrenia: paranoid type, disorganized type, catatonic type, and undifferentiated type. Strong evidence exists for the role of genetic factors in the development of schizophrenia. Studies of the brain have shown that brain atrophy (a loss of neurons in the cerebral cortex) and overactivity of the dopamine system may play roles in the development of schizophrenia. Psychological factors such as family dynamics and a high level of expressed emotion (high levels of criticism, hostility, and overinvolvement) may also play a role. Studies of sociocultural factors have indicated that the prevalence of schizophrenia is highest in lower socioeconomic populations.

Personality Disorders

People diagnosed with personality disorders exhibit stable, ingrained, inflexible, and maladaptive ways of thinking, feeling, and behaving. Studies of people with antisocial personality disorder have focused on the role of genetics and psychological factors such as classical conditioning and modeling to understand the development of that disorder.

Chapter Outline

Historical Perspectives on Psychological Disorders
  The Demonological View
  Early Biological Views
  Psychological Perspectives
      Today's Vulnerability Stress Model

Defining and Classifying Psychological Disorders
  What is "Abnormal?"
  Diagnosing Psychological Disorders
  Critical Issues in Diagnostic Labeling
      Social and Personal Implications
      Legal Consequences
      "Do I Have That Disorder?"

Anxiety Disorders
  Phobic Disorder
  Generalized Anxiety Disorder
  Panic Disorder
  Obsessive-Compulsive Disorder
  Posttraumatic Stress Disorder
  Causal Factors in the Anxiety Disorders
      Biological Factors
      Psychological Factors
          Psychodynamic theories
          Cognitive factors
          Anxiety as a learned response
      Sociocultural Factors

Mood (Affective) Disorders
    Depression
    Biopolar Disorder
    Prevalence and Course of Mood Disorders
    Causal Factors in Mood Disorders
        Biological Factors
        Psychological Factors
            Personality-based vulnerability
            Cognitive processes
            Learning and environmental factors
        Sociocultural Factors
        Applications of Psychological Science:Understanding and Preventing Suicide

Somatoform Disorders

Dissociative Disorders
    Psychological Frontiers: Dissociative Identity Disorder: A Clinical and Scientific Puzzle

Schizophrenia
    Characteristics of Schizophrenia
    Subtypes of Schizophrenia
    Causal Factors in Schizophrenia
        Biological Factors
        Psychological Factors
        Environmental Factors
        Sociocultural Factors

Personality Disorders
    Antisocial Personality Disorder
    Causal Factors
        Biological Factors
        Psychological and Environmental Factors
    Research Close-Up: Personality Disorders in Men Who Batter Women

Key Terms: *Write the letter of the definition next to the term in the space provided.*

Historical Perspectives on Psychological Disorders
Defining and Classifying Psychological Disorders

1. ___ abnormal behavior

    a. stresses that each of us have some degree of vulnerability to develop a psychological disorder, given sufficient stress

2. ___ competency
3. ___ insanity
4. ___ reliability

    b. predisposition to a disorder
    c. some recent or current event that requires a person to cope
    d. behavior that is personally distressful, personally dysfunctional, and/or so culturally deviant that other people judge it to be inappropriate or maladaptive

5. ___ stressor
6. ___ validity

    e. high levels of agreement in diagnostic decisions
    f. when diagnostic categories accurately capture the essential features of the various disorders

7. ___ vulnerability

g. refers to a defendant's state of mind at the time of a judicial hearing by which a person is judged as to his or her ability to understand the nature of the proceedings

8. ___ vulnerability-stress model

h. a legal judgement that a person was so severely impaired during the commission of a crime that they lacked the capacity to appreciate the wrongfulness of their acts or to control their conduct

Anxiety Disorders
Mood (Affective) Disorders

1. ___ agoraphobia

a. disorder in which the frequency and intensity of anxiety responses are out of proportion to the situations that trigger them

2. ___ anxiety

b. state of tension and apprehension

3. ___ anxiety disorder

c. strong and irrational fears of certain objects or situations

4. ___ biological preparedness

d. fear of public places and open areas

5. ___ bipolar disorder

e. excessive fear of situations in which a person might be evaluated and embarrassed

6. ___ compulsions

f. fears of specific stimuli

7. ___ culture-bound disorder

g. a chronic state of "free-floating" anxiety

8. ___ depressive triad

h. sudden, unpredictable, and intense anxiety

9. ___ dysthymia

i. disorders consisting of repetitive uncontrollable thoughts and behaviors

10. ___ generalized anxiety disorder

j. repetitive and unwelcome thoughts, images, or impulses that invade consciousness

11. ___ learned helplessness theory

k. repetitive behavioral responses

12. ___ major depression

l. a disorder in which a person experiences severe anxiety, flashbacks, numbness, and guilt

13. ___ mania

m. evolution makes it easier for us to learn to fear certain stimuli

14. ___ mood disorder

n. occurs when unacceptable impulses threaten to overwhelm the ego's defenses

15. ___ neurotic anxiety

o. disorder that only occurs in certain places

16. ___ obsessions

p. emotion-based disorders involving depression or mania

17. ___ obsessive-compulsive disorder

q. a type of depression that leaves people unable to function effectively in their lives

18. ___ panic disorder

r. a less intense form of depression that has less dramatic effects on personal and occupational functioning

19. ___ phobias

s. a disorder in which depression alternates with periods of mania

20. ___ posttraumatic stress disorder

t. a state of highly excited mood and behavior

21. ___ social phobia

u. theory that holds that depression occurs when people expect that bad events will occur and that prevention and coping are impossible

22. ___ specific phobia

v. the willful taking of one's own life

23. ____ suicide

w. a cognitive triad of negative thoughts concerning the world, oneself, and the future

Somatoform Disorders
Dissociative Disorders
Schizophrenia
Personality Disorders

1. ____ catatonic type

a. disorder that suggests a medical problem but has no known biological cause

2. ____ conversion disorder

b. disorder in which people become unduly alarmed about symptoms and are concerned that they will have a serious illness

3. ____ delusions

c. disorder in which people experience intense pain that is out of proportion to the medical condition they have or for which no physical basis can be found

4. ____ disorganized type

d. a somatoform disorder in which serious neurological symptoms suddenly occur with no apparent physical cause

5. ____ dissociative disorders

e. disorders that involve a breakdown of the normal integration of facets of the self

6. ____ dissociative identity disorder

f. a person responds to a stressful event with extensive but selective memory loss

7. ____ dopamine hypothesis

g. a dissociative disorder in which a person loses all sense of personal identity

8. ____ expressed emotion

h. a disorder in which two or more separate personalities coexist within the same person

9. ____ hallucinations

i. theory that the development of new personalities occurs in response to severe stress

10. ____ hypochondriasis

j. a psychotic disorder that involves severe disturbances in thinking, speech, perception, emotion, and behavior

11. ____ negative symptoms
k. false beliefs

12. ____ pain disorder
l. false perceptions

13. ____ paranoid type

m. type of schizophrenia that prominently features delusions of persecution and grandeur

14. ____ personality disorder

n. type of schizophrenia that features confusion, incoherence, and severe deterioration of adaptive behavior

15. ____ positive symptoms

o. type of schizophrenia that features striking motor disturbances

16. ____ psychogenic amnesia

p. type of schizophrenia in which people exhibit some schizophrenic symptoms but not enough to be diagnosed into a particular category

17. ____ psychogenic fugue

q. type of schizophrenia that is characterized by positive symptoms

18. ____ regression

r. delusions, hallucinations, and disorganized speech and thinking

19. ____ schizophrenia
s. type of schizophrenia that features negative symptoms

20. ____ somatoform disorder
t. normal reactions that seem to be missing

21. ___ trauma-dissociation theory
22. ___ Type I schizophrenia
23. ___ Type II schizophrenia

24. ___ undifferentiated type

u. hypothesis that the symptoms of schizophrenia are produced by overactivity of the dopamine system
v. a retreat to an earlier stage of psychosocial development
w. involves high levels of criticism, hostility, and overinvolvement
x. disorders in which people exhibit stable, ingrained, inflexible, and maladaptive ways of thinking, feeling, and behaving

Review at a Glance: *Write the term that best fits the blank to review what you learned in this chapter.*

Historical Perspectives on Psychological Disorders

The belief that abnormal behavior is caused by supernatural forces is called the (1) _____ view. Early biological views stressed that psychological disorders have the same causes as physical diseases. In today's (2) _____ - _____ model, each and every one of us has some degree of vulnerability for the development of a particular psychological disorder.

Defining and Classifying Psychological Disorders

When diagnosing psychological disorders, clinicians must use criteria that is both valid and reliable. (3) _____ means that clinicians using the system should show high levels of agreement in their diagnostic decisions, while (4) _____ means that the diagnostic categories should capture the essential featurs of the various disorders. The most widely used classification system in the United States is called (5) _____. Psychiatric diagnoses can have important legal consequences. A defendant's state of mind at the time of a judicial hearing is called his or her (6) _____. The presumed state of mind of a defendant at the time the crime was committed is determined in the legal (not psychological) determination of (7) _____.

Anxiety Disorders

Strong and irrational fears of certain objects or situations are called (8) _____. Fear of public spaces is called (9) _____; excessive fear of situations in which the person might be evaluated and possibly embarrassed is called (10) _____ phobia. Fears of dogs, snakes, spiders, airplanes and other objects are called (11) _____ phobias. When a person experiences a chronic state of "free-floating" anxiety that is not tied to any specific thing, that person is diagnosed with (12) _____ _____ disorder. Sudden, unpredictable, and intense anxiety is a symptom of (13) _____ _____. Repetitive, unwelcome thoughts images, or impulses that invade consciousness are called (14) _____, while repetitive behavioral responses are called (15) _____. When a person suffers from both, he or she is diagnosed as having (16) _____ - _____ disorder. People who have been exposed to traumatic live events may experience (17) _____ - _____ _____ disorder. The search for biological processes associated with anxiety disorders have pointed to abnormally low levels of the neurotransmitter (18) _____. According to Freudian psychodynamic theory,

(19) _____ anxiety occurs when unacceptable impulses threaten to overwhelm the ego's defenses. Social and cultural factors likely also play a role in the development of anxiety. Certain disorders that only occur in certain places are called (20) _____ - _____ disorders.

Mood (Affective) Disorders

A type of depression that leaves people unable to function effectively in their lives is called (21) _____ depression. A less intense form of depression is called (22) _____. In (23) _____ _____, periods of depression alternate with periods of (24) _____, a state of highly excited mood and behavior. A cognitive explanation of depression known as (25) _____ _____ theory suggests that depression occurs when people expect that bad events will occur and that there is nothing that they can do to prevent or cope with them.

Somatoform Disorders

In (26) _____, people notice and become unduly alarmed about any symptom they detect. People with (27) _____ disorder experience pain that is out of proportion to their medical condition or for which no physical problem can be found.
(28) _____ disorder is diagnosed for people in which serious neurological symptoms occur for no physical reason.

Dissociative Disorders

Dissociative disorders involve a breakdown of the normal integration of personality. In (29) _____ _____, a person responds to a stressful event with extensive but selective memory loss. (30) _____ _____ involves a loss of personal identity and the establishment of a new identity in a new location. A disorder formerly known as multiple personality disorder is known in DSM-IV as (31) _____ _____ disorder. An explanation of this disorder called (32) _____ - _____ theory suggests that the development of new personalities occurs in response to severe stress.

Schizophrenia

Schizophrenics sometimes have (33) _____, false beliefs that are sustained in the face of evidence to the contrary and (34) _____, false perceptions that have a compelling sense of reality. There are several types of schizophrenia. Delusions of persecution and grandeur are features of the (35) _____ type. Confusion, incoherence, and severe deterioration of adaptive behavior are characteristic of the (36) _____ type. The (37) _____ type involves striking motor disturbances. A predominance of positive symptoms is present in (38) _____ schizophrenia, while a predominance of negative symptoms occurs in (39) _____ schizophrenia. Schizophrenia is thought to have a biological basis, including the influence of genetic factors. Other researchers believe that an excess of the neurotransmitter (40) _____ is a cause of schizophrenia. Environmental factors may also play a role in the development of the disorder. Schizophrenics are more likely to relapse after treatment if they return to a home with a high degree of (41) _____ _____.

Personality Disorders

People with (42) _____ _____ disorder seem to lack a conscience.

Apply What You Know

1. Go to the web site "News of the Weird" at http://www.newsoftheweird.com and find three cases of behaviors that you would consider to be abnormal. Using the criteria for what an abnormal behavior is, explain why each behavior is "abnormal."

Stretching Your Geographies

1. Women are generally about twice as likely than men to suffer from both anxiety and mood disorders. Research the prevalence rates for both sets of disorders in the United States. Using what you have learned about biological, psychological, and environmental factors in the development of disorders, explain why you think this difference occurs.

2. "Abnormality" is a somewhat relative concept. Do some research to find five behaviors that are considered normal in U.S. culture but are considered abnormal in other cultures.

Practice Test

Multiple Choice Items: *Please write the letter corresponding to your answer in the space to the left of each item.*

_____ 1. A recent immigrant to the United States has been having some problems in living and after some initial hesitation, decides to see a therapist for some assistance. After the interview, the therapist makes a particular diagnosis and is discussing the case with a colleague when the colleague raises some concerns. She points out that the therapist may need to reconsider his diagnosis because the behaviors involved are much more common and are even considered "normal" in the country from which the person came. The views of the colleague are **most consistent** with the _____ perspective on psychological disorders.

    a. sociocultural
    b. behavioral
    c. biological
    d. cognitive

_____ 2. Sara lost both of her parents when she was a young child. Primarily because of this historical factor, she develops an anxiety disorder when she learns that the life of her best friend is threatened by cancer. This example provides the **best illustration** of _____.

    a. learned helplessness
    b. the vulnerability-stress model
    c. the demonological perspective
    d. the trauma dissociation model

_____ 3. During a psychological assessment, a client shares that she just lost her job and recently ended a long-term romantic relationship. Such information would be recorded on Axis _____ by the psychologist using the DSM-IV.

    a. I
    b. II
    c. III
    d. IV

_____ 4. When considering the term insanity, it is important to remember that _____.

    a. it is an Axis II disorder that has substantial overlap with other Axis I and II disorders
    b. while it has strong reliability, its validity has not yet been fully established
    c. it refers to a defendant's state of mind at the time of a trial, not when the crime was committed
    d. it is a legal term, not a psychological term

_____ 5. Roger is tense and anxious almost everyday. Though he is frequently worried and often has the sense that something bad is about to happen, he can't relate his anxiety to any particular situation or setting. He has difficulty getting restful sleep at night and often takes antacids for his upset stomach. Roger would **most likely** be diagnosed as having _____.

a. social phobia
b. an environmental or situational phobia
c. generalized anxiety disorder
d. post traumatic stress disorder

_____ 6. Annette is very afraid of germs and disease, so much so that she washes her hands over 100 times a day to make sure that she can avoid infection. Usually she doesn't show much anxiety but if she is in a place where she is unable to clean her hands, such as the wilderness, she can become very distressed and upset. Annette would most likely be diagnosed as having _____.

a. obsessive-compulsive disorder
b. schizophrenia paranoid type
c. generalized anxiety
d. a health-related phobia

_____ 7. Research conducted with people suffering from panic disorder has revealed that these individuals may possess an abnormal sensitivity to _____ that can trigger increased brain activity in the _____ brain hemisphere areas involved in negative emotional expression.

a. dopamine; right
b. GABA; left
c. lactic acid, right
d. epinephrine; left

_____ 8. Steve has a rather strong fear of social situations. He used to try to go to parties and other social events but his anxiety would usually overwhelm him. When experiencing these negative emotions, he would often leave parties early, a behavior that allowed him to reduce or eliminate his anxiety. According to the principles of operant conditioning, Steve's escape behavior is being _____ and this means that it will be more likely to occur in the future.

a. positively reinforced
b. negatively reinforced
c. aversively punished
d. response-cost punished

_____ 9. A person with a euphoric mood, a decreased need for sleep, and grandiose or exaggerated cognitions would **most likely** be diagnosed as having _____.

a. psychogenic fugue
b. schizophrenia
c. major depression
d. mania

_____ 10. Twin studies suggest that approximately _____ of the variation in clinical depression can be accounted for by genetic factors.

a. 10%
b. 50%
c. 67%
d. 80%

_____ 11. Martin Seligman has theorized that an increased focus on individuality and personal control and a loss of interest in traditional family and religious values have combined to produce a dramatic increase in _____ since 1960.

a. dissociative identity disorder
b. schizophrenia
c. anxiety disorders
d. depression

_____ 12. Jane has recently managed to earn a spot on her highly competitive high school basketball team. Research on psychological disorders suggests that if Jane is depressed, she will attribute her success to _____ while if she is not depressed, she will most likely attribute her achievement to _____.

a. external factors; external factors as well
b. external factors; personal factors
c. personal factors; external factors
d. personal factors; personal factors as well

_____ 13. All of the following are different types of somatoform disorders except _____.

a. conversion disorder
b. psychogenic fugue
c. hypochondriasis
d. pain disorder

_____ 14. After surviving a particularly violent tornado, Dean experiences a selective memory loss for specific traumatic events that occurred just before and during the disaster. Other than these specific memory losses, Dean's personality and subjective sense of identity are essentially unchanged. Dean is **most likely** to be diagnosed with _____.

a. psychogenic fugue
b. dissociative identity disorder
c. schizophrenia, disorganized type
d. psychogenic amnesia

_____ 15. Aaron has been diagnosed with schizophrenia. He appears to be confused most of the time and it is very difficult to communicate with him because it is often hard to understand exactly what he means. He frequently acts childlike and also displays inappropriate affect, such as the time that he laughed throughout the funeral of his uncle. Aaron would **most likely** be diagnosed with the _____ type of schizophrenia.

a. paranoid
b. undifferentiated
c. disorganized
d. catatonic

_____ 16. Many Vietnam veterans came back from the war suffering from a great deal of stress and anxiety. Psychiatrists would likely note that the stressful episodes the soldiers encountered during the war contribute to their current concerns about anxiety. The disorder that most approximates the problems of these soldiers is known as _____.

a. posttraumatic stress disorder
b. borderline personality disorder
c. schizotypal personality disorder
d. panic disorder

_____ 17. Constantly subjected to stress because he just can't catch that cursed roadrunner, apparently suffering from malnutrition because he spends all of his money on elaborate gadgets from the Acme company to catch the bird instead of spending it on food at the Canyon Wal-Mart Supercenter, and in constant pain from falling off cliffs and having anvils land on his head, Wile E. Coyote comes to have a sense of a lack of control over his life. Seligman (1975) would say that Wile E. is suffering from _____.

a. dysthymia
b. bipolar disorder
c. an internal locus of control
d. learned helplessness

_____ 18. In July, 1998, James P. Morrow, a recent resident of an Ohio penitentiary, filed a lawsuit in Dayton against Gov. George Voinovich and 300 other officials because they allegedly tried to "beam" security people down to confront Morrow every time he entered a courthouse. According to Morrow's petition, the only way he could bypass such beaming is if the court granted him "Wallydraggle, Mummery Feg Winple Soupcon-type relief." Copyright 1998 by Universal Press Syndicate.

Mr. Morrow seems to be suffering from _____, and the most likely diagnosis for his bizarre behavior would be _____.

a. dysthymia; dissociative identity disorder
b. a catatonic state; catatonic schizoprenia
c. delusions; paranoid schizophrenia
d. hallucinations; borderline personality disorder

_____ 19. Symptoms of schizophrenia include all of the following <u>except</u> _____.

    a. delusions of grandeur (false beliefs that a person is famous)
    b. disturbances of affect
    c. distortions of perception
    d. multiple personalities

_____ 20. Santa, trying to hurry through his rounds this Christmas Eve so that he can hurry home and get some home-cooked lovin' from Mrs. Claus, worries about staying clean because of all of those leaps down people's dirty chimneys. He also worries about smelling bad for Mrs. Claus because of all of the time he's spending around those reindeer. Thus, in every house that Santa delivers presents he takes a shower and helps himself to some cologne. If this behavior persists in Santa's daily life over the next year, Dr. Jack Frost is likely to diagnose Santa as having _____.

    a. generalized anxiety disorder
    b. obsessive-compulsive disorder
    c. a panic disorder
    d. bipolar depression

_____ 21. People with multiple personalities, such as Eve White (Eve Black, Jane), the subject of the movie "The Three Faces of Eve," are said to have _____.

    a. dissociative amnesia
    b. dissociative fugue
    c. dissociative identity disorder
    d. schizophrenia

_____ 22. The Grinch regularly steals everyone's Christmas presents, puts the stockings on his own feet, tells impressionable children that department store Santas aren't actually the real thing, rips decorations off of Christmas trees, and buys up all the local Christmas turkeys to use in place of bowling balls on his weekly bowling night. During all of these escapades, the Grinch feels no remorse whatsoever for his actions, despite the angry mobs that descend on his humble abode. We might most likely diagnose the Grinch as suffering from _____.

    a. catatonic schizophrenia
    b. residual schizophrenia
    c. obsessive-compulsive disorder
    d. antisocial personality disorder

_____ 23. When clinicians agree in their diagnostic decisions, _____ has been established.

    a. validity
    b. reliability
    c. DSM-IV
    d. Axis V of DSM-IV

_____ 24. Insanity is _____.

a. a legal definition
b. a term that refers to the defendant's state of mind at the time of a judicial hearing
c. the same thing as competency
d. a type of dissociative disorder

_____ 25. A fear of public spaces is called _____.

a. social phobia
b. specific phobia
c. generalized anxiety disorder
d. agoraphobia

_____ 26. According to Freud, neurotic anxiety occurs when _____.

a. the ego uses defense mechanisms
b. unacceptable impulses threaten to overwhelm the ego's defenses
c. a child reaches the oral stage of psychosexual development
d. a person experiences a panic attack

_____ 27. Loss of interest in normal daily activities is considered a _____ symptom of depression.

a. emotional
b. cognitive
c. motivational
d. somatic

_____ 28. Beck's depressive triad of negative thoughts concerns all of the following except _____.

a. the world
b. oneself
c. the future
d. perceptions of a strong self of self-efficacy

_____ 29. The most popular current theory for explaining dissociative disorders is called _____ theory.

a. trauma-dissociation
b. DID
c. Type I
d. Type II

_____ 30. Back in the 1970's, Texas Ranger pitcher Rogelio Moret suddenly became extremely rigid, not moving a muscle, one day in spring training. Moret was subsequently found to have schizophrenia and had to retire from baseball. Based on these symptoms, you would expect that Moret was diagnosed with _____ schizophrenia.

a. paranoid
b. disorganized
c. catatonic
d. undifferentiated

True/False Items: *Write T or F in the space provided to the left of each item.*

_____ 1. According to the demonological view, psychological disorders are diseases just like physical disorders.

_____ 2. Reliability means that the diagnostic categories accurately capture the essential features of the various disorders.

_____ 3. Competency refers to a defendant's state of mind at the time of a judicial hearing.

_____ 4. A fear of riding in airplanes would be a type of specific phobia.

_____ 5. The mood disorders involve depression and mania.

_____ 6. Conversion disorder is a type of dissociative disorder.

_____ 7. In psychogenic amnesia, a person develops multiple personalities.

_____ 8. Hallucinations are false perceptions.

_____ 9. Type I schizophrenia is characterized by negative symptoms.

_____ 10. There is no evidence for a biological basis for schizophrenia.

Short Answer Questions

1. What does the vulnerability-stress model argue?

2. What is "insanity?"

3. How is anxiety a learned response?

4. What are the differences between the three major types of mood disorders?

5. What are the main characteristics of schizophrenia?

Essay Questions

1. What is "abnormal?"

2. What are the psychological factors involved in causing anxiety disorders?

3. What biological factors cause mood disorders?

4. Describe the subtypes of schizophrenia.

5. What are the causal factors in schizophrenia?

Answer Keys

Answer Key for Key Terms

Historical Perspectives on Psychological Disorders
Defining and Classifying Psychological Disorders

1.	d	5.	c
2.	g	6.	f
3.	h	7.	b
4.	e	8.	a

Anxiety Disorders
Mood (Affective) Disorders

1.	d	13.	t
2.	b	14.	p
3.	a	15.	n
4.	m	16.	j
5.	s	17.	i
6.	k	18.	h
7.	o	19.	c
8.	w	20.	l
9.	r	21.	e
10.	g	22.	f
11.	u	23.	v
12.	q		

Somatoform Disorders
Dissociative Disorders
Schizophrenia
Personality Disorders

1.	o	13.	m
2.	d	14.	x
3.	k	15.	r
4.	n	16.	f
5.	e	17.	g
6.	h	18.	v
7.	u	19.	j
8.	w	20.	a
9.	l	21.	i
10.	b	22.	q
11.	t	23.	s
12.	c	24.	p

Answer Key for Review at a Glance

1. demonological
2. vulnerability-stress
3. Reliability
4. validity
5. DSM-IV
6. competency
7. insanity
8. phobias
9. agoraphobia
10. social
11. specific
12. generalized anxiety
13. panic disorder
14. obsessions
15. compulsions
16. obsessive-compulsive
17. post-traumatic stress
18. GABA
19. neurotic
20. culture-bound
21. major
22. dysthymia
23. bipolar disorder
24. mania
25. learned helplessness
26. hypochondriasis
27. pain
28. conversion
29. psychogenic amnesia
30. Psychogenic fugue
31. dissociative identity
32. trauma-dissociation
33. delusions
34. hallucinations
35. paranoid
36. disorganized
37. catatonic
38. Type I
39. Type II
40. dopamine
41. expressed emotion
42. antisocial personality

Answer Key for Practice Test Multiple Choice Questions

1. a
2. b
3. d
4. d
5. c
6. a
7. c
8. b
9. d
10. c
11. d
12. b
13. b
14. d
15. b
16. a
17. d
18. c
19. d
20. b
21. c
22. d
23. b
24. a
25. d
26. b
27. c
28. d
29. a
30. c

Answer Key for Practice Test True/False Questions

1. F
2. F
3. T
4. T
5. T

6. F
7. F
8. T
9. F
10. F

Answer Key for Practice Test Short Answer Questions

1. The vulnerability-stress model suggests that each of us has some degree of vulnerability for the development of a psychological disorder. The vulnerability may have a biological basis, such as genetics, a brain abnormality, or a hormonal factor. Personality factors, such as low self-esteem or pessimism, may also increase vulnerability. Finally, sociocultural factors can also increase vulnerability. Vulnerability combines with an experience with a stressor or stressors to trigger the appearance of a disorder.

2. "Insanity" is a legal rather than a psychological or psychiatric definition. It refers to the presumed state of mind of a defendant *at the time of a judicial hearing*.

3. From the behavioral perspective, anxiety disorders develop because of conditioning processes. For example, phobic reactions may occur because of associating a specific object or event (CS) with pain and trauma (UCS), producing a fear response. Phobias can also be acquired through observation (modeling). Finally, behaviors that produce anxiety reduction are negatively reinforced, which is an aspect of operant conditioning.

4. Major depression is a disorder that leaves people unable to function effectively in their lives. Dysthymia is a milder form of mood disorder which has less severe effects. Bipolar disorder is a disorder in which periods of depression alternate with periods of mania, a state of highly excited mood and behavior.

5. Schizophrenia is a psychotic disorder that involves severe disturbances in thinking, speech, perception, emotion, and behavior. It is characterized by delusions, hallucinations, disorganized speech and thought, and inappropriate, blunter, or flat affect.

Answer Key for Practice Test Essay Questions

1. Decisions about what behaviors are "abnormal" are surprisingly difficult to make. Most psychologists and psychiatrists would agree to examine the three "D's" in determining whether a behavior should be considered abnormal. Behaviors that are distressing to self or others, deviant (i.e. violate social norms), and dysfunctional (for person and/or society) are considered to be abnormal. If only one or two of the "D's" are present, judgements of abnormality are less likely.

2. According to Freud, neurotic anxiety occurs when unacceptable impulses threaten to overwhelm the ego's defenses. Cognitive theorists stress the role of maladaptive thought patterns in anxiety disorders. As mentioned in the answer to question #3 above, anxiety can be a learned response.

3. Both genetic and neurochemical factors have been linked to depression. Twin studies have shown that MZ twins have concordance rates of up to 67% for experiencing clinical (major) depression. Low levels of neurotransmitters such as serotonin, dopamine, and norepinephrine have also been found to be associated with mood disorders. One theory holds that when a person experiences low levels of these neurotransmitters, the brain regions responsible for reward and pleasure are not stimulated. Many drugs that treat mood disorders work by increasing neurotransmitter levels.

4. The paranoid type of schizophrenia is characterized by delusions of persecution and grandeur. Suspicions and anxiety often accompany the delusions, and hallucinations may occur. The disorganized type is characterized by confusion, incoherence, and severe deterioration of adaptive behavior. The catatonic type is characterized by severe motor disturbances ranging from muscular rigidity to random or repetitive movements. The undifferentiated category is for people who exhibit symptoms of schizophrenia but do not neatly fall into any of the first three categories. Type I schizophrenia is characterized by the predominance of positive symptoms, such as delusions and hallucinations, while Type II schizophrenia is characterized by the absence of normal behaviors, which are known as negative symptoms.

5. Strong evidence exists for a biological basis for schizophrenia. The disorder tends to run in families, and twin studies show higher concordance rates between MZ twins than between DZ twins. Brain studies have indicated brain atrophy in the brains of schizophrenics. According to the dopamine hypothesis, excess levels of dopamine may cause schizophrenia. Freud believed that the disorder was caused by regression to early stages of psychosexual development because of life stress. Cognitive theorists believe that schizophrenics have a defect in attentional mechanisms. Stressful life events seem to precede much schizophrenic behavior. Family dynamics, particularly the level of expressed emotion, may play a role. Finally, sociocultural factors may play a role. Schizophrenia tends to be found more among those in lower socioeconomic classes. It is not clear if being in that class causes or influences the development of schizophrenia or whether schizophrenics are just more likely to end up in lower socioeconomic classes.

Chapter 15
TREATMENT OF PSYCHOLOGICAL DISORDERS

Learning Objectives: *These questions, with a few additions (indicated with an asterisk), are taken from the directed questions found in the margins of the chapter. After reading the chapter, you should be able to answer these questions.*

1. What two treatment elements combine in treatment of behavior disorders?

1.1* Who do people usually consult with when dealing with mental health problems? What percentage of the population has consulted with a professional counselor or therapist?

1.2* What are the different types of mental health professionals?

2. What is the major therapeutic goal in psychoanalysis?

3. How are free association and dream analysis used in psychoanalysis?

4. How do resistance and transference reflect underlying conflicts?

5. What are interpretations, and how are they used by analysts?

6. What two research results favor the use of brief therapies over classical psychoanalysis? How do brief psychodynamic therapies differ from it?

7. What is the goal of humanistic therapies, and how do the therapies try to achieve this goal?

8. Define the three important therapist attributes described by Rogers.

9. How is gestalt therapy derived from gestalt psychology principles?

9.1 Note the similarities and differences of Rogers' and Perls' approaches to therapy. What factor may have accounted for the decline in popularity of gestalt therapy?

10. What do ABCD stand for in rational-emotive therapy, and how is this model used in therapy?

11. Which disorders have responded most favorably to Beck's cognitive therapy? What is the focus of the therapy in these disorders?

11.1* What basic assumptions about psychological disorders are made by the behavioral approach to therapy?

12. What are the classical and operant conditioning procedures used in exposure therapy? How was this procedure tested with agoraphobics?

13. How does systematic desensitization differ from exposure in terms of its (a) underlying principle and (b) specific techniques?

14. How does classical conditioning underlie aversion therapy? What additional training can enhance its effectiveness?

15. How do token economies work, and what evidence is there for their effectiveness?

16. Under what conditions is punishment used as a behavior modification technique? What evidence is there for its effectiveness?

17. How is modeling used in social skills training? How is self-efficacy involved in its effectiveness?

18. What clinical observation stimulated the development of family therapy, and what are its key assumptions?

18.1* What are some of the characteristics of successful marriages?

19. How has acceptance been integrated into marital therapy?

20. What is eclecticism? Give an example of an integration of therapies.

21. Which specific attributes of VR make it potentially useful in therapy? What evidence is there that VR can work therapeuticaly?

22. What factors serve as barriers to therapy for ethnic minorities?

23. What skills are found in culturally competent therapists?

23.1* What factors might account for the greater prevalence of psychological disorders in women?

24. What is the "specificity question" in psychotherapy research?

25. What types of measures are used to assess the outcome of therapy?

26. Describe Eysenck's challenge to therapy effectiveness and the data on which it was based.

27. Summarize desirable standards for designing psychotherapy research studies with regard to design, treatment standardization, and followup.

28. How has meta-analysis been used to assess therapy effects? What have meta-analyses shown about overall effectiveness and the effects of different forms of therapy?

29. What client variables are important to treatment outcome?

30. Define and give examples of common factors.

31. Which therapist factors affect treatment outcome?

32. What were the major findings of the CR survey? On what bases were its conclusions criticized?

33. How do antianxiety drugs achieve their effects? Do they have any drawbacks?

34.   How do the three classes of antidepressant drugs achieve their effects biologically? How effective are they compared/combined with therapy?

34.1*   How do antipsychotic drugs achieve their effects?

35.   What s tardive dyskinesia, and how is it caused?

36.   Which disorders do and do not respond favorably to ECT?

37.   What was the rationale and the effects of prefrontal lobotomy?

37.1*   What is a cingluotomy and with what disorders is it used?

37.2*   Describe the results that Lewis Baxter obtained in his work with people suffering from obsessive-compulsive disorder.

38.   What is the rationale for deinstitutionalization? What prevents it's achieving its goals?

39.   Define the two major approaches to prevention.

Chapter Overview

The Helping Relationship

The goal of all therapy is to help people change maladaptive thinking, feeling, and behavioral patterns. Therapeutic techniques vary widely and depend on the theories that therapists use to understand psychological disorders.

Psychodynamic Therapies

The goal of psychoanalysis is to help clients achieve insight, the conscious awareness of the psychodynamics that underlie problems. Freudian Psychoanalysts use free association techniques and dream interpretation in therapy. Clients may experience resistance to dealing with unconscious conflicts but eventually will transfer the conflicts associated in dealing with others to the therapist. Psychoanalytic therapists provide interpretation to the clients in an effort to help them achieve insight. Brief psychodynamic therapies utilize basic concepts from psychoanalysis, but conversation between therapist and client typically replace free association and therapy occurs more frequently than it does in traditional psychoanalysis.

Humanistic Psychotherapies

Client-centered therapy, developed by Carl Rogers, focuses on unconditional positive regard, empathy, and genuineness (therapist consistency of feelings and behaviors). The characteristics of therapists have indeed been found to have important effects on therapeutic outcomes. Gestalt therapy is another approach to helping people get in touch with their selves.

Cognitive Therapies

Cognitive therapies focus on maladaptive ways of thinking about oneself and the world. Ellis' rational-emotive therapy stresses the roles of activating events, belief systems, emotional and behavioral consequences of appraisal in the development of psychological disorders and the importance of disputing, or challenging, erroneous beliefs in treatment. Similarly, Beck's cognitive therapy is designed to help clients point out logical errors in thinking that underlie disturbances such as mood disorders.

Behavior Therapies

Behavior therapies use basic principles of classical and operant conditioning in therapy. For example, anxiety responses can be eliminated through extinction procedures. Systematic desensitization is a technique used for treating anxiety disorders. Aversion therapy is used to reduce deviant behaviors. Behavior modification techniques such as the use of positive reinforcement and punishment can also be used in therapy. The modeling of social skills can be used to help people to function effectively in society.

Group, Family, and Marital Therapies

Sometimes, the family rather than the individual is treated because of the importance of family dynamics in the development of some disorders. Marital therapy focus on communication, understanding needs, and problem-solving skills. A recent addition to marital therapy is a focus on acceptance of the partner.

Integrating and Combining Therapies

To an increasing extent, therapists are becoming eclectic in their use of treatments and theoretical orientations to help people in therapy.

Cultural and Gender Issues in Psychotherapy

Cultural factors play a number of roles in the use of psychotherapy. Cultural norms can affect the likelihood of turning to professionals in time of need. A lack of access to services and a lack of skilled counselors who can provide culturally responsive forms of treatment can hinder people in getting treatment. Therapists must understand the external barriers deeply embedded in the culture that may be involved in the development of psychological disorders in women.

Evaluating Psychotherapies

Today, researchers use the specificity question: "Which types of therapy, administered by which types of therapists to which types of clients having which kinds of problems, produce which kinds of effects. This question stresses the interactions between all variables in producing successful therapy. Randomized clinical trials and placebo control groups are considered critical for good research into the effectiveness of psychotherapy. Meta-analyses are used to combine the results of many studies.

Biological Approaches to Treatment

Antianxiety drugs such as Valium and Xanax are used to help people deal with anxiety. Antidepressant drugs fall into three major categories: tricyclics, MAO inhibitors, and SSRIs (selective serotonin reuptake inhibitors). Electroconvulsive therapy (ECT) is a technique used for treating major depression. Psychosurgery refers to surgical procedures that remove or destroy brain tissue.

Psychological Disorders and Society

A deinstitutionalization movement began in the 1960's to transfer the primary focus of treatment from the hospital to the community. Unfortunately, many patients have been released into communities that are unable to care for them, resulting in an increase in the homeless population and a revolving door phenomenon involving repeated hospitalizations and releases. Preventive mental health programs focus on both situation-focused prevention, which is directed at reducing or preventing environmental causes of disorders and competency-focused prevention, which is designed to increase personal resources and coping skills.

Chapter Outline

The Helping Relationship

Psychodynamic Therapies
    Psychoanalysis
        Free Association
        Dream Interpretation
        Resistance
        Transference
        Interpretation
    Brief Psychodynamic Therapies

Humanistic Psychotherapies
    Client-Centered Therapy
    Gestalt Therapy

Cognitive Therapies
    Ellis's Rational-Emotive Therapy
    Beck's Cognitive Therapy

Behavior Therapies
    Classical Conditioning Procedures
        Exposure: An Extinction Approach
        Systematic Desensitization: A Counterconditioning Approach
        Aversion Therapy
    Operant Conditioning Treatments
        Positive Reinforcement
        Therapeutic Use of Punishment
    Modeling and Social Skills Training

Group, Family, and Marital Therapies
    Family Therapy
    Marital Therapy

Integrating and Combining Therapies
  Psychological Frontiers: Virtual Reality as a Therapeutic Technique

Cultural and Gender Issues in Psychotherapy
  Cultural Factors in Treatment Utilization
  Gender Issues in Therapy

Evaluating Psychotherapies
  Psychotherapy Research Methods
    What is a Good Psychotherapy Research Design?
    Meta-analysis: A Look at the Big Picture
  Factors Affecting the Outcome of Therapy
  Research Close-Up: The Effectiveness of Psychotherapy: Feedback From the Consumer

Biological Approaches to Treatment
  Drug Therapies
    Antianxiety Drugs
    Antidepressant Drugs
    Antipsychotic Drugs
  Electroconvulsive Therapy
  Psychosurgery
  Mind, Body, and Therapeutic Interventions

Psychological Disorders and Society
  Deinstitutionalization
  Preventive Mental Health
  Applications of Psychological Science: When and Where to Seek Therapy

Key Terms: *Write the letter of the definition next to the term in the space provided.*

The Helping Relationship
Psychodynamic Therapies
Humanistic Therapies
Cognitive Therapies
Behavior Therapies
Group, Family, and Marital Therapies

1. ____ aversion therapy

2. ____ behavior modification

3. ____ counterconditioning

4. ____ eclectic

5. ____ empathy

a. conscious awareness of the psychodynamics that underlie problems

b. Freud's technique asking clients to verbally report without censorship any thoughts, feelings, or images that entered awareness

c. defensive maneuvers that hinder the process of therapy

d. occurs when the client reacts to the therapist as if he or she were an important figure from the person's past

e. any statement by the therapist intended to provide the client with insight into behavior or dynamics

6. ___ exposure

7. ___ free association

8. ___ genuineness

9. ___ insight

10. ___ interpersonal therapy

11. ___ interpretation

12. ___ psychodynamic behavior therapy

13. ___ resistance

14. ___ response prevention

15. ___ social skills training

16. ___ stimulus hierarchy

17. ___ systematic desensitization

18. ___ token economy

19. ___ transference

20. ___ unconditional positive regard

21. ___ virtual reality

f. a brief psychodynamic therapy that focuses on a client's interpersonal problems

g. communicated when therapists show clients that they genuinely care about and accept them without judgement or evaluation

h. willingness and ability to view the world through the client's eyes

i. consistency between the way a therapist feels and the way he or she behaves

j. presenting the feared CS in the absence of the UCS

k. a technique to keep the avoidance response from occurring

l. a learning-based treatment for anxiety disorders

m. a procedure in which a new response that is incompatible with anxiety is conditioned to the anxiety-producing CS

n. an ordering of anxiety-producing events

o. therapy in which the therapist pairs an attractive stimulus with a noxious UCS in an attempt to condition an aversion to the CS

p. treatment techniques that involve the application of operant conditioning procedures

q. a system for strengthening desired behaviors through the application of positive reinforcement

r. learning new skills by observing and imitating a model who performs a socially skillful behavior

s. combining treatments and making use of various orientations and therapeutic techniques

t. Wachtel's integration of psychodynamic and behavior therapies

u. involves the use of computer technology to simulate real experiences

Integrating and Combining Therapies
Cultural and Gender Issues in Psychotherapy
Evaluating Psychotherapies
Biological Approaches to Treatment
Psychological Disorders and Society

1. ___ common factors

2. ___ competency-focused intervention

3. ___ cultural competence

a. ability to use knowledge about the client's culture to achieve a broad understanding of the client, at the same time understanding how the client may be different from the stereotype

b. "Which type of therapy, administered by which kinds of therapists to which kinds of clients, having which kinds of problems, produce which kinds of effects?"

c. symptom reduction in the absence of any treatment

4. ___ deinstitutionalization

d. studies in which individuals are randomly assigned to an experimental condition which receives the treatment or to a control condition

5. ___ deterioration effect

e. the group which gets a treatment they think will be effective but does not actually work

6. ___ effect size statistic

f. a statistical technique that allows researchers to combine the results of many studies to arrive at an overall conclusion

7. ___ effectiveness

g. represents a common measure of treatment effectiveness in meta-analysis

8. ___ efficacy

h. clients' general willingness to invest themselves in therapy and take risks

9. ___ electroconvulsive therapy

i. refers to ability to experience and understand internal states, to be attuned to relational processes with therapists, and to apply what is learned in therapy to life

10. ___ meta-analysis

j. as a result of hostile interchanges between therapist and client, the client gets worse

11. ___ openness

k. shared by diverse forms of therapy that might contribute to therapeutic success, such as a caring therapist

12. ___ placebo control group

l. refers to whether therapy can produce scientifically-demonstrated positive outcomes

13. ___ psychosurgery

m. outcomes that psychotherapy has in real-life settings of clinical practice

14. ___ randomized clinical trial

n. a severe movement disorder produced by antipsychotic drugs

15. ___ self-relatedness

o. seizure induction effective in treating major depression

16. ___ situation-focused intervention

p. procedures to remove or destroy brain tissue to change disordered behavior

17. ___ specificity question

q. a movement to transfer the primary focus of treatment from the hospital to the community

18. ___ spontaneous remission

r. directed at reducing or eliminating the environmental causes of behavior disorders or enhancing situational factors that help prevent the development of disorders

19. ___ tardive dyskinesia

s. designed to increase personal resources and coping skills

Review at a Glance: *Write the term that best fits the blank to review what you learned in this chapter.*

Psychodynamic Therapies

The goal of psychoanalysis is to help clients achieve (1) _____, the conscious awareness of the psychodynamics that underlie their problems. Freud asked his clients to recline on a couch and to verbally report their thoughts, a technique called (2) _____ _____.
Through this technique, as well as (3) _____ _____, Freud believed that the

therapist could help the client understand the unconscious motivations of their behavior. Clients were expected to engage in defensive maneuvers called (4) _____ that hinder the process of therapy. If therapy is successful, (5) _____ should occur. In a brief psychodynamic therapy called (6) _____ therapy, the therapist focuses on the client's current interpersonal problems.

Humanistic Psychotherapies

In client-centered therapy, (7) _____ _____ _____ is communicated when therapists show clients that they genuinely care about and accept them. A second vital factor in therapy is called (8) _____, the willingness and bility of a therapist to see the world through the client's eyes. The third important therapist characteristic is (9) _____, which refers to consistency between a therapist's feelings and his or her behaviors.

Cognitive Therapies

Ellis' rational emotive therapy is embodied in his (10) _____ model. (11) _____ cognitive therapy revolves around pointing out logical errors in thinking that underlie emotional disturbance.

Behavior Therapies

Classical conditioning approaches are often used in treatment of psychological disorders. In the extinction approach called (12) _____, the feared CS is presented without the UCS while using (13) _____ _____ to prevent the response from occurring.
(14) _____ _____ is a technique developed by Joseph Wolpe to treat anxiety disorders, particularly phobias. In this procedure, the client is first trained in relaxation techniques and is then helped to construct a (15) _____ _____ of low-anxiety to high-anxiety scenes relating to the fear. The client then practices the relaxation techniques while progressing through the stimulus hierarchy. In (16) _____ therapy, the therapist pairs a stimulus that is attractive to a person with a noxious UCS in an attempt to condition an aversion to the CS. (17) _____ _____ techniques are operant conditioning treatments that involve trying to increase or decrease a specific behavior. In (18) _____ _____ training, clients learn new skills by observing and then imitating a model who performs a behavior.

Integrating and Combining Therapies

Today, therapists use a wide variety of techniques and approaches in treatment, which is called the (19) _____ approach. For example, (20) _____ _____ therapy involves an integration of psychoanalysis and behavior therapy.

Cultural and Gender Issues in Psychotherapy

Stanley Sue (1998) suggests that (21) _____ _____ therapists are able to use their knowledge about the client's culture to achieve a broad understanding of the client while at the same time being attentive to how the client might be different from the cultural stereotype.

Evaluating Psychotherapies

Good research designs to evaluate the effectiveness of psychotherapy involve both
(22) _____ _____ trials and (23) _____ _____ groups. The
statistical technique of (24) _____ - _____ allows researchers to combine the
results of many studies to arrive at an overall conclusion. Several factors have been found to
affect the outcome of therapy. (25) _____ involves client's willingness to invest
themselves in therapy, while (26) _____ - _____ refers to ability to experience
and understand internal states, to be attuned to relational processes with therapists, and ability to
apply what is learned in therapy to life outside treatment. Hostile interchanges between therapists
and clients can lead to a (27) _____ effect in therapy. Various therapies tend to enjoy
similar success rates, suggesting that there are (28) _____ _____ shared by these
therapies.

Biological Approaches to Treatment

Valium, Xanax, and BuSpar are examples of (29) _____ drugs. Antidepressant drugs fall
into three major categories: (30) _____, (31) _____, and
(32) _____. (33) _____ drugs are used to treat schizophrenia. These drugs can
produce a severe movement disorder called (34) _____ _____.
(35) _____ therapy, or ECT, is used to treat severe major depression. (36) _____
refers to procedures to remove or destroy brain tissue in an attempt to change disordered
behavior.

Psychological Disorders and Society

Concerns about the inadequacies of mental hospitals and the ability of antipsychotic drugs to
"normalize" patients' behavior led to a (37) _____ movement to transfer the primary
focus of treatment to the community from the hospital. Preventive mental health programs have
become increasingly important. In (38) _____ - _____ prevention, the focus is
on reducing or eliminating the environmental causes of behavior disorders or on enhancing
situational factors that help to prevent the development of disorders. (39) _____ -
_____ prevention programs are designed to increase personal resources and coping
skills.

Apply What You Know

1. Think of three behaviors that you would like to change. Describe each of them. Using what you have
learned in this chapter, describe which forms of therapy would be most effective in helping you make the
desired changes.

Stretching Your Geographies

1. Stanley Sue's and others' work have suggested that cultural factors can play a role in treatment utilization and therapeutic interventions. Interview two clinical psychologists in your area to determine what cultural factors play a role in these processes in your area of the country.

Practice Test

Multiple Choice Items: *Please write the letter corresponding to your answer in the space to the left of each item.*

_____ 1. The primary therapeutic goal of _____ is to help a person achieve greater insight, which is the awareness of the underlying dynamics of their problems.
   a. humanistic therapy
   b. cognitive therapy
   c. behavior modification
   d. psychoanalysis

_____ 2. Susan has an anxiety disorder and has sought help from a therapist, Dr. Jones. Dr. Jones believes that Susan's anxiety is related to her unconscious fear of her unmet sexual impulses and that in order for Susan to get over her anxiety problem, she needs to have greater awareness of this unconscious dynamic. Dr. Jones is most likely associated with the _____approach to therapy and appears to be trying to produce positive changes by fostering more _____.

   a. psychodynamic; transference
   b. interpersonal; empathy
   c. psychoanalytic; insight
   d. humanistic; unconditional positive regard

_____ 3. A therapist who takes to a humanistic approach to psychotherapy would **most likely** have the goal of creating a therapeutic environment that _____.

   a. encourages insight
   b. challenges irrational thoughts
   c. reinforces desired behaviors
   d. allows for self-exploration

_____ 4. Josh is visiting a friend when he accidentally breaks a valuable plate. He begins to berate himself for his clumsiness and stupidity and almost instantaneously he starts to feel embarrassed and upset. According to Ellis' ABCD model of emotion, the breaking of the plate would represent the _____.

   a. A
   b. B
   c. C
   d. D

_____ 5. Exposure therapies operate on the assumption that _____ is the most direct way to reduce or eliminate a learned anxiety response.

   a. classical extinction
   b. positive reinforcement
   c. operant extinction
   d. response cost punishment

_____ 6. Janice has a phobia of dogs and decides to consult with a behavior therapist in order to get some help. The therapist first teaches her a muscle relaxation technique. After she has learned this, they create a list of increasingly fearful situations involving dogs. Starting with the least feared situation, the therapist has Janice imagine it and then use her relaxation training to eliminate any anxiety that arises. This therapist is using the general technique called _____ and the list that they have created is an example of _____.

a. aversive conditioning; a punishment
b. systematic desensitization; a stimulus hierarchy
c. exposure therapy; flooding
d. behavior modification; positive reinforcer

_____ 7. Great flexibility and an increased sense of what is called presence are characteristics of _____, which has recently been used to treat a limited number of psychological disorders.

a. systematic desensitization
b. psychodyanamic behavior therapy
c. virtual reality
d. aversion therapy

_____ 8. The process where some individuals experience complete symptom reduction in the absence of any treatment is known as _____.

a. the placebo effect
b. natural recovery
c. spontaneous remission
d. automatic adjustment

_____ 9. Dr. Stone designs a study to test the effectiveness of a new treatment for anxiety disorders. After making sure that her participants are roughly similar on important demographic variables, people are randomly assigned to receive her new therapy or another therapy technique that has already been proven to be effective. Of the following statements, the one which **best describes** Dr. Stone's study is that her study _____.

a. uses randomized clinical trials and it has a placebo control group
b. uses randomized clinical trials but does not have a placebo control group
c. does not use randomized clinical trials but it does have a placebo control group
d. does not use randomized clinical trials and it does not have a placebo control group

_____ 10. Modern meta-analyses comparing the effectiveness of various types of therapies have concluded that _____.

a. behavioral and psychodynamic therapies are the most effective
b. client-centered therapies are the most effective
c. most therapies are no more effective than receiving no treatment at all
d. with some exceptions, most different therapies are equally effective

_____ 11. The fact that vastly different types of therapies often produce similar outcomes has led some researchers to search for what are called _____, which are similar elements shared by each of the approaches that may account for their common successes.

a. meta-factors
b. joint components
c. common factors
d. shared components

_____ 12. Tricyclics, MAO inhibitors, and SSRIs were all mentioned as drug treatments for _____.

a. anxiety disorders
b. schizophrenia
c. depression
d. somatoform disorders

_____ 13. The "placebo effect" largely influences _____ in therapy outcomes.

a. therapeutic technique
b. client expectancies
c. neurotransmitter levels
d. primary appraisal

_____ 14. The main goal of psychoanalysis is to help clients achieve _____.

a. insight
b. free association
c. dream analysis
d. resistance

_____ 15. When clients project their anxieties, fears, or other impulses onto the therapist during psychoanalytic therapy, _____ has occurred.

a. insight
b. free association
c. transference
d. resistance

_____ 16. Of the following, the one which is not part of humanistic psychotherapy is _____.

a. unconditional positive regard
b. conditions of worth
c. empathy
d. genuineness

_____ 17. In Ellis' rational-emotive therapy, the key to changing maladaptive emotions and behaviors is thought to be _____.

a. dream analysis
b. insight
c. disputing erroneous beliefs
d. somatic therapy

_____ 18. In extinction, the phobic object is _____.

a. the UCS
b. paired with a noxious UCS
c. presented in the absence of the UCS
d. the UCR

_____ 19. In aversion therapy, the behavior to be changed is _____.

a. paired with a noxious UCS
b. considered to be a UCS
c. presented in the absence of the UCS
d. negatively reinforced

_____ 20. Token economies _____.

a. use aversion therapy procedures
b. use extinction procedures
c. don't work
d. use operant conditioning techniques to strengthen desired behaviors

_____ 21. Studies of punishment with severely disturbed autistic children have found that _____.

a. self-destructive behaviors can be controlled through punishment procedures
b. punishment makes autistic behavior more likely to occur
c. punishment is ineffective in changing autistic behavior
d. punishment doesn't work nearly as well with autistic children as it does with mentally retarded children

_____ 22. Eclectic therapists _____.

a. use psychodynamic behavioral therapy exclusively
b. believe strongly that therapists should use a single theoretical orientation in their therapy
c. believe strongly that therapists should use a single therapeutic technique in their therapy
d. use several different orientations and techniques in their therapy

_____ 23. The question: "Which types of therapy, administered by which kinds of therapists, to which kinds of clients, having which kinds of problems, produce which kinds of effect?" is known as the _____ question.

a. therapeutic
b. therapist
c. specificity
d. clinical trial

_____ 24. A _____ allows researchers to combine the results of many studies to arrive at an overall conclusion.

a. placebo control group
b. randomized clinical trial
c. meta-analysis
d. correlational study

_____ 25. Common factors in successful psychotherapy include _____.

a. faith in the therapist
b. a lack of self-efficacy
c. a lack of self-relatedness
d. a decreased optimistic outlook on life

_____ 26. _____ is a scientific term that refers to whether a therapy can produce positive outcomes exceeding those in appropriate control conditions.

a. Meta-analysis
b. Placebo
c. Effectiveness
d. Efficacy

_____ 27. MAO inhibitors _____.

a. reduce the activity of the enzyme that breaks down neurotransmitters in the synapse
b. decrease levels of monamine oxidase
c. decrease levels of serotonin
d. have less severe side effects than the tricyclics

_____ 28. SSRIs _____.

a. increase MAO levels
b. decrease MAO levels
c. have more serious side effects than either tricyclics or MAO inhibitors
d. increase levels of serotonin in the synapse

_____ 29. ECT is used to _____.

    a. increase MAO levels
    b. treat severely depressed people when other measures fail
    c. surgically remove parts of the brain
    d. place patients in a vegetative state

_____ 30. Procedures that are used to increase people's self-efficacy are part of _____.

    a. ECT
    b. competency-focused intervention
    c. situation-focused intervention
    d. deinstitutionalization

True/False Items: *Write T or F in the space provided to the left of each item.*

_____ 1. Freud believed that dream interpretation was "the royal road to the unconscious."

_____ 2. Interpersonal therapy, a brief psychodynamic therapy, focuses on the client's current interpersonal problems.

_____ 3. Genuineness refers to a therapist's ability to view the world through a client's eyes.

_____ 4. In Ellis' ABCD model, the "C" stands for cognitions.

_____ 5. Systematic desensitization is a learning-based treatment for anxiety disorders.

_____ 6. Family therapy had its roots in the clinical observation that clients who had shown improvement in therapy suffered relapses when they returned home and began interacting with their families.

_____ 7. Clinicians who are eclectic stick to one tried-and-true technique in therapy.

_____ 8. A placebo control group is used to control for client expectations of improvement.

_____ 9. A meta-analysis allows researchers to combine the results of many studies to arrive at an overall conclusion.

_____ 10. Self-relatedness refers to a client's willingness to invest themselves in therapy and to take the risks required to change themselves.

Short Answer Questions

1. What is free association?

2. What are the processes of client-centered therapy?

3. How is social skills training accomplished?

4. How is virtual reality being used as a therapeutic technique?

5. What is electroconvulsive therapy?

Essay Questions

1. How do cognitive therapies work?

2. What is systematic desensitization?

3. What is a good psychotherapy research design?

4. Describe the factors affecting the outcomes of therapy.

5. Describe preventive mental health programs.

Answer Keys

Answer Key for Key Terms

The Helping Relationship
Psychodynamic Therapies
Humanistic Therapies
Cognitive Therapies
Behavior Therapies
Group, Family, and Marital Therapies

1. o
2. p
3. m
4. s
5. h
6. j
7. b
8. i
9. a
10. f
11. e

12. t
13. c
14. k
15. r
16. n
17. l
18. q
19. d
20. g
21. u

Integrating and Combining Therapies
Cultural and Gender Issues in Psychotherapy
Evaluating Psychotherapies
Biological Approaches to Treatment
Psychological Disorders and Society

1. k
2. s
3. a
4. q
5. j
6. g
7. m
8. l
9. o
10. f

11. h
12. e
13. p
14. d
15. i
16. r
17. b
18. c
19. n

Answer Key for Review at a Glance

1. insight
2. free association
3. dream interpretation
4. resistance
5. transference
6. interpersonal
7. unconditional positive regard
8. empathy

21. culturally competent
22. randomized clinical
23. placebo control
24. meta-analysis
25. Openness
26. self-relatedness
27. deterioration
28. common factors

9. genuineness
10. ABCD
11. Beck's
12. exposure
13. response prevention
14. Systematic desensitization
15. stimulus hierarchy
16. aversion
17. Behavior modification
18. social skills
19. eclectic
20. psychodynamic behavior

29. antianxiety
30. tricyclics
31. MAO inhibitors
32. SSRIs
33. Antipsychotic
34. tardive dyskinesia
35. Electroconvulsive
36. Psychosurgery
37. deinstitutionalization
38. situation-focused
39. competency-focused

Answer Key for Practice Test Multiple Choice Questions

1. d
2. c
3. d
4. a
5. a
6. b
7. c
8. c
9. b
10. d
11. c
12. c
13. b
14. a
15. c

16. b
17. c
18. c
19. a
20. d
21. a
22. d
23. c
24. c
25. a
26. d
27. a
28. d
29. b
30. b

Answer Key for Practice Test True/False Questions

1. T
2. T
3. F
4. F
5. T

6. T
7. F
8. T
9. T
10. F

Answer Key for Practice Test Short Answer Questions

1. Free association refers to verbal reports without any censorship of thoughts, feelings, or images that enter awareness. It was a technique pioneered by Freud.

2. Three things are important in client-centered therapy. First, the therapist should communicate unconditional positive regard. Second, the therapist should express empathy for the client's point-of-view. Finally, the therapist, should be genuine and make sure that there is congruence between his or her feelings and his or her behaviors.

3. In social skills training, clients learn new skills by observing and then imitating a model who performs socially skillful behaviors.

4. Virtual reality involves the use of computer technology to create highly realistic environments in which behavior and emotions can be studied. Virtual reality is highly flexible, meaning that it can be used to create a number of environments in which a therapist can study a client's reactions.

5. Electroconvulsive therapy (or ECT) is a technique in which a person receives electric shock to the brain. This shock, which lasts less than a second, causes a seizure of the central nervous system. Such treatments can help people with major depression but may cause permanent memory loss in some cases.

Answer Key for Practice Test Essay Questions

1. Cognitive therapies stress the importance of maladaptive thought processes in the development of psychological disorders. As such, the therapies attempt to change the thought processes. Clients are given help in identifying the maladaptive thoughts, are encouraged to challenge the thoughts, and change them. Both Ellis's rational-emotive therapy and Beck's cognitive therapy work this way.

2. Systematic desensitization is a counterconditioning technique that is most useful in treating anxiety disorders, particularly phobias. The first step in the technique is to train the client in the skill of muscle relaxation. The client then constructs a stimulus hierarchy of ten to fifteen scenes relating to the fear. Then, while practicing the relaxation techniques he or she has just learned, the client progresses through practicing behaviors in the stimulus hierarchy, starting with the least anxiety-provoking ones.

3. Sound psychotherapy research designs use both randomized clinical trials and placebo control groups. Randomized clinical trials involve making sure that both experimental and control group participants are similar on various variables that might affect the response to treatment. Placebo control group participants receive an intervention that is not expected to work but controls for client expectancies because the client <u>does</u> believe that the treatment will work. Treatment is standardized through manuals containing procedures that therapists involved in the study must follow exactly. Finally, sound designs include follow-ups to determine the long-term effects of the treatment.

4. Openness involves willingness to invest in therapy and take risks necessary for change. Self-relatedness refers to ability to experience and understand internal states. Common factors shared by successful therapies include faith in the therapist and treatment, receiving a plausible explanation for problems, alternative ways of looking at problems, a protective setting, an opportunity to practice new behaviors, and increased optimism and self-efficacy.

5. Preventive mental health programs are designed to prevent problems from occurring. Situation-focused prevention is directed at reducing or eliminating the environmental causes of behavior disorders or enhancing situational factors important in the prevention of the development of disorders. Competency-focused prevention programs are designed to improve people's personal resources and coping skills.

Chapter 16
PSYCHOLOGY AND SOCIETY: FROM BASIC RESEARCH TO SOCIAL APPLICATION

Learning Objectives: *These questions, with a few additions (indicated with an asterisk), are taken from the directed questions found in the margins of the chapter. After reading the chapter, you should be able to answer these questions.*

1.   How do theory, research, and interventions all influence one another? Provide an example of each of the six possible influences.

2.   What four important scientific and policy questions can be answered through good program evaluation research?

2.1*   According to psychologist James Garbarino, why are so many children at risk for various psychological and behavioral problems?

3.   What are two factors that might have limited the outcomes from Project Head Start? How did such speculation influence later childhood interventions?

4.   What were the major outcomes of the Abecedarian early intervention project? What evidence suggests that such interventions must occur before school age?

5.   What social and educational outcomes were found in the 22-year follow-up of the Perry Preschool Program?

6.   What is the goal of the Penn Optimism Project. What techniques does it use, and what effects have been found?

7.   What changes have occurred in the major causes of death during the 20th century? How do these changes suggest the potential contributions of health psychology?

8.   What are the two-major categories of health-related behaviors? Give an example of each type.

9.   What are two major assumptions of the Stages of Change model in terms of the process of behavior change?

10.   Distinguish between the stages of precontemplation, contemplation, and preparation.

11.   What is needed in order for people to be able to move through the action, and maintenance stages to termination?

12.   What are stage-matched interventions? How do they move people from precontemplation to action?

13.   What is aerobic exercise? What evidence is there that it promotes health and longevity?

14.   How large are exercise dropout rates? What factors do and do not predict dropout?

15.   Why is yo-yo dieting a risk factor for death from cardiovascular disease?

16.   What are the major behavior-change techniques used in behavioral weight control programs?

17.   What is the scope of the worldwide AIDS crisis?

17.1* What are some of the key characteristics of the AIDS virus and how is the disease transmitted?

18.   Summarize the four features of most AIDS prevention projects, and the outcomes of a program directed at homosexual men. How do cultural factors influence outcomes?

18.1* What is the current fastest growing population of people with the AIDS virus?

19.   Summarize the comparative effects of abstinence and protected-sex messages to high-risk adolescents.

19.1* On what continent are the majority of AIDS cases found?

19.2* Cite some relevant statistics on the harmful effects of alcoholism and smoking.

19.3* Which psychological perspective has had the most recent success in effectively treating substance abuse?

20.   How are classical conditioning principles applied in aversion therapies for smoking and drinking? What are the outcomes for alcoholics?

21.   What kinds of behavior change procedures are employed in multimodal treatments for substance abuse?

22.   What are the major goals and techniques in motivational interviewing? How effective is this approach?

23.   How severe is the problem of relapse in substance abuse treatment?

24.   What is the difference between a lapse and a relapse? How does the abstinence violation effect contribute to relapse?

25.   How does relapse prevention treatment try to keep lapses from becoming a relapse? How effective is this approach?

26.   What is a harm reduction approach, and how does it differ from an abstinence-based one?

27.   How serious are the consequences of heavy drinking among college students?

28.   What methods and outcomes occurred in Marlatt et al.'s alcohol harm reduction study with high-risk college students?

29.   What evidence indicates that violence and bullying, especially by young people, is a major social problem? What sex differences occur in bullying behavior?

30.	What are the roles of negative and positive reinforcement in violent behavior? Cite examples of each.

31.	What can be done to reduce violent behavior in people for whom emotions like anger are a strong antecedent?

31.1*	Describe the goals and intervention strategies of MTV's <u>Real Life</u> series.

32.	How do cultural beliefs contribute to violence against women?

32.1*	What has been determined regarding the biological factors involved in aggression?

33.	How do the results from the Oak Ridge study demonstrate the important role of personality in response to treatment for violent behavior?

34.	What are the major assumptions of multiculturalism?

35.	What four factors influence the extent to which the effects predicted by the contact hypothesis actually occur? How are these factors incorporated into cooperative learning programs like the Jigsaw Program?

36.	How have the four contact hypothesis factors been applied within the interactive problem solving workshops conducted in the Israeli-Palestinian project?

36.1*	What are the key aspects of Marie Jahoda's concept of positive mental health?

36.2*	Research in what particular areas led to the development of a psychology of optimal living?

37.	Summarize the personal and environmental factors that make some children highly resilient to stressful environments.

Chapter Overview

Linkages Between Theory, Research, and Interventions

> Theories, research, and interventions designed to solve practical problems are systematically related to each other. Research into the effectiveness of programs is called program evaluation research.

Enhancing Children's Development

> Head Start, the Abecedarian Program, and the High/Scope Perry Preschool Project are examples of programs that were developed to enhance children's development. Early studies of Head Start indicated disappointing results, but participants in the Abecedarian Program and the High/Scope Perry Preschool Project, which focused on providing children with stimulating learning experiences, have shown important long-term effects in IQ and standardized test scores for disadvantaged students. Intervention programs for preventing teenage depression, such as the Penn Optimism Project, have found that cognitive treatments for depression can help teens cope with depression.

Health Promotion and Illness Prevention

The field of health psychology studies psychological and behavioral factors in the prevention and treatment of illness and in the maintenance of health. Health-enhancing behaviors (e.g. exercise) serve to maintain and increase health, while health-compromising behaviors (e.g. smoking, unhealthy diets) are those that promote the development of illness. Prevention programs for AIDS have focused on reducing risky sexual behaviors that can increase the chances of contracting HIV.

Combating Substance Abuse

Psychological approaches to treatment and prevention of substance abuse focus on the use of aversion therapies and multimodal treatments, which involve relaxation and stress management techniques, applying self-monitoring procedures, coping and social skills training, marital and family counseling to help with conflicts, and positive reinforcement procedures to strengthen change. Motivational interviewing techniques help abusers to increase their awareness of problems, to give them a greater desire to take action, and to help them develop a greater sense of self-efficacy. Such techniques are designed to prevent both lapse and relapse. Harm reduction is a prevention strategy designed to reduce the harmful effects of a behavior once it has occurred.

Reducing Violence

Both negative and positive reinforcement can strengthen violence, so treatments often focus on the elimination of such reinforcements. Rage and violence are responses to emotional antecedents. People who develop rage and other emotional reactions to stimuli can be treated through programs that focus on reducing physiological arousal, such as relaxation training. The mass media can be used to help reduce violence through programs that focus on the understanding of causes of violence and methods of coping with anger and frustration. Cultural beliefs that encourage violence are often targeted by intervention programs. Biological treatment programs focus on altering brain chemistry through drugs.

Psychology in a Multicultural World: Increasing Understanding and Reducing Conflict

Multiculturalism is a movement that promotes diversity and the treatment of all with respect and equality. Cooperative learning programs involve children of different ethnic groups in learning groups, where equal status, the reinforcement of positive interactions, and groups working together for mutual achievement are stressed. Such interactive problem-solving techniques have been applied to other groups, such as Israelis and Palestinians, to help them solve their problems.

Chapter Outline

Linkages Between Theory, Research, and Interventions

Enhancing Children's Development
    Early Childhood Interventions
    Promoting Psychological Well-Being
        Preventing Teenage Depression

Key Terms: *Write the letter of the definition next to the term in the space provided.*

1. ___ abstinence violation effect
2. ___ aerobic exercise

3. ___ contact hypothesis

4. ___ cooperative learning programs
5. ___ harm reduction
6. ___ health-compromising behaviors

a. evaluates whether an intervention works
b. situations marked by poverty, crime, violence, child abuse, family disintegration, low levels of social support, lack of helpful and friendly interactions among neighbors, and physical danger
c. studies psychological and behavioral factors in the prevention and treatment of illness and in the maintenance of health
d. behaviors that serve to maintain or increase health
e. behaviors that promote the development of illness
f. sustained activity that elevates the heart rate and increases the body's need for oxygen

7. ___ health-enhancing behaviors

8. ___ health psychology

9. ___ interactive problem solving

10. ___ interventions

11. ___ lapse

12. ___ motivational interviewing

13. ___ multiculturalism

14. ___ multimodal treatment approaches

15. ___ program evaluation

16. ___ relapse

17. ___ relational aggression

18. ___ socially toxic environments

19. ___ yo-yo dieting

g. dieting, stopping dieting and gaining weight, then dieting again

h. involves multiple treatments such as relaxation, stress management techniques, self-monitoring procedures, coping, social skills training, marital and family counseling, and use of positive reinforcement procedures

i. a technique for helping abusers increase their awareness of problems, desire to take action, and self-efficacy

j. a return to an undesirable behavioral pattern

k. a one-time "slip" when confronted with a high-risk situation

l. becoming upset over a lapse, and coming to believe that the lapse is proof that temptation can't be resisted

m. a prevention strategy designed to reduce the harmful effects of a behavior when it occurs

n. involves spreading of vicious rumors, exclusion from peer groups, and withdrawal from friendships

o. a social-intellectual movement that promotes the value of diversity as a core principle and insists that all cultural groups be treated with respect and as equals

p. suggestions that direct contact between the races could set the stage for greater multicultural understanding and a reduction in prejudice and discrimination

q. involve children of different ethnic groups in contact, with one-on-one interactions, cooperative activities, and social norms for intergroup contact

r. a process designed to enable parties to explore each other's perspective, develop joint ideas, and transfer ideas into policy

s. systematically applied applications designed to solve a practical problem

Review at a Glance: *Write the term that best fits the blank to review what you learned in this chapter.*

Linkages Between Theory, Research, and Interventions

How do we know whether an intervention works, whether the benefits of the program outweigh its costs, and whether the program is the most efficient way to use limited resources? All of the these questions are the focus of (1) _____ _____.

Enhancing Children's Development

An increasing number of children grow up in environments marked by poverty, crime, violence, abuse, family disintegration, low levels of social support, lack of helpful and friendly interactions among neighbors, and physical danger. Such environments are called (2) _____ _____ environments. Early childhood interventions such as the Head Start program, the

Abecedarian Program, and the High/Scope Perry Preschool Project were designed to help children overcome living in such disadvantaged environments.

Health Promotion and Illness Prevention

The field of (3) _____ _____ studies psychological and behavioral factors in the prevention and treatment of illness and in the maintenance of health. Health-related behaviors fall into two categories. (4) _____ - _____ behaviors serve to maintain or increase health. (5) _____ - _____ behaviors are those that promote the development of illness. Exercise is an example of a health-enhancing behavior. (6) _____ exercise is sustained activity that elevates the heart rate and increases the body's need for oxygen. Weight control is important in maintaining health. The accumulation of abdominal fat is increased by (7) _____ - _____ dieting.

Combating Substance Abuse

A therapy for combating substance abuse based on the classical conditioning model is called (8) _____ therapy. Today, such therapy is sometimes part of a (9) _____ _____ _____, that involves multiple treatments. A new technique called (10) _____ interviewing helps abusers increase their awareness of problems, desire to take action, and self-efficacy for doing so. High dropout rates are often a problem in substance abuse programs. (11) _____ are one-time "slips," while (12) _____ are a return to the undesirable behavior pattern. When a person becomes upset and feels that a lapse is proof that he or she will never be able to resist temptation, the (13) _____ _____ effect has occurred. Sometimes the focus of treatment shifts from preventing a problem to dealing with the aftereffects of it. (14) _____ _____ is a prevention strategy that is designed to reduce the harmful effects of a behavior when it occurs.

Reducing Violence

Many violent acts are maintained by (15) _____ reinforcement resulting from the removal of some unpleasant or aversive stimulus. Other violent acts result in tangible rewards, meaning that they are (16) _____ reinforced.

Psychology in a Multicultural World: Increasing Understanding and Reducing Conflict

"A social-intellectual movement that promotes the value of diversity as a core principle and insists that all cultural groups be treated with respect and as equals" is called (17) _____. Much work has been done to try to create greater tolerance between groups. According to Gordon Allport's (18) _____ hypothesis, direct contact between the races could set the stage for greater multicultural understanding. Research on the contact hypothesis has led to programs called (19) _____ _____ programs, which involve children of different ethnic groups in activities that place children at equal status and require the responsibility of all to achieve some common purpose. Another approach, called (20) _____ _____ _____, is a process designed to enable parties to explore each other's perspective, develop joint ideas, and develop policies based on the ideas.

Apply What You Know

1. Describe a program evaluation study that could be used to evaluate the effectiveness of the Head Start program.

Stretching Your Geographies

1. Many programs are developed to aid children from disadvantaged backgrounds. Conduct some library research to determine how programs like Head Start, the Abecedarian Program, and High/Scope Perry Preschool Project have helped children from such backgrounds. Describe what you find.

Practice Test

Multiple Choice Items: *Please write the letter corresponding to your answer in the space to the left of each item.*

_____ 1. A marital therapist has developed a unique, new, model about the particular factors involved in domestic violence. To test this model, he conducts a study where the key variables specified by the model are measured and statistical tests are used to see if the relations between the variables conform to the model. Given the information presented, this example **best illustrates** how _____.

    a. theory can influence interventions
    b. research can influence interventions
    c. theory can influence research
    d. research can influence theory

_____ 2. Dr. Scully has introduced a new program into a local high school designed to reduce the number of high school dropouts. To assess the effectiveness of the program, she not only looks at drop out rates but also at measures designed to shed light on the particular aspects of her program that are most effective and at the relative financial and social costs of implementing the program. Dr. Scully's research is **best described** as an example of _____.

    a. basic research
    b. correlational research
    c. program evaluation
    d. observational research

_____ 3. Researchers evaluating the effectiveness of the Abecedarian early intervention project concluded that _____.

    a. children who received the program early (age 2-3) and late (age 5-8) appeared to benefit equally from it
    b. while both late and early programs were highly effective, children who received the early program (age 2-3) benefited the most
    c. the children who received the early program (age 2-3) showed substantial benefits while the program appeared to have little effect when given late (age 5-8)
    d. both the early (age 2-3) and late (age 5-8) program were largely ineffective

_____ 4. Program evaluation of the Perry Preschool program revealed that _____.

    a. despite its promise, the program was largely ineffective
    b. the program produced a few immediate positive changes but the benefits did not last past grade school
    c. the program was effective but was not considered to be cost effective in the long-term
    d. the program was effective and was shown to be highly cost effective in the long-term

_____ 5. Assume that you are being consulted by educators who are designing a Head Start program for at-risk children in their school district. Based solely on the results of the Perry Preschool program, the **best recommendation** to make is to _____.

a. Start the program when the kids are 5- to 6-years old
b. Start the program when the kids are 7- to 8-years old
c. Have the program be 5 days a week
d. Have the program be 2 days a week

_____ 6. Follow-up analyses concerning the effectiveness of the Penn Optimism study have revealed that _____.

a. at the 10 year follow-up, children who received the intervention have lower rates of depression
b. children who received the program tended to have higher incomes as adults
c. at the two year follow-up, children who received the intervention have lower rates of depression
d. children who received the program were less likely to have criminal records as adults

_____ 7. The two main types of health-related behaviors are called _____.

a. positive and negative health behaviors
b. protective and endangering behaviors
c. health-enhancing and health-compromising behaviors
d. situation-focused and competency-focused health behaviors

_____ 8. Regular medical check ups, exercise, and a healthy diet are all considered to be examples of what the text called _____ behaviors.

a. competency-focused health
b. situation-focused health
c. protective health
d. health-enhancing

_____ 9. Research on the Stages of Change model has indicated that _____.

a. there is little or no support for the validity of this model
b. people tend to change their behaviors after going through only one cycle of the stages
c. people only move forward through the stages as they change their behaviors
d. people tend to move forward and backward through the stages as they change their behaviors

_____ 10. _____ has been shown to increase the amount of abdominal fat, which is a known significant risk factor for cancer and cardiovascular disease.

a. Anorexia
b. Random dieting
c. Yo-yo dieting
d. Excessive fasting

_____ 11. Of the following statements regarding AIDS, the one which is **false** is that _____.

a. The incubation period for the disease may be as long as 10 years
b. The AIDS virus is fatal because the virus attacks specific key organs
c. One of the ways it can be contracted is through blood transfusions
d. The AIDS virus mutates quickly, making it difficult to treat

_____ 12. Suppose you are a drug rehabilitation counselor and are considering what treatment to use with a client that you are about to meet for the first time. If your funds are limited and you don't have much time, research suggests that you would be **best off** using _____.

a. Antabuse
b. motivational interviewing
c. the multimodal treatment approach
d. shock therapy

_____ 13. Harold has been receiving treatment for alcoholism for over a year and treatment has been going very well. However, two moths ago, after a particularly bad day at work, some friends invited him to go with them to a bar and Harold had five beers. The next day when he thought about what had happened, he started to feel badly but them remembered some things he'd spoken about with his counselor about the problems associated with excessively blaming himself and being negative. As a result, Harold was able to put this incident behind him and he was able to remain abstinent for the next 3 months. In this example, Harold's behavior would **best** be defined as an example of _____.

a. the contact effect
b. the abstinence violation effect
c. a relapse
d. a lapse

_____ 14. A politician argues that it is very difficult if not impossible to eliminate such problems as drug and alcohol abuse and asserts that what is important is for us to reduce the negative consequences associated with these behaviors, such as unsafe sex and criminal behavior. This politician's views are **most consistent** with the _____ model.

a. relapse prevention
b. abstinence
c. harm reduction
d. tolerance

_____ 15. _____ involves acting aggressively by doing such things as withdrawing friendship, spreading vicious rumors, and excluding specific kids from peer group and it is used _____.

a. Relational aggression; more often by girls
b. Social aggression; more often by girls
c. Interpersonal aggression; equally by boys and girls
d. Expressive aggression; more often by boys

_____ 16. Systematically applied applications designed to solve a practical problem are called _____.

    a. interventions
    b. program evaluations
    c. environmental manipulations
    d. toxic environment engineering

_____ 17. The field of _____ psychology studies psychological and behavioral factors in the prevention and treatment of illness and in the maintenance of health.

    a. stage of change
    b. program evaluation
    c. intervention
    d. health

_____ 18. Of the following, the one which is not a health-enhancing behavior is _____.

    a. exercise
    b. using condoms during sexual activity
    c. breast self-examination
    d. eating fatty diets

_____ 19. Aerobic exercise _____.

    a. elevates the heart rate and decreases the body's need for oxygen
    b. has been found to have few physiological benefits
    c. increases the body's need for oxygen
    d. does not promote longevity

_____ 20. Dropout rates of _____ percent have been typical of virtually all exercise programs implemented.

    a. ten
    b. twenty
    c. thirty
    d. fifty

_____ 21. AIDS interventions are designed to _____.

    a. eliminate HIV
    b. motivate people to change their sexual behaviors and convince them that they can do so
    c. change homosexual but not heterosexual behaviors
    d. increase higher-risk sexual behaviors

_____ 22. Aversion therapies rely on principles of _____.

    a. classical conditioning
    b. modeling
    c. observational learning
    d. multimodal treatment approaches

_____ 23. A new technique designed to help abusers increase their awareness of problems, desire to take action, and self-efficacy for doing so is called _____.

    a. aversion therapy
    b. multimodal treatment
    c. motivational interviewing
    d. relapse prevention

_____ 24. Self-blaming failure to prevent an undesirable behavior and believing that the failure indicates an inability to resist temptation is called _____.

    a. a lapse
    b. a relapse
    c. increased self-efficacy
    d. the abstinence violation effect

_____ 25. A return to the undesirable behavior pattern is called _____.

    a. a lapse
    b. a relapse
    c. the abstinence violation effect
    d. harm reduction

_____ 26. The removal of some unpleasant person or other stimulus seems to _____ aggressive and violent behavior.

    a. positively reinforce
    b. negatively reinforce
    c. positively punish
    d. negatively punish

_____ 27. Studies of abused Russian women have indicated that half of these women maintain that they "deserve" it. Thinking back to a concept you learned in Chapter 12, these women seem to be using the _____.

    a. principle of deindividuation
    b. just-world hypothesis
    c. ABCD model
    d. principle of social loafing

_____ 28. The _____ suggested that direct contact by itself between the races should create greater understanding and less prejudice and discrimination.

    a. contact hypothesis
    b. cooperative learning programs
    c. jigsaw program
    d. interactive problem solving model

_____ 29. Studies of the contact hypothesis have found that _____.

a. contact between groups reduces prejudice
b. contact between groups reduces discrimination
c. cooperative activities between groups helps to reduce both prejudice and discrimination
d. it is important that one group have a higher status than the other to increase feelings of mutual understanding

_____ 30. A process designed to enable parties to explore each other's perspective, to develop joint ideas for how to resolve their conflict, and to transfer those ideas into actual policies is called _____.

a. the contact hypothesis
b. the jigsaw program
c. H.O.P.E.
d. interactive problem-solving

True/False Items: _Write T or F in the space provided to the left of each item._

_____ 1. Theories, research, and interventions are intimately related to one another.

_____ 2. Studies of the Abecedarian program showed that children in the preschool condition had lower I.Q.s and lower standardized test scores at the age of 15 than did children in the control group.

_____ 3. The Penn Optimism Project is attempting to teach cognition and behavioral coping skills that should reduce the likelihood of later depression.

_____ 4. Engaging in unprotected sexual activity is a type of health-enhancing behavior.

_____ 5. In the Stages of Change Model, people recognize that they have a problem in the precontemplation stage.

_____ 6. The AIDS epidemic threatens to overwhelm our health care financing and delivery systems.

_____ 7. Motivational interviewing was developed to help abusers increase their awareness of problems, desire to take action, and self-efficacy for doing so.

_____ 8. A one-time "slip" into a problem behavior is called a relapse.

_____ 9. Relational aggression typically involves physical battering.

_____ 10. It is important for two groups to be of equal status if prejudice and discrimination are to be reduced.

Short Answer Questions

1. What factors can help prevent teenage depression?

2. What is aversion therapy?

3. What is motivational interviewing?

4. What are the antecedents of violence?

5. What did the contact hypothesis say?

Essay Questions

1. What is the stages of change model?

2. What is multimodal treatment?

3. What are harm reduction approaches to prevention and how do they help to combat substance abuse?

4. Describe the biological approaches to violence reduction.

5. How can interactive problem solving techniques be used to help solve international conflicts?

Answer Keys

Answer Key for Key Terms

1. l
2. f
3. p
4. q
5. m
6. e
7. d
8. c
9. r
10. s

11. k
12. i
13. o
14. h
15. a
16. j
17. n
18. b
19. g

Answer Key for Review at a Glance

1. program evaluation
2. socially toxic
3. health psychology
4. Health-enhancing
5. Health-compromising
6. Aerobic
7. yo-yo
8. aversion
9. multimodal treatment approach
10. motivational

11. Lapses
12. relapses
13. abstinence violation
14. Harm reduction
15. negative
16. positively
17. multiculturalism
18. contact
19. cooperative learning
20. interactive problem solving

Answer Key for Practice Test Multiple Choice Questions

1. c
2. c
3. c
4. d
5. c
6. c
7. c
8. d
9. d
10. c
11. b
12. b
13. d
14. c
15. a

16. a
17. d
18. d
19. c
20. d
21. b
22. a
23. c
24. d
25. b
26. b
27. b
28. a
29. c
30. d

Answer Key for Practice Test True/False Questions

1. T
2. F
3. T
4. F
5. F

6. T
7. T
8. F
9. F
10. T

Answer Key for Practice Test Short Answer Questions

1. For example, the Penn Optimism Project is designed to teach cognitive and behavioral coping skills that will help teenagers cope better with psychosocial stressors and reduce the likelihood of developing depression. Negative beliefs about selves are replaced with more constructive and realistic ones. Pessimistic attributions for successes and failures are replaced with optimistic ones.

2. An aversion therapy uses the techniques of classical conditioning to treat things like substance abuse by pairing cigarettes, alcohol, or other substances with negative stimuli, like electric shock or nausea-inducing drugs.

3. Motivational interviewing is a technique developed to help abusers increase their awareness of problems, to increase their desire to take action, and to give them self-efficacy for doing so.

4. Antecedents to violence are the internal and external stimuli that precede the violent act. Such antecedents may include other people, environmental stimuli, and rage, among others.

5. The contact hypothesis stated that direct contact between the races could set the stage for greater multicultural understanding and a reduction in prejudice and discrimination.

Answer Key for Practice Test Essay Questions

1. The Stages of Change Model states that people go through six major stages as they learn to change negative behavior. The first stage is precontemplation, in which people have no desire to change behavior and don't recognize that they have a problem. In the stage of contemplation, the person recognizes that a problem exists, but there is no decision to take action. In the preparation stage, people have decided to change, but they have not actively begun to do so. In the action stage, people actively begin to modify their behavior and their environment. A person enters into maintenance as they try to control their behavior and prevent relapse. The final stage, termination, occurs when the change in behavior is so ingrained and under personal control that the original problem behavior will not reoccur.

2. Multimodal treatment involves multiple treatment elements such as:

   • Teaching relaxation and stress management techniques
   • Applying self-monitoring procedures
   • Coping and social skills training
   • Marital and family counseling
   • Use of positive reinforcement procedures

3. Harm reduction techniques are designed reduce the harmful effects of a behavior after it has occurred. Needle and syringe exchange programs have helped to reduce the spread of HIV infections. Methadone maintenance program have helped to reduce criminal activity among heroin users.

4. Biological approaches to violence reduction focus on brain chemistry. Increasing serotonin levels via drugs has been found to act as a braking mechanism on acts of impulsive aggression.

5. Interactive problem-solving techniques are designed to enable parties to explore each other's perspective, to develop joint ideas as to how to resolve the conflict, and to transfer their ideas and insights into the policy process. In the first step, each party describes the conflict from its own perspective. Then the parties are encouraged to work together the develop ways to satisfy the conflict in a mutually satisfactory way, a solution called "win-win."